Thinking NEGATIVELY

National Library of New Zealand Cataloguing-in-Publication Data

Richardson, Mark, 1971-

Thinking negatively / Mark Richardson. 1st ed.

ISBN 1-86971-029-0

1. Richardson, Mark, 1971- 2. Cricket.

3. Cricket—Psychological aspects. I. Title.

796.358092—dc 22

A Hodder Moa Book

Published in 2006 by Hachette Livre NZ Ltd

4 Whetu Place, Mairangi Bay

Auckland, New Zealand

Designed and produced by Hachette Livre NZ Ltd

Printed by Everbest Printing Co. Ltd, China

Front & back cover: Photosport

Thinking NEGATIVELY

Mark Richardson

Hodder Moa

Contents

Acknowledgements

To Mum, Dad and my sister Penny

This book is not about some street kid who started with nothing, fought dogs in the street for food, found a discarded cricket bat in the rubbish bin and worked his way up to test stardom. No, I come from a distinctly middle-class family. Mum and Dad — Carolyn and Howard — sold shoes for a living. They worked hard so they could give me and my older sister Penny pretty much all we needed: a private-school education, holidays at the beach, values and morals. But most importantly for me, they recognised that I was a cricketer and gave me nothing but support — as well as many a lift to the cricket ground when I was too young to drive. They have been great parents and deserve the life of retirement they have created for themselves in Havelock North. However, although they retired from the shoe trade quite some time ago they reckon they could only finally put their nerves to rest the day I announced my retirement from cricket. My whole family have lived the ups and downs of my career as much as I have — and experienced the same highs and lows. Anxiety was a constant companion when it came to watching their son and brother play test cricket, and when I was batting they couldn't watch — Dad would go out to the garden while Mum cleaned the house, and Penny just felt sick. I'd bet that on the times they did pluck up the courage to attend a game in person it was probably as mentally arduous for them as it was for me!

To my wife Mary

When I first met my wife I had been playing test cricket for about a year. She knew nothing about the game but instantly understood the most important thing: *cricket was a hell of a lot more to me than just a game.* She understood that tours were not holidays and accepted the emotional hold that the game had over me. I could never switch off between games and couldn't help but take my work home, but she allowed me the space for my many moments of self-pity, frustration and even delusions of grandeur — and that takes a very special person. When I think back to when we first met it makes me laugh that she went out and bought herself a cricket skills coaching book — a wise move, but a book on amateur psychology might have proved more useful for what lay ahead.

To my many coaches, particularly David Trist, Mark O'Donnell and Gilbert Enoka for their contributions to this book

I can't say I was the easiest person to manage. I was a huge drain on the time and patience of my coaches and I expected a lot from them. They have my utmost respect for the work they put into the game and I trust that they enjoyed our many discussions of techniques and tactics as much as I did.

To the guys I played alongside

I was moody, selfish, demanding, argumentative — and bloody awful in the field — but for the most part you all put up with me.

Foreword One

We used to call him 'Donut'

Why? Because as a left-arm spin bowler — and this was how Richie started out his career — his antics on the field could only have been carried on by someone who possessed a hole in their brain! But seriously, Richie was an intense competitor back in the days of our youth, although I had to remind him more than once that the competition was between him and the bloke he was bowling to at the other end. On many an occasion the fiery left-arm spinner would be chastising himself so badly that he was actually in breach of the code of conduct on sledging. But sledging yourself? Hence 'Donut'. The left-arm bowling thing died a natural death for Mark in the end, but he was a prodigious turner of the ball and I always felt that he was a better bowler than he gave himself credit for.

Batting, on the other hand, was something he could always do. Even though in the early days he was placed down in the depths of any batting line-up, he was no fool. On display when he was at the wicket was an excellent technique and he always showed the hallmark of any great player — scoring off the back foot. However, in my opinion there was one element that stunted his growth with the bat and made Richie the sort of character that could've been seen travelling the Yellow Brick Road hand in hand with the Tin Woodman as they both went off in search of a heart! By that I mean, if the bowling was over 130 kph then he didn't want to know.

Now it's this last fact that baffles me the most. How did a guy who openly acknowledged that he was scared of the ball transform himself into one of New Zealand's best-ever openers, and while he was at the peak of his game, one of the best openers in the world? Harmison, Ahktar, Lee, Donald — he's countered them all.

As with anything Richie does, he'll do it *his* way, and it was just unfortunate he was never picked for New Zealand earlier in his career. Whether or not the selectors didn't take him seriously enough or they put him in the 'too hard basket', I don't know, but he came through the hard way by forcing his way into the Black Caps by sheer weight of runs domestically.

Armed with a tenacious attitude for a fight, this gutsy competitor takes us on a journey through his fascinating mind in this book. The freeways, the side roads, the back roads and the long roads — Richie's journey is one which we can all enjoy.

Chris Cairns
Black Cap

Foreword Two

The importance of the mind in sport

The mind is the most untapped domain in the ongoing quest for consistent 'best performance'. What is known — that it controls all human behaviour, triggers all human emotions, manages all our interactions with the environment — is reduced in significance when we factor in our own, probably limited, understanding of it. Anybody as intrigued as I am with the search for sporting excellence and the enduring quest for fulfilment of potential, will find it impossible to bypass this most crucial domain — they know it is not just the body that must be conquered.

While elite athletes can spend countless hours training their bodies — fine-tuning their energy systems, building their mechanical structures and refining their skill components — far too often, little time or attention is devoted to preparing the mind for the challenges and demands of sport. Because an athlete's state of mind can significantly affect his or her performance or the eventual outcome of competition, developing strong mental skills can assist athletes at all levels searching for a competitive advantage.

Things impacting on an athlete's state of mind may include the pressure and desire to win, hectic travelling and playing schedules, past successes or failures in competition, as well as the myriad expectations that are part and parcel of the performance landscape — from coaches, family, media and the general public. Consistent success, then, is an 'inside job'. It is about managing the multitude of shifts that occur in your state of mind, from moment to moment, day to day, and week to week. Master this skill and you take a gigantic step forward in the 'consistent performance stakes'. I have worked with many sportspeople in my time and Mark presents as one of those few who have truly mastered this art. He has gained an understanding of how the mind impacts on performance and how, with measured application, you can use your mind to get the best out of yourself in the cauldron of international sport.

In his early career he was 'chewed over and spat out'; he then remodelled and transformed himself into an extremely successful international cricketer — as an opening batsman. Along this journey Mark has become a true disciple and a wonderful example of how the application of mental management systems can enhance performance. This is so, because of how he worked hard to understand himself and how he responded inside and outside the 'contest moment'; because he worked hard at practising routines and regimes which ensured that he delivered 'in the moment'; and above all *because he believed in what he was doing*. Mark's methods will serve as a great example to sportspeople from all codes who have the drive and desire to be the best that they can possibly be in their chosen field of endeavour.

I will remember Mark Richardson for his unashamed honesty, his dedication to the rituals and regimes that worked for him, his sense of humour, his willingness to share his knowledge with those who listened, and for his celebration of the fact that the 'difference factor' for 'Mark the cricketer' was deeply rooted in a sense of understanding about the relationship between his mind and his body. If, like me, you believe that harnessing the mind's power is a performance bastion yet to be conquered consistently, then this book will serve as a tremendous insight into how to set about accomplishing the task.

Thank you Mark for what you have given to cricket, to sport itself, and in particular to highlighting the value of systematic training of the mind and its role in consistent champion performance.

Gilbert Enoka
Sports Psychology Consultant

Why I Wrote This Book

In December 2004 my first-class cricket career came to an end. It was a strange feeling as I walked off the ground. Just two weeks earlier I had left the Adelaide Oval at the conclusion of my test career. My mind had been made up about my retirement and it felt like a massive burden had been lifted from me — but it was a very private moment. This time it was public knowledge that I was taking part in my last game of competitive cricket. There were a few notable people in attendance and my Auckland team-mates applauded me off the field, but all up it was a very low-key affair. I remember thinking as we were in the field and needing one last wicket to win the match, 'Hurry up and get this over with — I've had enough of this shit!' and I guess that pretty much sums up how I felt — worn out by the game. There was no heroic test century with a standing ovation from 40,000 fans at Eden Park, but rather a quiet stroll to a tent on the boundary of an empty public park. It was fitting really, and I left feeling that the game had finally beaten me — it had won the battle, as it should have. I finished up six runs short of 10,000 first-class runs, which had been a goal, played poorly in my last innings and gave my wicket away to a very uncharacteristic shot. In the dressing-room afterwards I sat down and thought, 'Well, that's that then,' took my gear off, packed my bag and buggered off. There was no elation but rather quiet satisfaction.

I was not one of the all-time great cricketers. I was a Kiwi battler who played a minor part in the history of the game, but a part that seemed, for a long time, to be unlikely. I didn't win many battles against the world's best players, but I competed hard and, in a short career at the top level, made the grade. However, there was one battle which I fought on a regular basis and won on many occasions and that was the battle with myself. New Zealand captain Stephen Fleming once said to me during a particularly challenging time at the crease, 'Don't you dare give in to yourself!' That was a constant challenge, and although I reckon I eventually did give in, I did so when *I* felt ready to and that left me feeling satisfied.

The inner battle began in the early 1990s, but before that the balance between cricket and myself could not have been more natural or synergistic. In a match between St Kentigern College and Auckland Grammar, played in 1987, I turned my hand to spin bowling and the positive results which followed came as naturally as they had from the first day I'd had a go at the game. New Zealand Under 18, Under 19, Under 20, National Development Squads, and Auckland First-Class Team selections followed, all signalling that I was on a logical path of progression to the New Zealand team as a left-arm spin bowler. There was no doubt in my mind that this would be the case; all it would take would be to show up, run in smoothly, transfer that momentum in a fluid bowling action, spin the ball hard, and watch it drift, drop and turn — it was all so easy. However, in 1991 nothing could have seemed more difficult and my mind was as out of control as my bowling delivery. From this point on I began a nine-year struggle to achieve my life's major driving goal — to play cricket for New Zealand. I eventually did achieve that goal but it definitely didn't occur naturally.

Cricket was my life and many things motivated me to stick at it, but it was my ability to take control of my mental game that finally allowed me to achieve my goal. Taking control of my mental game was a learned skill and I had a very good teacher in Alex McKenzie. Alex was the sports psychology professional I contacted to help with my cricket and he was instrumental in my development as he introduced me to the techniques I employed to bring about positive change in my game. In this book I outline in my own words the techniques and processes which we developed together but use Alex's more expert perspective as a means of summarising each of the three sections I have chosen to use to describe my cricket career.

They say the game at the top level is 90 per cent mental and I'd agree with that, but I think very few individuals understand what they are really saying when they make that statement. As a bowler I couldn't cut it mentally, but as a batsman I developed some true mental strength. My mental game was not just about handling myself during competition, nor was it about playing with a smile and not feeling nerves, but rather it covered every aspect of my drive toward cricketing success. Mental toughness was not just about turning up on match day, gritting my teeth and giving it my all on that day — rather, being mentally tough was about identifying what I needed to do to succeed, training according to those requirements, staying focused on those imperatives and letting them take hold during competition. Being mentally tough is all about preparation; preparing repetitively, and most importantly intelligently, for the coming season, practice, game, delivery. Ten per cent of your success might be down to natural ability, and perhaps underneath it all I did have a little natural ability with the bat, but it is what you *do* with that ability that matters and that is where the mental element comes into play. It takes cricketing intelligence to understand and develop your technique, cricketing smarts and discipline to carry out appropriate tactics, and then emotional control and focus to keep the nasties that want to stop you from applying them at bay — all 100 per cent mental.

I've divided this book into three distinct sections. The first section is all about me. I don't believe that my career in cricket is deserving of an extensive autobiography because I just wasn't that big — albeit in New Zealand my story of failed bowler to successful batsman did capture the imagination of many. In this section I share the reasons why I couldn't walk away from cricket even when the game was tormenting me and success at the top level couldn't have seemed more improbable. It follows my progression from bowler to test-match batsman and outlines my major motivations along the way and explains why I eventually retired from the game earlier than many would have expected.

The second section is about the process I put myself through to turn myself from a useful first-class middle-order batsman into a test-match opening batsman. It was an extensive, detailed, and at times anally retentive process, but one that made the highly unlikely a reality. It was *my* process and I don't profess to say it is everyone's cup of tea, but I'm sure that people from all disciplines can gain some kind of insight from it. When it comes to mental approaches to achieving I believe there is no singularly best model, and while some approaches preach a 'step back and let it happen' method, my way was 'head down, bum up and make it happen'.

In the third section I deal with the 'big four' — the 'demons' that ripped my bowling to shreds and tried their best to destroy my personal process and batting. They are the same demons that I can almost guarantee everybody from all walks of life faces from time to time and I hope that my reflections on them provide perspective for others.

I achieved my goals through perseverance, hard work and focus, but most importantly I learnt *how* to succeed. In cricket circles you would have described me as a grafter and, in contrast to my efforts as a young bowler, there was little by way of natural beauty when I plonked myself at the batting crease. However, I learnt how to get the most out of an average ability. I hope this book provides a little inspiration and insight for those who consider themselves less than gifted but who are nevertheless serious about getting the best out of themselves.

Section One
From Failure to Success

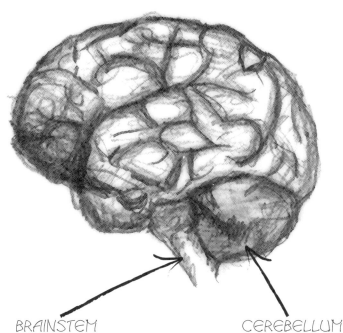

BRAINSTEM
Controls the things we
don't think about

CEREBELLUM
Responsible for voluntary
muscle movement

Chapter One

How the hell did all this start?

It was 27 November 2004 and I was in my hotel room, lying on my bed and bawling my eyes out. I'd just failed against Australia again, this time in the first innings of the second test at Adelaide. This innings was going to be 'it'. It was going to be the innings where I finally proved to myself I could cut it with the best, that my average in the mid-40s and all the accolades I had received over the last four years were in fact a true reflection of my credentials as a test batsman. I'd stepped up at Lord's a few months earlier, so why not do it again at another of the world's most picturesque and historic cricket grounds — the Adelaide Oval. But what eventuated was the straw that finally broke the camel's back — or perhaps in my case the plough that dragged the draught horse down: 59 balls for nine runs; a lot of playing and missing on a great batting surface; being given not out when I was very clearly out; and — most disturbing of all — losing my composure after I'd set an important tour goal of not reacting to Shane Warne's endless pathetic ramblings.

Cricket had reduced me to tears on many, many occasions, but this time it felt different. Whereas previously my tears had come out of frustration or simple disappointment, this time I had experienced an overwhelming sensation of helplessness. The game had finally won. It had me close to a nervous breakdown. It was taking all my willpower to keep my composure around my team-mates but as soon as I was alone I would lose control. I knew I couldn't continue to function in this manner. The last time I'd felt this way was during the last series I'd played in Australia — f**king Australians! It was during the VB series of 2002, which was a one-day tri-series involving New Zealand, South Africa and, of course, Australia. After failing in my first two innings in One-Day International cricket I figured I had one last chance to make the grade in this format, and the third game was in front of a full house at the Sydney Cricket Ground (SCG) against Australia. But my innings that day was a sheer embarrassment as I took 71 balls to reach a mere 26. I don't know how I even got the 26 runs because it felt like I had played and missed at every ball. Slumped in tears in the showers the water couldn't wash away the humiliation I was feeling. We actually won that game, but emotionally I felt like someone who had lost everything they cared for. Later that night as I sat in my Sydney hotel room I decided that this had to stop. The game had no right to affect me like this, and in fact if I was going to continue playing and aim to succeed I had to get control of my emotions. I never did . . .

Now, two years on, I had come to the same conclusion, except this time I knew what I had to do. There was only one decision I could make. It was to walk away from my playing days while I still had some self-respect. The alternative — to continue helplessly riding the emotional rollercoaster I was on and risk destroying all the other parts of my life I valued — was not worth contemplating. Immediately the tears stopped. My next — and final — innings in test cricket, while only 16 scratchy runs, was the first and only time in 15 years of first-class cricket that I played without nerves. That innings also very quickly confirmed to me that I simply could not operate at my best without nerves.

How could a mere game have such a profound effect on a person? It hadn't started out that way, and if I could have foreseen what it would do to me as an adult perhaps I would never have picked up a bat as a kid, but I did — so why?

Is it because Dad had played?

My dad had been a cricketer — a pretty good one too; well, good enough to play minor association cricket for Hawke's Bay. You'd think he and his old team-mates were recalling great test victories whenever they get together — and they bloody well go on about it enough! Fair's fair though, they *were* test matches for them; and whatever level you play at, for competitive people, winning is always something to celebrate. However, there I'll be, sitting round the table at Mum and Dad's, 157 first-class games and 38 tests to my name, and I dare not say anything critical about the games he played.

As a youngster Dad probably had more potential as a soccer player. He turned out for Seatoun in their 'glory years' and reckons he had a chance to play for New Zealand until a case of hepatitis buggered him up. In photos he looked pretty fit too, but I don't know, how far are you going to go in a game that requires real speed and agility when you have the genes that created a son nicknamed 'Rigor Mortis'? Anyway, what I'm trying to say here is that Dad was a sportsman; he valued sport and sportspeople. And I'm his son so I guess I've just followed suit. Ever since I can remember we've talked sport and not much else — the soppy stuff is Mum's domain — and Dad has done everything in his power to ensure I could participate in sport. Whether *he* chose cricket and soccer for my childhood or I did, I don't really know — perhaps it was a bit of both — but what I do know is that the first minute I played cricket, cricket chose me.

My first real memory of playing cricket comes from when I was about five years old, around Christmas time on the Lowry's farm in Hawke's Bay. Mr Lowry had put in a cricket pitch in one of his fields and each year he would stage a game. This day is still vivid in my mind because of two things, both of which occurred during the lunch break. Firstly there was an aerial lolly scramble with Dad dressed as Santa throwing out the lollies from Mr Lowry's crop-duster. After the goodies were bailed out Mr Lowry landed in secret, dropped Dad off, took off again and performed some aerobatics for the crowd — Mum nearly had a fit! However, secondly, and most importantly, it was during this same lunch break that Richie Singleton, my long-time backyard test-match opponent, and I went out onto the cricket pitch to play. I was bowling and sent down what was to be, in my mind, the 'perfect' ball. It's the first ball I can remember bowling and it landed at my feet and rolled towards the wickets at the other end. (Incidentally, I served up a similar ball in my first first-class game for Auckland, although the accuracy of my very first ball impressed me a hell of a lot more than the one delivered 13 years later impressed Auckland captain Jeff Crowe.) Anyway, upon Richie's swing and miss, it 'cannoned' into middle stump with so much force that I think it caused the bails to vibrate — a little! 'You're out! My turn to bat!' 'No I'm not,' came the reply, 'the bails have to come off.' After a brief discussion in which both points of view were put forward (this day was also the occasion of my first sledging match) the matter was referred to the 'third umpire' (also a first) in the form of Lloyd, Richie's father, who judged in favour of the batsman. Upon receiving the not-out decision I promptly led my team from the field in protest (yes, I've always been in favour of neutral umpiring). I was only five years old and the game had already pissed me off. And so began my 28-year love-hate relationship with cricket.

Is it because I was competitive?

I believe competitiveness is an inherent quality, something everyone has to a degree. Some people are competitive about some things and not about others, while some — like Dion Nash — are competitive about absolutely everything. I seem to be competitive about the things I think I am good at. When I look for the answer as to why cricket became my passion, the idea nags away in the back of my mind that the direction my life was to take was somehow tied up with the direction the ball took that I bowled, at the age of five, on that farm cricket pitch. It went straight, and because of that I think the seed was planted in my mind, telling me I was good at cricket. There are many other things I enjoy doing — for example, sports like surfing — but if I don't see myself as good at them I just cannot be bothered being competitive about them. That's not to say I don't invest a huge amount of time in trying hard and aiming to get as good as I can at them. For instance, I think nothing of getting up at three o'clock in the morning to drive two hours to Raglan to surf, but if someone wants the wave I'm paddling for I'll probably let them have it. I also had a brief foray into rugby, and actually one of my highlights in the code was tackling All Black flanker Mike Brewer. It was during my university days and at the height of my bowling 'yips'. I had already played briefly at under-19 level at Waikato, but got back into it around 1993 when at Otago.

Dunedin is a rugby town. It is rugby, rugby, rugby all the way, and that passion is fuelled heavily by the students. It's very hard when you're a student at Otago University not to get swept up in the rugby culture. The Otago team players quite simply *are* 'the men'; the senior club players 'think' they are 'the men'; and going out with a good rugby player is a real status symbol for the women. I was single at the time so what other option did I have but to join a rugby club, become a great rugby player and score myself a bimbo bombshell. So I joined Pirates Rugby Club in St Kilda, mainly because it had a cool name, and played in black. My God did I try and train hard. In retrospect, it probably helped get my cricket back on track because I got super-fit. I never missed training and worked diligently by myself on perfecting my pass — I was a halfback, incidentally. I even wrote down a comprehensive list of goals setting out my development right up to All Black selection, but really I knew I was crap. I did manage to make reserve for the premier senior team, but my lack of speed and natural aptitude was all too evident and I never had the competitive mongrel factor you see in all good halfbacks. Cricket was different, however, and like I said, from my very first cricket experience I believe I nurtured an innate belief that I was good at the game and would one day show the world. My competitiveness, therefore, stemmed from the belief that to show the world I had to beat the world. Team-mates had to be made aware that I was the best and thus I had to outperform them.

I still remember my first game of proper cricket. I was about eight years old by this time, and Dad took me down to Glover Park in Auckland's eastern suburbs. This was where the University St Heliers Cricket Club's junior teams were based. I made six runs in my first innings of Saturday morning cricket. I also made six runs in my first test innings and finished six runs short of my last documented goal of 10,000 first-class runs. So naturally my final meaningful act on a cricket field was when I went back down to Glover Park a few weeks after my last ever first-class game, walked out onto the very pitch it all began on, hit my wife for six, walked off and put it all to bed.

Anyway, I made six runs first up and thought I'd done pretty well until I looked in the scorebook the coach was keeping and saw to my horror that other kids had scored a heap more than me. Next Saturday, I determined there and then, *I* would be the top scorer.

Is it because it was fun?

Cricket *was* fun. It was fun because I was good at it. I bowled all the time and got heaps of wickets. Things came easily to me and I loved all the kudos I got from being singled out at school assembly following a triumphant Saturday performance. But I was actually a bit of a nerd at school. I wasn't really interested in the parties that the rugby or rowing team guys went to, preferring to spend my Friday nights preparing for Saturday and my Saturday nights reflecting on Saturday afternoon and watching tapes of past test matches and One-Day Internationals. All I really wanted to do at school was play cricket at lunch time, and hang out for home time so I could go to cricket practice. Nevertheless, although I wasn't social, I was always accepted, and I didn't get picked on because I was good at something and people gave me credit for it.

What I loved best about cricket was the bowling. I just couldn't wait to get the ball in hand and bowl. Sure wickets came, but what I really loved was the very act of bowling. Every time I ran in it was a chance to bowl a better ball than the last. And if I wasn't bowling in a game I would spend hours bowling to a stump and playing out an imaginary game in my head. Accuracy was my forte, which was developed out of a requirement to save the living-room window. My pitch was a downhill stretch about 16-and-a-half metres long, with the target being an area of brick wall between two windows, about a metre-and-a-half wide. Success on this pitch was all about finding the right line. It was a safety issue. Summer holidays spent in Hawke's Bay playing backyard cricket with Richie Singleton saw full 50-overs-a-side matches complete with official scorebooks and replica New Zealand beige and English blue World Series uniforms. Poor Richie often had to bowl his full quota of overs while my bowling prowess more often than not saw me take his 10 wickets well within the fifty.

Yep, I was a cricketer all right, but was not really any different from any other kid who showed talent and was achieving at their sport. I loved it, wanted to be the best, and had the support of my parents. Nor, from ages eight to eighteen, was there a doubt in my mind that I was headed to the top — and let's face it, I was the best cricketer in my junior grade teams. I was the kid who bats where he wants, usually first, scores 50 most games, bowls the most overs, and on whose performance the team relies. I also made most of the rep teams along the road from junior to senior cricket; it wasn't always as the same type of player but that really doesn't matter. From age eight to twelve I was a top-order batsman who bowled slow mediums; by under-14s I was a fast bowler and middle-order batsman. At the under-16 level I'd realised I was only a medium pacer — but a bloody good one — and a lower-order batsman extremely scared of the fast bowlers. Finally, by the end of school cricket and the under-19 level I was a left-arm spinner and a totally gutless lower-order batsman. But whatever my style I was one of, if not the most, promising players in the team. Every game I took part in felt like another natural step along the path to national selection. Success came with ease. Bear in mind though that the volume of training I did was incredible, but training was fun anyway. If the players I played against weren't so good, I saw them as easy but necessary wickets; if they were good I lifted my level of competition. If they were older and in higher teams, well it didn't matter because I would soon overtake them, and if they had it over me a little, well that didn't matter either because they would probably play for New Zealand alongside me. Competition was great fun, but then again I was not just competing against myself.

In retrospect, whatever I did as a junior cricketer didn't really matter, but what did matter was vitally important — and that was that I was a true cricketer. I get angry when I see parents and coaches identify and pigeonhole a young player who might show promise at one particular skill and make statements about how this kid will go on to play for New Zealand. That kid might go on to play for their country one day, but who knows as what type of player? Dan Vettori started off as a left-arm quick, Ian Smith as a bowler and John Aiken, the Auckland and Wellington left-handed opening batsman, as a right-handed batsman. What I do know is that if a kid is not a true cricketer, he or she will fizzle out. A true cricketer is someone who has a natural aptitude for the game and an indescribable desire to succeed. These two attributes combined will see them develop their skills and style along the way, but also see them practise every day. Their desire will see them stick with the game through thick and thin. They will find a way to keep playing and training even when they need to get a job. They will find a way to get to training even if it is across the other side of town and they don't have a car. Nothing will get in the way of achieving at the game they are good at. They live it, breathe it and think about it constantly. These are the kids our junior programmes should be identifying. I was one of these kids. And even though I don't play any more, I will always be a true cricketer.

However, while I always knew that cricket was 'it' for me, I did have a back-up plan which was to become a pilot and I was considering joining the air force. Much later on, while in Dunedin and after having gained a commercial pilot licence, I looked into that option again only to find out I had an astigmatism in my left eye and that they weren't really looking for a blind fighter pilot. Interestingly, while the sharpness of my vision is quite poor, my hand-eye coordination is extremely good. Make of that what you will.

Truth be told, my plans to join the air force when first out of school were squashed earlier when, in the sixth form, I discovered my total lack of ability at physics which was, of course, a prerequisite for acceptance into the air force. Fortunately, I was able to opt out of attending physics class for another class's physical education session without getting found out for two whole terms. My eventual mistake was to go back to physics class one day. The physics teacher — his name escapes me now but he was a dead ringer for Fred Flintstone — duly gave me a bollocking. I responded by saying that I didn't really care because I was going to be a professional cricketer anyway. 'Bullshit, you won't amount to anything,' was his response. I'd like to track him down one day and give him 'the bird' for that.

I did become a professional cricketer, of course, but my road to eventual success was not to be the fun and games it had been when I was a child and a teenager.

Chapter Two

Losing it

Everyone has had this experience at some time in their life. It is the time when you manage to cock up something that until now you have done naturally without any conscious thought. You know, like when you fall over getting out of bed. Or put both feet through the same leg hole in your underpants. Or, instead of putting the cereal spoon in your mouth, you try to ram it through your cheek. Or you ram a hole in the garage wall because you put the car in reverse instead of drive. Usually you just laugh it off (except perhaps the car one), call yourself a clumsy git and get on with the day. But what if you don't laugh it off? What if you actually think you did it because you believe something is fundamentally wrong with you and the way you have been doing it in the past? All of a sudden the natural becomes the unnatural as you take a simple task and turn it into a self-conscious rigmarole. I had this experience once: it was in October 1992. At the time I described this moment as *The day I woke up and had forgotten how to bowl*. In retrospect, I now describe this moment as *The day I woke up and discovered self-doubt*. It was an experience that completely changed my life.

This might sound a little exaggerated but things did go downhill alarmingly quickly from the day that I first questioned my natural ability. It was the start of the 1991/92 season and all through the winter the ball had not been coming out of my hand quite like normal. While I never really found that much rhythm in the nets as I was always so preoccupied with technical things, I'd usually get the ball pretty much in the right place. This time though it had been coming out really high and slow with absolutely no spin or fizz on it — the type of ball cricketers would describe as 'powder-puff'. The harder I tried to get some spin and pace on the ball the worse it seemed to become, and onto a good length was the last place it wanted to go. It was frustrating me a little but I sort of shook it off thinking, 'Oh well, it will come good in competition', but nagging away in the back of my mind was some disturbing doubt.

In October the club season began and my club, University St Heliers, took on East Coast Bays at Papatoetoe. Early-season cricket in Auckland is always 50-over matches played on artificial pitches, and there are only so many of them around, so both teams found themselves miles from their home grounds in South Auckland. Having had a poor winter of training it may have helped to get an environment I was comfortable in to kick things off on the right track, but Papatoetoe was not that place. For a start, their artificial pitches are miles from the changing-rooms. Furthermore, given the theft problem there, you had to lock the changing-rooms, take all your gear to the boundary and share one park bench with the whole team. This is also a ground where locals like to cut through on their way back from the supermarket — the most direct route being right through the middle of the ground holding the artificial wicket. Being told to 'f-off' by a bunch of skinny white guys dressed in nerdy white clothing is not high on the agenda of these unwelcome participants, who normally respond by walking through the game painfully slowly or responding in kind.

Then there was the artificial wicket, which I disliked bowling on immensely. It's not because they don't spin, actually they offer good spin and great bounce, but the run-up going from grass to concrete was what always put me off. I always found it hard to find a rhythm on uneven run-ups or even bowling over other bowlers' footmarks, a bit like a racehorse that gets freaked out by shadows maybe (perhaps when it came to playing on artificial pitches I could have tried blinkers). On top of all that, it was a cold, blustery day with a south-westerly and scattered showers. It all made for a pretty crappy setting

— being out in the middle of nowhere, on a plastic pitch, with testosterone-charged South Aucklanders wandering through the ground — it just didn't feel like senior club cricket.

However, the constants that matter were still there: I had the ball in hand and the pitch was still 22 yards long and that should have been enough. There was something missing though, something that had for the most part been a constant for the last 15 years and that was very important — I didn't want to bowl. I didn't want to bowl because I wasn't confident of what was going to happen when I let the thing go. My hands were sweaty and my mind was churning with all sorts of negative thoughts. 'Shit, this isn't much fun!' I thought. Problem was, I did bowl. I bowled my 10 overs for 92. God knows why the captain kept me on. Perhaps it was because of what I had done in the past. Reputation was something that was to haunt me from that day forward.

This was the 10-over spell that transformed my whole outlook on the game. I had lost rhythm and control in my bowling on a handful of occasions previously. During a half season for Cornwall Cricket Club, and in an under-18 tournament in Dunedin, I had struggled to find my length and had been lacking in confidence. In fact, looking back at these periods I can see they were when I first confronted my arch-enemy, a force that I never came to grips with and a bastard you will hear all about later on in the book. These little glitches came and went and I never really worried too much about them. However, this latest glitch was different, in a major way. I *expected* to bowl poorly and accepted it and its consequences. In 10 overs my whole self-image changed. It didn't feel like simply a bad day to be shrugged off, it felt more like I had hit a brick wall on my road to cricketing stardom. I recall a young left-arm spinner called Mark Haslam was playing for East Coast Bays in this game. As I sat there red-faced and confused about my performance I watched him bowl 10 very impressive overs and thought to myself, 'This guy is going to get my spot in the Auckland team.' Mark did indeed get my spot that year and then very soon after was selected for New Zealand.

Up until my second season for Auckland and especially during my school and under-20 days I'd seen my bowling through rose-tinted glasses. Bad balls just didn't register, probably because the standard of batting wasn't good enough to put them away. I was super-confident and boy, was I cocky. When

St Kentigern played a game against a touring first XI from Adelaide I had bowled from one end as usual for most of the innings, turned it square and got five for bugger all. The coach from the Australian team was umpiring at my end. After collecting my man of the match award at the end of the game he had come up to me and said, 'You have promise, kid. I've never seen a finger spinner turn the ball like that, but if I had been batting I would have waited for that one short ball you bowl an over and hit you for four through cover point.' I just nodded appreciatively and thought, 'F**k off, you senile old prick! What short ball?'

The fact was, that if you could turn the ball away from the bat in schoolboy and under-age cricket, and on dry and dusty or soft and wet pitches as they always are, it didn't really matter what you threw down — the batsmen would just crap themselves and self-destruct. In fact, the general pattern was: push forward and play and miss; watch the long hop go past; freak out at how much they both turned; panic, run down and slog at the next ball; get out stumped — and with Adam Parore behind the stumps you had no chance. However, if you did happen to show any sort of application, the fast in-swinging arm-ball would do the trick. When I think back, it amazes me how often this was the case and it wasn't a hell of a lot different in club cricket for the most part.

However, my thought patterns began to change a little from the time I made my first-class debut. I was selected to play for a New Zealand President's XI against the touring Indian team in the 1989/90 season. In those days they didn't have a regular 'A-team' programme but there was often the equivalent sides selected under the 'President's' or 'emerging' banners. As usual there are always a couple of young bolters picked from obscurity in these selections, and myself and Adam Parore were such players, by virtue of our youth and our Auckland 'B'(yes, this was before the days of political correctness — the good old days) team performances.

I didn't have a bad debut really, when you consider it was against India on a flat wicket, a small ground, and that they aren't the worst players of spin. I didn't get any wickets in the first innings, which was a novel experience, but bowled okay. I did make 26 not out with the bat which was my highest first-class score for quite some time. In our second innings in the field, before I knew it I had three wickets for very little — good wickets too in Manoj Prabhakar, Sachin Tendulkar and Kapil Dev. However, Tendulkar was 16 years old at the time and Prabhakar and Kapil were later accused of match fixing. After I got my third wicket, Gavin Larsen, who was at this stage a promising all-rounder, came up and said, 'You probably can't quite believe what is happening,' and I thought, 'What do you mean, this is what usually happens.' About six or seven overs later I hadn't got any more wickets and was getting hit around a bit. Martin Snedden, who was the captain, sensing I was losing focus a little, came up and asked how I was. I said something about how I couldn't stop these guys from hitting me round, to which he looked me straight in the eyes and said, 'Well stop bowling half volleys then!' He may as well have hit me over the head with a sledgehammer.

Prabhakar and Kapil had slogged out to me; Tendulkar, well I was too good for him; but Mohammad Azharuddin and Kiran More had sat patiently, worked out I bowled a scoreable ball an over and put it away when it came. I had just experienced what quality cricket was all about — organisation. All of a sudden I realised that turning the ball and having good flight was all well and good, but it means very little at the top level if you do not have enough control and accuracy to put pressure on the batsman. When you face up to a bowler you have to quickly assess their merits. A very basic plan might be to organise your defence in the first few overs and while doing so, assess what scoring options this bowler may allow you. If the bowler is very accurate, or puts so much pressure on your defence that by looking to defend you will eventually succumb for very few runs, you may decide to attack him, possibly by using the sweep or using your feet proactively to upset the length. If, on the other hand, you are comfortable in defence, or the bowler is prone to a regular loose one, you may just sit and wait and take the scoring option as offered up. Being a finger spinner and having a delivery that was quite slow through the air, I did not get the severe spin and drift that wrist spinners like Shane Warne or Stuart McGill get, so I was not able to put as much pressure on good batsmen's defensive techniques. Consequently, organised players soon realised they could sit on me and feed off the occasional bad ball.

Nevertheless, in my first full season of first-class cricket my bad ball was not that frequent and the positive qualities of my bowling — my drift and sufficient turn — were good enough to get a reasonable job done. It was no surprise that I tended to have most success against Central Districts because those cowboys always tried to bash me everywhere with very little thought. Slowly but surely though, my focus was shifting from my flight and turn to my bad ball, and with that commenced my slide into the mental hell that is 'the yips'. Probably helping to accelerate the process was one of my boyhood heroes, Jeff 'Chopper' Crowe.

Chopper

Jeff Crowe was captain of Auckland and New Zealand during my time as a bowler in the Auckland side. I always admired the battlers for some reason and Chopper was a battler. Players like John Reid, Bruce Edgar, John Wright, Ewen Chatfield and Chopper were my favourite players to follow and featured regularly in my imaginary backyard cricket games. I regarded them as honest triers, not naturally gifted stars, and I can't tell you why but that really appealed to me. If a player was struggling a bit or had even been recently dropped I made a point of picking them in my backyard eleven.

Chopper played a lot of his early first-class career for South Australia under the captaincy of Ian Chappell. He idolised Ian Chappell who by all accounts was one tough son of a bitch and a ferocious competitor. Chappell played back and across and is revered as one of the world's great hookers and pullers. Like all good apprentices Chopper must have modelled himself on his South Australian master, and when he first returned to New Zealand he also had the back and across technique going and was good on the pull, hook and cut. Later on, after a few seasons on our goat-track pitches, he still went back and across but his game had become a lot less expansive.

When I came to play with Chopper my memories of him as a batsman were of a quiet man, probably because his teeth were so tightly clenched together, who plonked himself at the crease and refused to be intimidated or removed. I just could never fathom how he could get hit in the inner thigh, shoulder, forearm, chest, wherever, and not even flinch. He scored a lot of runs for Auckland. But Chopper did not suffer fools and the first way to lose his respect was to show any sort of mental weakness. In my first game for Auckland it was a thrill to play with such a hero of mine; in my second, I was starting to get a little concerned; and after my third, I was petrified.

In that first game, my grip slipped as I was just about to deliver the ball. I tried to hold on to the ball and not bowl it, but it came out anyway. It landed at my feet and dribbled down towards Central Districts' wicketkeeper batsman Tony Blain. Tony looked around, picked his spot and hit the now stationary ball for four. Everyone was in hysterics, including me — but Chopper? Well, he was expressionless. In the second game I was fielding under the helmet at short leg when the batsman got a thick inside edge onto his pad and the ball ballooned about three metres into the air and lobbed down towards me. You will never get an easier catch. I lined the ball up, like you would had someone lobbed it underarm at you, and celebrated the early wicket. The ball never even brushed a finger. In fact, my attempt was so bad that you couldn't help but find it amusing, and most on the park did. At the end of the over, as Chopper changed ends on his way from first slip to first slip, I said, 'What a joke.' He looked at me in a way I've never forgotten and in a disturbingly low voice said, 'Who's f**king laughing?' In my third game he opened up a little more and I left the field in tears.

Chopper's handling of me was often put forward as the reason behind my bowling falling to bits. I don't entirely agree. He definitely accelerated the process, but to hold him fully accountable is unfair; there were many factors that contributed to my downfall. When placed in charge of a group of cricketers Chopper expects an impeccable standard of behaviour and the level of unwavering dedication and toughness that he demands of himself — no doubt the same standards he learned from Ian Chappell. It is no surprise that now his playing days are over he has found himself as a Black Caps manager and, more recently, an International Cricket Council (ICC) match referee. I consider Chopper a 'leader of men', but if he does have a weakness in his style it would be his inability to relate to players who might respond to or indeed need a softer, more tolerant style of management. Under pressure I was definitely one of these players, but I feel that all Chopper really saw in me was an emotionally unstable, immature, brainless, spoilt little kid. To be fair, I didn't really do anything to prove him wrong.

Quite simply, there was no way Chopper was going to change his captaincy style to accommodate this young idiot the selectors kept pushing on him. From his position at first slip he made his displeasure in my bowling plainly obvious as he stood disinterested and silent until the loose ball came along when a very audible yell of 'For f**k's sake, Richie!' could be heard for quite some distance. In fact, this turn of phrase is still in currency around the cricket fraternity whenever Richardson-Crowe relations are mentioned. I even drew on it heavily in my 'first tour speech', a tradition whereby on your first tour for New Zealand you must give an impromptu two-minute speech (although as a result of the kind of language generally used, the tradition has sort of faded away these days). Mine was given at a public barbecue in Zimbabwe on the topic of 'What impact has Jeff Crowe had on the development of your career?' Chopper just happened to be our manager at the time too. Years later, and upon announcing my retirement from all cricket, I received an email from Chopper which was entitled 'For f**k's sake, Richie!'

Still, Chopper had his uses for me, which most of the time involved carrying the drinks — which I hated because at this stage I still believed I could bowl and wanted to prove it. If I did play I didn't bowl much, which was understandable given we had the incumbent New Zealand off-spinner in Dipak Patel. In the early '90s first-class cricket was played over three days, and often to get an outright result the captains had to get together to set the game up. This is when I would get to bowl, with everyone round the bat, and it was to our advantage if the opposition scored quick runs. The reality of this situation went over my head about as often as the ball seemed to. Later in the summer when the pitches were drier I often became a legitimate and important member of the team. I lived for these opportunities, but the more of them I got, the more nervous I became. Runs mattered now and it seemed every loose ball I bowled was welcomed by Chopper about as fondly as a serious case of haemorrhoids; which is probably what I was to him, a pain in the arse. Now I was acutely aware of my bad ball and instead of running in looking to 'rip the shit' out of it, all I wanted to do was land it somewhere near a good length and not get yelled at.

My fear of Chopper was well known round the traps and was a laughing matter for some. Once, when travelling to Auckland from Dunedin with the Otago team, Chopper was on our flight. My team-mates thought it would be funny to fix the seating so I would have to sit next to him. They succeeded and I don't believe a flight from Dunedin to Auckland has ever been longer, nor the seats been as uncomfortable, nor has there been as much childish sniggering from the passengers. It is important for you to understand though that I did not hate Jeff Crowe, it is just I was extremely scared of him — a bit like a dog who wants nothing more than to please its master but always ends up getting a clip round the ears. I would have to wait another seven years before I finally had another chance to please my master.

In the winter of 2000 I got selected in the New Zealand 'A' Team to tour England. To emphasise the importance of this tour the coach and manager would be the top team's coach and manager — David Trist and Jeff 'Chopper' Crowe. 'Shit!' I thought, 'this will be a test of my bottle.' While I was a completely different cricketer now and a hell of a lot more mature, I still found the presence of my old Auckland captain disconcerting. This trip was a 'rip, shit or bust' moment in my career and I wasn't going to let a ridiculous fear stand in my way. I really was a different cricketer, and while as time went on I still felt uncomfortable around Chopper I began to relate a hell of a lot better to him. I suspect this was because he was quite astonished with my turnaround and was growing a little respect for me as a cricketer, although he still took enormous sadistic pleasure from my lack of fielding ability, especially at high catching practice. Throughout my time in the Black Caps when he was manager I still had the odd 'little Richie' moments, but he seemed to tolerate them a bit better now. Perhaps he appreciated the way I was prepared to get hit by the ball from time to time.

In his last test as Black Caps' manager Chopper presented the caps to the playing eleven and delivered a little speech. In it he named his greatest New Zealand test team made up of players he had seen play cricket, players whose abilities and dedication to the 'black cap' were the greatest he'd seen. He named me as John Wright's opening partner. This was one of my finest moments in cricket because this dog had finally received the pat on the head it had been yearning for.

Losing my Auckland spot

In my early days in the Auckland team, while the 'for f**k's sakes' were coming my way from time to time and were helping to foster anxiety, I still had enough skill and confidence to bowl all right. I don't recall ever bowling with any great rhythm during my time at the bowling crease, but my action was holding together enough to get a reasonable job done. My first full season for Auckland, in 1990/91, was my best as a bowler, but cricket was changing. It was hard and for the most part the batsmen I bowled to had a level of organisation I was not used to. The 1991/92 season began badly and just got worse.

After my 10-over spell at Papatoetoe my confidence had taken a huge hit. Unfortunately, the confidence the selectors had in me had not been similarly affected. I continued to be selected, but bowling was now a harrowing experience. All I cared about was not sending down a really bad ball. Rhythm was a thing of the past and my action got jerkier and jerkier. If you're a golfer you may have experienced this feeling. You're putting or chipping and just at the point where the club should be accelerating through the shot it stops, loses momentum, and in an effort to follow through you sort of lunge at the ball. It's called 'the yips' and is a hideous illness to contract and I now had it bad. The Papatoetoe game that heralded the beginning of my fall from prominence was a low-profile encounter. However, a few short months later I would make a very high-profile statement that I was officially now 'rubbish'.

I was selected in the New Zealand Emerging Players team to play England in the opener of their 1992 tour of New Zealand and World Cup campaign. My selection was a straight case of reputation over reality. Obviously in the eyes of the selectors I was still a prospect for national honours, but if they had seen what my eyes were seeing every over I'm sure they would have run a mile. At this time I was also struggling with a rotor-cuff injury. The rotor-cuff is a small muscle in your shoulder, but it has a big influence on your throwing power. At warm-ups I mentioned to the coach of our team that I had a dodgy throw at the moment. He asked, 'Are you injured?' If I had said yes I would have been made twelfth man. It would have been so easy to admit it, but there was still this driving desire to play and a mistaken belief that with a small adjustment to my action it would all come back in one ball. I said that I was fine. I wish I hadn't.

The game was played at Seddon Park in Hamilton (now known as Trust Bank Park). In the early '90s it was a flat track, and as such, slow bowling played a big part in most games. I was the only spin bowler in our team and thus would be needed if we were to restrict a very good English batting line-up. I bowled on a turning wicket and it would have been a lot worse had our captain and wicketkeeper Ian Smith not asked the batsmen to go easy on me. I don't think this was out of genuine concern for me, rather it was more that he could sense I was approaching a complete nervous breakdown and as captain didn't want to have to deal with that. I was following half-track long hops with chest-high full tosses to the likes of Graeme Hick, Graham Gooch and Alan Lamb; but worst of all, Hamilton was the home of Matthew Hart who was at this stage a very good left-arm spinner and my main competition for the next level. I was disgracing myself in front of his home crowd and they did not hold back in letting me know it. It was really hurting. I bowled so badly that even my grandparents, who had come up from Rotorua and who would normally say 'well done' regardless of what had happened, avoided me. In the changing-rooms at the end of the game Mickey Stewart the England manager was asked to talk to me. He was trying to offer some advice and all I kept saying over and over was, 'It's just shit, all of it, it's just shit.'

In addition to my deeply humilating bowling experience there was something else that played on my mind for quite some time and which in fact I still think about. I was batting quite high in the order at seven (jeez, the selectors had an inflated opinion of me), and after two terrible displays of batting and cowardice against fast-medium bowler Chris Lewis, as I left the ground for the last time I heard Robin Smith say as he joined his team-mates in the huddle around the wickets, 'That guy should have been batting at No. 11.' Bowling long hops is bad enough, but being labelled a 'jack' is a real blow to any bloke's testosterone.

As the season progressed I lost my place in the Auckland team, the Auckland second XI, and should have been dropped from my club team but for the fact they just didn't have the heart. Meanwhile, both Mark Haslam and Matthew Hart went on to play for New Zealand.

Cricket was making me miserable. So why stick with it? I was well on my way to a Bachelor of Management Studies at Waikato University and so could have easily turned my attention towards aiming for a corporate career. This is a question I would ask myself many times over the next seven years and I would always arrive at the same answer. It wasn't really a firm answer; it was more of a feeling, a feeling deep inside that I couldn't explain but one that would not let me walk away just yet. Things had certainly gone sour and I was asking myself serious and disturbing questions about my ability, but I always felt I was only one good ball away from it all coming back.

Chapter Three

Trying like hell to find the answer

By the end of the 1991/92 season my 'yips' were at their worst. I felt like I was having some sort of recurring nightmare and yet I still felt like I could get it back and so kept running in. Only a year or so back I had been so close to being selected for New Zealand and I was not ready to let go of that dream just yet. On the advice of the two young professionals from Sussex County Cricket Club who at the time were playing for University St Heliers in their off season, I decided to travel to England to play league cricket. One of these young professionals was Andy Cornford. He was a good all-rounder who was trying to forge out a county career but never quite made it and is a fireman now. Andy's club team was Brighton & Hove, who played in the Sussex League, and he said they would welcome a left-arm spinner. So off I went, 'yips' and all, to England. I had wanted to go there a few years earlier but the then Auckland coaching director, John Bracewell, had advised me to go to university first. It was sound advice, but after two years of my studies I was facing a crisis and cricket took priority.

England 1992

I hated my first taste of life in league cricket, but surprisingly, by the end of it I was bowling better than I ever had. I stayed with Brighton and Hove club captain Ray Bieber. Biebs was a bachelor who had started from very little to become a successful money broker in London. He is a very intense fellow with some quite distinct mannerisms, but has a heart of gold and is often misunderstood by those who do not know him. He is possibly the most disliked man by opposition teams in the Sussex League, but that is only because cricket is a driving obsession for him and he plays with real intensity. Even now, in his forties, hip replacement and all, playing for the club's top team is his major priority. Biebs and I are quite different people and we must have seemed like the original 'odd couple'. We annoyed the hell out of each other. Biebs is meticulous and I was a 21-year-old student; need I say any more. But Biebs became, and will always be, a lifelong friend. Being an MCC member, Biebs was in the crowd when I scored my hundred at Lord's, which made that innings that much more special for me.

In 1992 the Sussex League was an amateur league, and the NZ$600 I had saved up was not going to go far so I needed to find a job. I found work as a breakfast waiter at the Royal Albion Hotel, which was perfect because I would finish work at 11 a.m. and, since league cricket started in the afternoon in Sussex, be free to play every game on offer. That didn't mean I liked the job though. I would get up six days a week at 5 a.m., put on a tuxedo, walk an hour down to the hotel because I was too tight to pay for the bus, and serve groups of rude French and German tourists their fried eggs and deep-fried bread. All of which I could cope with, but it was the hotel management I couldn't stand.

The waiting staff in the hospitality industry in England seems to be mainly made up of European and antipodean immigrants or students. The work is considered beneath the respect of an Englishman, pub owners aside, and we were treated like crap. It was a dreadful environment. I am not a violent man at all, but when the hotel manager manhandled me as I walked through the restaurant, off duty and without my bow tie on, it was the closest I've come to making a huge mistake. A few years back the hotel burned down and, had I still been in England at the time, I would have understood if I had been fingered as a prime suspect for arson.

If I wasn't playing cricket in the afternoons I would coach as part of the Sussex Schools' coaching programme. What would happen is I would get lumped with a whole class of about 30 primary-school kids while the teacher had a cup of tea or caught up on some marking or something. However, I was a professional cricket coach, not a bloody schoolteacher! English kids have some real behavioural problems which I think are probably due to them being cooped up inside so much. There was no middle ground. The kids from the state schools were generally totally unruly, while the private-school kids were impeccably behaved but doomed to a future of cravats, smoking jackets and MCC memberships. This was not how I'd imagined the life of a professional cricketer.

On the positive side, I was making a bit of coin and playing really well. I had got off to a shaky start, mainly through nerves, but all of a sudden got some feel with my bowling which got better and better. Which would have been fine, except there was a problem, and that was that I was bowling with an action that was nothing like my natural one.

A change of action

In my first year of school cricket I was playing in the top third-form team as a left-arm seamer. One day a visiting English professional told me I had a perfect action for spin bowling. When I relayed the information to my school coach, the former Black Cap and forever-to-the-point Ross Morgan, he responded: 'Bullshit, what would he know? Besides, left-arm spinners are a dime a dozen!' A year later Ross Morgan was the first XI coach and towards the end of the school season on a crumbly Auckland Grammar pitch he suggested I might like to try my hand at a few left-arm spinners. Oh, and that English professional, well he was a chap called Clive Radley who went on to run the MCC Young Players programme at Lord's for many years.

While my seam bowling action did convert to the slow stuff quite well I carried over with me a slight pause on my back foot as I loaded up on my front side. This pause probably stopped me from converting much momentum into speed, but it wasn't so much of a hindrance when generating turn. However, it required precise timing to get my release on the correct trajectory. Timing takes rhythm, and rhythm I now believe to be mental, but buggered if I was aware of this then. When the timing, rhythm, head and sanity went sour I buried myself in technique. I was convinced that I could find out what was wrong with my action and fix it. So began a 12-year tussle of technical trial and error that only ended when I retired. Actually, it still hasn't bloody ended because when I bowl a few overs in the odd social match I've played since pulling the pin I'm still preoccupied with technique. I know it's wrong but I just can't kick the habit. It seems to be an addiction I'm cursed with for life.

At the time I was losing my bowling, the English left-arm spinner Phil Tufnell was 'the man'. I loved his bowling action, especially the momentum he took from his bounding approach to the crease into his bowling delivery. This was the answer, I thought. If I could just get rid of this destructive pause on my back foot everything would be okay, and imitating Tufnell was the way. I studied hours of footage of his bowling. I would slow it down, analyse it frame by frame and then try to convert myself into a Tufnell clone (minus his extracurricular activity, which I just could never get close to). Over in England, and after a few weeks of bowling rubbish in games but bowling well in the nets using the Tufnell action, I decided to commit fully to this new style and give it a go in the middle. It worked and it felt great.

As far as I was concerned I was cured and I couldn't wait to get back to New Zealand to reclaim my mantle of 'most promising' cricketer. I know now that I wasn't cured at all. The 'yips' virus is a mental not a technical one. Yes, I had confidence again and I was accelerating through my action, but the drug I'd used, a change of action, wasn't an antidote at all. In retrospect it was a temporary pick-me-up which when it wore off would leave me virtually incurable.

The reason for my remission while in England was indeed mental, only I didn't recognise in what respect. It was the change of environment. All I was to Brighton & Hove Cricket Club was a young Kiwi lad who wanted to play cricket. Representative selection wasn't an issue, the club wasn't paying me, there was no expectation and I just fitted in as another guy in the team. I was just another club cricketer trying to do my bit to win games for my mates and enjoying the competition. I was in a new air space and as a consequence a new head space, but the minute the wheels touched down back in New Zealand they fell off again.

Going to Dunedin

A lot of cricketers and administrators who knew of my promise as a young bowler were under the misconception that I was given a rough deal from Auckland, but they were wrong. I got dropped because I was rubbish. It was because of this misconception that while I was in England I was approached by the Wellington and Otago Cricket Associations. A move south was on the cards and I went way south to Dunedin. To tell you the truth, the main reason I chose Dunedin over Wellington was because Dunedin had better waves. Surfing is and will always be my salvation, but you have to have a great wife to get away with that one.

Dunedin is a wonderful little city although I think the people there can be a little defensive when it comes to the rest of the country, in particular 'Auckland wankers'. I reckon it took all of about four years before the papers stopped referring to me as an Aucklander. Even when I was selling radio advertising the mere mention of my big-city upbringing could spoil the most certain of sales.

So here I was, new city, new team, and most importantly, new action, one that wasn't churning out long hops and full tosses. Change of environment worked in England so no reason it shouldn't work here, right? Wrong! Lurking around in the arrivals hall waiting for me to come home were my old buddies — reputation and expectation — and they were pretty keen to hitch a ride down to Dunedin with me. Upon arriving in Dunedin, the Otago Cricket executive director, Warren Lees, picked me up from the airport and on the way into town was telling me how they were really excited to have a left-arm spinner. Prior to me they had had Stephen Boock who played 30 tests taking 74 wickets at 34.64. Not bad, but his first-class record, of which the vast majority was played for Otago, is quite unbelievable: 164 games, 640 wickets at 22.36. That is outstanding and his contribution at the bowling crease was a massive feature in many Otago successes. He retired shortly before I arrived in the south and Otago were keen to replace him. 'Jeez-arse,' I thought, 'I haven't even dropped my bags off and I'm already getting hit with a very heavy dose of expectation.'

Come my first practice session I marked out my run, bounded in very Tufnell-like and delivered a horrible 'half-tracker'. 'Shit, that didn't feel so great,' I thought. A little red-faced, I picked the ball up, turned and walked back to my mark, trying very hard to ignore the crowd of administrators, selectors and players gathering to watch their new slow bowler in action. 'Tufnell, Tufnell, Tufnell,' I was desperately saying to myself as I ran in again and delivered a waist-high full toss. And I was gone once more.

I had been promised the first few games for Otago that year and was told I wasn't on trial, but that was no real comfort. So I played, and played poorly, until the Otago selectors had no option but to drop me. For the second half of the 1992/93 season I played a combination of second XI and first-class cricket. I could still turn the ball, and that alone gave me some success at the lower level, but at the top provincial level my lack of consistent line and length found me out time and time again. It was during this period though that I began to understand one of the reasons I wanted to succeed at cricket so badly.

Motivator 1: Fame and fortune

Jeff Wilson, a name that needs no introduction in New Zealand, was just starting out on his cricket career about the time I arrived on the scene in Dunedin. He hadn't done anything extra special at this stage, and in terms of rugby had not even played his first senior club game, but anyone you talked to about him had the same message: 'This kid is going to be a great double international.' He was a star even before he walked out onto a field and I was extremely jealous. Over the next year, a year that I was in the complete cricketing wilderness, Jeff went on to play cricket for New Zealand and then make a sensational debut for the All Blacks; and all you heard when walking down the streets of Dunedin was, 'Wilson this, Wilson that'. Every time I heard the public accolades it grated on me badly. Silly really, because I could never dream of being anything like the athlete and sportsman that Jeff is and I quite like the bloke. He's pleasant enough, annoyingly competitive to play against, but a pretty stand-up guy. So why did his success annoy me so much? Simple really: he had what I desired — fame!

My flatmate in my first year in Dunedin was Justin Paul. Justin was an up-and-coming off-spinner and had come through the youth system. He told me the story of how at a youth training camp when the young talent were asked to say why they wanted to play cricket for New Zealand, everyone said the usual things like, 'To see how far they can go' or 'To realise their potential' and 'To win games for their country', but when it was Stephen Fleming's turn he apparently stood up and quite unashamedly said, 'For fame and fortune.' If this is true I respect his honesty and celebrate the fact that he has most certainly achieved that goal. Let's face it, we'd all like a little recognition from time to time and a bit of cash to go with it wouldn't go amiss either. I'm not sure about the fortune bit, but I was definitely with Flemo on the fame part and I wanted it bad.

It's hard to say exactly why I was so desperate for public kudos, but it could be put down to a couple of things. Before I really knew who was who, my dad would point out famous cricketers to me. They were important people to him and thus these were the sort of people who seemed to take on special significance to me. Later, as I began to play and watch copious amounts of cricket, these people began to become my idols. I would see them on TV or watch them from the stands, and once I even stood outside the players' tunnel at Eden Park just to see what Greg Chappell looked like close up. The smirk on his face as he emerged (he must have just shared a joke with someone) made me think he was a smart-arse and I've never liked him since. As I began to realise I had some potential at the game it dawned on me that *I* could become one of these people and that others would regard me in the same kind of superhuman light in which I held my cricketing idols.

However, the second reason for my desire for public recognition is a bit less healthy. As a youngster and at school my identity was my cricket success. Never a social person, as I've said, I was never part of the 'in' crowd, although my cricketing prowess saved me from being regarded as a 'geek'. When I went to university though, my social awareness began to develop. I started to notice girls; well, really I started to notice whether or not girls were noticing me. It began to dawn on me that if you wanted to have any success in the breeding stakes you needed to stand out from the crowd. I was never a great physical specimen; in fact, I was decidedly middle of the road in the looks department and a little on the non-muscular side. My self-image was very much 'Mr Average'. But if you were no Brad Pitt there was another way to become popular in your early university days — drink and be silly. So I joined a club of drinking buddies called 'The Poo-Shooters'. God knows where that name came from, but we identified ourselves with T-shirts that featured an ugly-looking dog firing poo out its arse and we thought we were so cool. Our exploits seemed to give us a profile and I enjoyed being part of the club, but underneath I knew my real chance to differentiate myself from the rest of New Zealand's hormone-charged youths was to become a cricket star.

My university days were fun, however, and it's no surprise I couldn't bowl a hoop down a hill at this stage of my life as I was drunk most of the time. Having cross-credited my grades from two years' work at Waikato down to Dunedin I graduated with a Bachelor of Commerce degree majoring in Management in 1995. Quite frankly though, I have no respect for my degree at all. As far as I'm concerned, university provided a forum for having fun and learning to mature socially. Graduation meant very little to me and having a degree is something I did because I could. It was clear in my mind how the world would work for me: get a profile and use it to get a job, and cricket was to be my vehicle for that.

I know it's not the done thing to admit it, but bugger it, we all know it's true — fame is cool. These A-list celebrity types make me laugh. They say they hate the intrusiveness of the public spotlight and despise the paparazzi and yet it is the very thing they need and crave to maintain the profile they use to sustain the life they have striven to build up in the first place. As my cricket career began to flourish and my profile began to build, fame became a reward for success that I loved and needed more and more. I always read my own press and got a buzz out of any compliments I received. I loved it when people in the street congratulated me for a good performance and I welcomed the attention. Nevertheless, I've since realised that while a bit of recognition can be flattering, it does not produce happiness, nor personal contentment, and it very quickly became less of a motivational factor for me; and besides, an average New Zealand cricketer is not that big anyway. I still do enjoy the limelight when I'm in it, however, and have no doubt that that enjoyment has led me to seek out a career in commentary and the media. It was most definitely the motivating factor for those lycra-clad sprinting races I came up with.

The 'end of series sprint race' was one of my most cunning successes. They were a great profile-generator, especially seeing as they were generating profile from something I was not renowned for — agility and speed. Purely as a cricketer I was no attention-grabber. Sure, my story of bowler to batsman was well known by those who followed cricket closely, but to the general population my name really only meant that opening batsman guy who bats really slowly. My sprinting antics were something that differentiated me from the rest of the team.

Running fast is a primal, hormone-charged activity, and the ability to do it is a much-admired attribute. If you are slow you must accept the public humiliation that comes with it. As one of the slowest players around the field, I was used to taking this criticism but was prepared to fight my case, and that was that I was okay over 100 metres, it was just the short stuff that I struggled with. Seeing as my protests were generally laughed off I had one option and that was to prove it.

Aaron Barnes, the Auckland stalwart — who was an aging gentleman like myself in the 2003/04 season — was the first to be challenged. Barnes was soundly beaten in front of a small but influential group of onlookers. Richard Boock, the main cricket writer for the *New Zealand Herald*, made mention of the amateur track event in his report on the game we had just completed and Black Cap team-mate Scott Styris, a man who seemed to take endless delight in my athletic misfortune, enjoyed the event so much he felt it deserved international status. Pakistan was our next international opponent and a match-up between me and Pakistan's slowest member, Danish Kaneria, was duly organised to take place at the conclusion of the 2003 Boxing Day test. At first I thought that it was all a bit silly but the boys seemed excited about it and so were the Pakis. Actually, I suspect the Pakis may have had a few US dollars on the event, and judging by the degree of apprehension Kaneria was exhibiting at the starting line it would suggest the Pakistan Mafia had got involved as well. However, once the race was run, and won by me of course, it was very noticeable how much enjoyment the event had given everyone.

I have never really worried about people laughing at me and have actually always encouraged this sort of humour. In this case I'd taken something for which I was habitually ridiculed and turned it into a positive, simply by being able to laugh at myself. Once the media got hold of it they immediately blew it up as some kind of long-standing tradition and it came to be an expected and anticipated finale to a test series. Always keen to add to the humour, I donned a lycra sprinting suit in the brown and beige colours made famous by our 1980s One-Day International players which took the self-deprecating spectacle to a new level of infamy. There were times when I thought, 'What the hell am I doing!?' but when I saw the entertainment I was providing I quite enjoyed being the centre of attention.

When Lance and I went at it

Unfortunately, my change of province was not resurrecting my cricket career and I was growing more and more desperate as the 1992/93 season progressed. In and out of the team I would go, while all the time searching for that little technical alteration that would propel me back on the path to cricketing fame. It was this misguided belief that my problem was technical, perhaps fuelled by my short-lived improvement while in England, together with the undying drive for recognition, that would not allow me to step back. In fact, the worse I got the stronger became my resolve to sort it out. So I buried myself in my training, in particular bowling in the nets.

I was always a big trainer, but this was a bit different — this was more like a form of self-torture. I bowled in the nets as a youngster because I loved to, but this time I was bowling because I felt I had to. It became a masochistic ritual. What I was doing was not going to help me, but I just couldn't stop doing it. After disappointing Saturdays I would bowl in the nets until it grew dark; during lunch breaks I preferred to roll a few down in the middle than have lunch; and on non-cricket days I would bowl for hours by myself or with any batsman I could line up. My spinning finger was raw before even bowling one down in a match and I am surprised I didn't give myself a stress fracture during this time, but if I had I probably would have kept bowling anyway. All the time I was searching for that magical little alteration that would solve all my problems. Little did I know that all I was doing was destroying any remnants of my natural action — and helping me every step of the way was Lance Cairns.

Lance Cairns was the man who eventually put me on the road to recovery — but not before he'd helped me reach rock-bottom. I believe Lance to be a very good technical coach, but unfortunately that was not what I really needed. Lance loves cricket and loves to think about technique in depth. He has a tremendous work ethic when it comes to working with cricketers, and used in the right manner he could be very helpful to New Zealand cricket.

Lance believes everything can be whittled down to some sort of technical explanation. Essentially I agree, but I strongly believe that technique can be massively influenced by psychological factors as well. It's a bit like the chicken-and-egg conundrum. Lance was the new coach of Otago when I came to the province and he was dead set on grabbing this coaching opportunity with both hands. Lance loved to coach, and while his deafness-induced slurred speech and the rather primitive way he played his cricket misled some people as to his intelligence and thoughtful nature, he loved to analyse cricket and in me he had a perfect subject on which to work. What a challenge I was to provide for Lance over the next couple of seasons!

We worked through every possible technical solution we could. Most of it revolved around my tendency to pause on my back foot before moving onto my bowling foot. High jumps, no jumps, quickly through, slowly through my delivery stride — we tried it all. We'd get it working okay in the nets and Lance would breath a sigh of relief at a job well done, then come match day he'd be back to scratching his head and 'belching' out his bemused disappointment. While I couldn't let the search for technical perfection go, Lance was even more absorbed in the struggle and we continued to go hammer and tongs, morning and night.

One morning, following a rather late night on the town, I was woken by Lance banging on the front door of my flat. He had had an idea and at 8.30 a.m. it was time to put it into practice. So with a pounding head and queasy stomach I went down to the local park with him for a bowl. As usual, it worked. I can't remember what it was we tried now, there had been so many attempted solutions, and of course it would have all fallen to bits out in the middle.

But in 1993 Lance finally pronounced, in his boisterous, distinctive slur, 'Work on your batting, because your bowling's f**ked.' He was right. I had no natural action or ability with the ball left, but I was still not fully committed to accepting this fact. At the start of the 1993/94 season I had no choice though as I was dropped from Otago. Losing my place in a first-class team for the second time was the slap in the face that finally brought me to my senses and I took a much-needed break.

Chapter Four

Yes it's me, but not as you knew me

A few club games into the 1993/94 season I was well aware that I had no chance of being selected for the Otago team. I was bowling rubbish with a different action every second ball, but this time I was resigned to the truth. I was still at university and the end of the academic year was approaching, and as club cricket often took a break during the Christmas period I decided that would be my chance to get away and forget my cricket worries for some time.

I had a 1982 Subaru 4WD wagon, a cool car and one I loved. So I packed it with my surfboard and a $50 tent from The Warehouse and hit the road on 'surf safari'. The idea was to head up the east coast of the South Island, over the Strait to see some friends in Wellington, work my way up through Taranaki to Raglan, stop at Auckland for Christmas with my folks, then have New Year's in the far north, head back south down the east coast of the North Island before ending up back in Dunedin just before the varsity year began again and to take my time doing it. The plan went without a hitch. As far as summers go it was a novelty and a memory I will always cherish.

Most importantly, I didn't think about cricket much at all on this surf safari, apart from on one occasion. I met some friends up north and camped on Ninety Mile Beach for New Year's. We drank, ate and surfed and I was more carefree than I'd been for quite some time. However, the realisation that I wasn't quite ready to give up cricket altogether came during a game of beach cricket. I hadn't swung a bat or bowled a ball for the sheer enjoyment of it for a long time, and in that brief moment while the surf was not good or we had run out of beer I rediscovered one of the reasons I first got involved in the game: I actually derived fun from the act of playing it.

Motivator 2: Fun and enjoyment

During my 15 years of first-class cricket I sat through a lot of team and pep talks. Some good stuff would come out mixed with some bollocks but there was one thing in particular I would sneer at with total cynicism. The content of many of these speeches would often follow the lines of: 'Okay boys, get out there, play straight, look to turn the strike over by working the singles, don't let the bowlers settle, make sure one of the top three gets a hundred, show some ticker, take it on the body if you have to . . . but above all enjoy yourselves.' Enjoy yourselves, enjoy yourselves, bloody well enjoy yourselves — I'll tell you right now, I found precious little to enjoy about cricket at top level!

I remember playing for the University St Heliers Under 14s and I couldn't wait to get the ball in hand or get out to the middle. If I was batting No. 3 or 4 the guys in before me were a pain in the arse and using up my batting time. I couldn't wait for them to get out so I could have my turn. I really couldn't tell you when this all changed but I can promise you it changed, and changed dramatically.

I did enjoy how cricket made me feel following a success and I particularly enjoyed the things that came with success. I've always loved staying in hotels and having someone make my bed and cook me breakfast, and cricket has allowed me to see some interesting places around the world. I've also met some interesting people along the way and I love the camaraderie and dressing-room banter involved in a cricket team. But playing the game? No, I never enjoyed the actual act of playing cricket, well not at the senior level anyway.

As a bowler playing for Auckland and Otago I would get sweaty palms and a nauseous feeling the second the captain gave me the nod to warm up, and then later as a batsman much of my time was spent overcoming the fear of failure or physical harm, anxiety, self-doubt and the desire to go for a 'nervous one' every five minutes. These feelings are uncomfortable and not much fun, but simply had to be endured if I was to get to the enjoyable part, which was success and the benefits I derived from that. However, my summer of 1993/94 had clearly shown me that you could still enjoy life without having to be a great cricketer and also that cricket was just a game, and as such why play it if you don't enjoy it? It was a feeling that wouldn't last, but while it did it put me on a new path, a path that would ultimately lead to a great deal of satisfaction.

When I returned to Dunedin it was like I was a different cricketer. I decided I was going to play cricket for the sake of playing in a team and trying to win games for that team. I would not look beyond the team, which was the North East Valley Club, and would try to play my part, whatever that would be. I was still able to throw some spinners down that were good enough to be effective at the club level, but because I wanted to get involved in the whole game I started to take my batting a little more seriously. Cricket now was about doing the job required, not simply realising my potential as a bowler, and all of a sudden my natural cricketing gifts began to show through. It was like I was back playing kids' cricket again. I found I wanted to score runs more than take wickets, perhaps because I was a recovering 'bowlerholic' and didn't want to go back down that road, and success with the bat began to make me feel great. I would always be first to training and loved smashing all the lower-grade bowlers all over the place. In games, while there were always nerves, I relished playing good shots. Dominating with the bat made me feel great and I wanted to score more and more runs. Luckily for me, Lance Cairns was right; I did have some potential with the bat.

When the club season of 1993/94 came to an end I had been named Dunedin Club Cricketer of the Year, which I wasn't actually aware of and to tell you the truth didn't really care that much about anyway, I was just having good fun. I was fit, enjoying my sport, and most importantly, wasn't taking myself too seriously. It was about this time that I discovered that taking the piss out of myself helped with my enjoyment on the field. For example, I had a fluorescent blue batting helmet with the words 'Avoid this' stencilled on the front. I didn't really like the short stuff, but wearing my helmet seemed to make a joke of it and helped lighten the atmosphere.

At the start of this summer I had walked away from the game but now, at the end of it, I was definitely back, but in a very different way. My attitude was good and for this summer, my first foray into top-order batting, it was about *playing* cricket and competing because I simply enjoyed it. That said though, I confess that enjoyment of the act of playing is something I struggled with for most of my career. As I said earlier, I can attribute enjoyment of what success gave to me or the dislike of what failure did to me as major motivators for playing well and sticking at it. Nevertheless, in this case I can definitely say that the enjoyment I was deriving from playing in the 1993/94 season was the motivator that kick-started my batting renaissance.

1994/95 season

As the 1994/95 season rolled round I was looking forward to getting back out on the field — well as much as you can during the early season in Dunedin given the rather hypothermic conditions you are asked to play in. North East Valley was a good team and I enjoyed mixing with some of the characters we had. My resurgence as a cricket force had caught the eye of the Otago selectors, but they must have only had one eye open. I was scoring runs, yes, but because of the rubbish cricket pitches we played on and some equally poor club batting (most teams in Dunedin only really had five or so half-decent premier-grade cricketers in them) I was also getting a hell of a lot of wickets too.

Generally the major provinces will organise practice games against each other pre-first-class season to get players in form or trial new blood. Wellington came down to Dunedin for a game and I was given a shot batting up the order and I failed. It brought back all the horrible feelings I had experienced in the past but this time as a batting hopeful. I wasn't prepared to go through the same torment again, and yet I knew I had to continue once more as, whether I liked it or not, cricket had a hold on me.

A week later, two Otago teams, a first and a second team, went up to Canterbury to play their counterparts. I was in the Otago Second XI side and we were to play a Canterbury Second XI at Geraldine. I was disappointed I had blown a chance as a batsman but I was now pissed off as the selectors obviously still saw me as a bowling prospect, given they were playing me as a bowler in this game. As far as I was concerned this was a waste of my time, as I had no interest in playing trial cricket as a bowler. I was happy to bowl for my club because I wanted them to win, but Otago Second XI in a trial match?

I didn't really give a shit. We did in fact win this match, and if you could look back on your life and pick out a few moments of such consequence that they changed the direction you were heading in, this was definitely a big one for me. My game of beach cricket up north was a quiet moment that said, 'Hey, why not give cricket another go?' but this match at Geraldine was a very loud moment that said, *'Check my shit out!'*

We bowled first and I bowled my 10 overs. It went okay and I think I got no wickets for about 30, but I knew my delivery was not up to first-class level, nowhere near in fact. The Canterbury Second XI got a good total, somewhere around 240 if my memory serves me correctly, and we chased it pathetically. By the time I came in to bat at No. 8 we needed about 100 from 10 overs. With one over to go we needed 33 to win — and we got them! I managed to hit five sixes in a row and then edge the last ball through backward point for three. It was a surreal experience as I just kept running down the wicket and hitting the bowler, left-arm spinner Hamish Kember, for six. Possibly the easiest ball to hit for six was the last one; it was right in the slot, but I tried too hard to smash it out of sight, took my eyes off it and miss-hit it. I've always rued not hitting the whole over for six — but hey, I can't be too disappointed. Up the road in Timaru the First XI was getting thumped and as a consequence of my implausible last-over heroics I won a place in the Otago Shell Cup (one-day) team for the first few Shell Cup matches. It was a freakish thing, but it was good enough to earn me my first game at provincial level as a batsman.

However, things didn't go overly well at first and after three Shell Cup games I was on the scrap heap once again. This first-class cricket thing was just not working. It's funny how things happen though, sometimes they just choose you, you don't choose them. That's how I feel about my career as a batsman. It began in earnest the next game after my dumping. The playing schedule had three one-day games first up and then it went into the Shell Trophy (four-dayers) before intermixing the two competitions. I was not down to play the first Shell Trophy game. I know this due to circumstantial evidence as my boarding pass for the plane ride and my hotel room both featured the name 'James Allan'. James was a hard-working top-order batsman, and lucky for me, an academic. University graduation clashed with the cricket schedule and James obviously considered his graduation to be a higher priority than playing first-class cricket — thank God for that, I say! So at the eleventh hour I got the call-up. Batting at No. 5 for Otago versus Central Districts at McLean Park in Napier I scored my first century at any level. It was the first time I experienced that magnificent feeling of relief mixed with elation that you achieve when you get to a hundred and I definitely wanted more of it. Most importantly, it paid the lease when it came to Otago selection for a while. I really shouldn't have got the opportunity but now I was back in business.

Back in business all right and probably reborn. All of a sudden I was back in a first-class team, but this time my bowling didn't really matter, as I was a batsman. All the nerves and apprehension was still there, but for some reason I could handle them a lot better and that was exciting for me. My success against Central Districts gave me a little confidence and that transferred over into the one-dayers as well. Lance even gave me a crack at opening in the one-dayers for a while, but my best success came in the middle order where I was playing quite well late in our turn at bat.

As the 1994/95 season progressed I began to establish myself more and more as a batsman, but it wasn't until late in the season that I did something that really made people sit up and take notice. The sixes at Geraldine were certainly interesting, my first ever hundred was definitely encouraging, but a century against the West Indies was simply astounding.

Otago cricket knew some time out that they would be given a first-class game against the touring West Indies. Those games are fantastic for provincial cricketers, especially the grinders who will never go on to higher honours. They benefit everyone. Obviously the tourists get reasonable practice too, and up-and-coming local players get the chance to push for national inclusion while your run-of-the-mill provincial player gets an opportunity to measure themself against a test team. There has been a tendency for New Zealand Cricket to take these games away from the major provinces and give them to 'A' selections, but the newly formed New Zealand Cricket Players Association (NZCPA) has fought hard for these games to return to the provincial teams, and I think fair enough. Why should the young hotties get all the chances to shine and get the extra match fees while first-class stalwarts get no reward for their toil? In fact, some of these players are still on the improve in their late twenties.

Anyway, the Windies were coming to Dunedin and I became more and more excited about it as I became more and more firmly cemented in the Otago middle order.

Of course, I was quite petrified of fast bowling at this stage, but the chance of facing the West Indies quickies was an experience that had a masochistic appeal. I had been visualising myself facing up to the likes of Curtly Ambrose and Courtney Walsh and seeing myself getting peppered, but also imagining myself taking it on the chest and helmet and coming back for more. I was also excited about playing against the great Brian Lara. Lara was the new 'king' of batsmen. He had the highest test individual score of 375 against England and had recently smashed 501 not out for the English county side of Warwickshire to break the first-class record as well. Man, was I excited!

The day of the match finally dawned and we were as prepared as we were going to get. The night before, Lance Cairns had got some psychiatrist lady to come in and give us some techniques for coping with fear. Good old Lance, always thinking. My fear was put on hold for a day and two sessions after the Windies won the toss and batted. Unfortunately, during their turn at bat my enthusiasm for Brian Lara took a little turn for the worse after he let down a lot of people who had come especially to see him bat. He played himself at No. 8, scratched around for a while and then missed a straight ball. Rumour has it he had been up all night shagging some student, which was a popular activity for many touring sports stars while in the university town of Dunedin. I was enjoying my cricket during these early days of my batting career and one thing I especially enjoyed was a bit of on-field banter. Well, I bit off a little more than I could chew when it came to having a crack at the great man.

Lara had participated in a charity match in Australia before coming on to New Zealand. In this match he managed to get out to Australian women's star Zoe Goss. I decided to remind him of the fact that he had got out to a woman. He was facing up to the Otago all-rounder Chris Finch who probably bowled about 100 kph — a woman's pace (sorry girls, but you're just not that quick). So I yelled out, 'Come on Zoe!' to Finchy. Harmless really and quite humorous if you ask me, but oh what a mistake! I've since come to realise that the one thing more important to a West Indian cricketer than runs or wickets is his bravado.

Later on, I came out to bat about 15 minutes before the end of the second day's play with the fall of our fourth wicket, and what happened next was totally unexpected and chilled me to the core. Brian Lara went out of his way to greet me as I arrived at the crease, walking up to me and calling me every name under the sun with most names beginning with a word that rhymes with 'ducken' and ending with one that rhymes with 'punt'. After he had finished telling me what type of person I was he then told me his fast bowlers were going to kill me. 'Charming little man!' I thought to myself as, with hands and legs shaking, I ducked and weaved my way through a couple of overs to be eight not out overnight.

That night I couldn't sleep. One of my cricketing idols had it in for me and it had me shaken. I played computer games at the local amusement arcade till closing, drove around a bit and I think finally got a few hours' kip at about 3 a.m. Upon waking I got a feeling that I can't explain — I've had it a couple of times in my career, the last time being my first test match at Lord's — but it is a feeling of total surety in something that hasn't yet happened. I won't try to analyse it now, I'll have a crack later on in the book, but for now let's just say that from the moment I woke up I knew that this day would be one that would be career defining.

I got out in the last over before lunch for 103. My hundred came off 115 balls and it was one of the most fluent and aggressive innings I've ever played. I was helped by the fact that the lethal West Indies pairing of Walsh and Ambrose were rested and Lara could only really call on Kenny Benjamin as the man most likely to 'kill me', and did that poor bastard get bowled into the ground. I think it also helped that Lara's continual name-calling between overs helped keep my mind off things between balls and also his game plan of 'knock the smart-arse honky's head off' played into my back-foot strengths as I cut my way to glory. At lunch I then talked my way to infamy.

Obviously I was fizzing at the break; it was without doubt the highlight of my career so far. Somehow the media had got wind of my little tiff with Lara and what better time to ambush me than while still in a euphoric state. I told the whole story, the truth and nothing but the truth, and boy did it gain some attention. Lara came out smelling of roses given that I had technically started it. But sure, he overreacted and turned it all nastier than it needed to be.

The lesson it taught me was that I should be very careful with what I take off the field and think twice before taking on the 'big fish'. I've always struggled with the 'big fish', however. I guess I just don't like arrogance.

Naturally enough, when I struck Kenny Benjamin for four to bring up my century against the West Indies it not only shocked me, but all of a sudden it forced the New Zealand cricketing fraternity to start to believe what they really didn't want to — I was now no mean batsman. That was great but also unfortunate, as the New Zealand selectors were far too hasty in believing I was an accomplished batsman as well.

I had scored two hundreds and a few fifties in the season and because of that I was selected to play in the New Zealand Emerging Players team that took on South Africa and Sri Lanka. While everyone wants their chance at the big time and I was thrilled to be included in this team, I really had no idea what I was doing. I was just walking to the crease and belting runs off bowlers who couldn't quite believe I was there and who were more bent on knocking my head off than getting me out. I just hooked and cut my way to runs with a lot of misses in-between. But this was the early to mid '90s, and to put it bluntly, the New Zealand Cricket Team was a shambles. It was a time when just about every opening bowler from every province was given a crack and anyone who made a hundred or whacked a few runs was looked at. So I was looked at along with the rest.

In the first game against South Africa we played at Nelson on a wicket that was a little fresh to say the least. It wasn't long before I was staring down Alan Donald, the great South African quickie, who was near his peak in terms of pace. It was the first of only two occasions on which I confronted bowling that was just too fast for me, the second being against Shoaib Akhtar in Pakistan. It was embarrassing as I was either hit or stood on the crease and played and missed. I was not out at lunch on not many and simply sat in the dressing-room dreading the thought of going back out to bat. I knew I had to do it. I also knew it was going to hurt, but at least it wouldn't last for long — and it didn't, in either innings.

Our group of 'emerging' players breathed a sigh of relief as we packed our bags, fortunate that with no broken bones we still could, and headed for the relative safety of the Sri Lankan attack. We knew they had no one who even remotely resembled Alan 'White Lightning' Donald, and by god, that was a comforting thought. We all planned on making our mark in a safer environment, but that didn't quite happen. While Donald had made me look out of my depth, Muttiah Muralitharan simple made me look an idiot. I always thought it was a stroke of genius for New Zealand Cricket to put their young up-and-coming batsmen on a fresh green pitch against a quality seam attack with one of the world's fastest bowlers, and then follow that up by banging them onto a known 'turner' at Palmerston North, against a team with no nasties other than a very threatening spin attack. Over the three days of the game against Sri Lanka, Murali made us all look like fools. There was one exception, however, and that was Nathan Astle whose well-thought-out 80 launched his international career.

I made 8 and 18 and in the process managed to play and miss at a whole over from Murali and in the second innings fell flat on my face as I was bowled round my legs by the great off-spinner. I picked myself up, dusted myself off — and there was a lot of dust on this pitch (well done, New Zealand Cricket) — and trudged off to howls of laughter from the Sri Lankan players. The internal tour didn't go well, but what was worse was that I had started to develop a dodgy reputation with New Zealand Cricket.

Our coach for these games was the then New Zealand selector, Bevan Congdon. I believed Congo to be a dead ringer of Hugh Hefner — in appearance anyway. I don't think his personality would be quite as flamboyant as Hef's though, and he most definitely didn't encourage flamboyance in your approach to cricket. I don't think I particularly endeared myself to Congo. Firstly, I was prepared to refute his outrageous assessments of the standard of cricket and cricketers in 'his day' and secondly, I then turned a blind eye to his attempts to help my batting.

After our first innings against the Sri Lankans in which Murali had bamboozled us, Congo called all the batsmen to his room to develop a batting plan to help us deal with the Sri Lankan spin bowlers. Batting plan! Who the hell needs a batting plan? So I just didn't bother turning up. Apparently, during this meeting Michael Parlane, the Northern Districts and later Wellington batsman, stated that he simply had no idea how to deal with the spin so he would go out first and slog at the opening bowlers, get as many as he could early on and then get out to the spinners — and he effected his plan perfectly.

So the 1994/95 season ended on a bit of a low point, but really, who was I to complain? At the beginning of it I was being trialled as a spin bowler and by the end I was being looked at as a batsman for national honours, and all because of one over of madness at Geraldine. Hamish Kember, I wouldn't have a clue where and what you are doing now, but thanks for lobbing them up that day, mate!

1995/96 season

It was a great feeling to be a certainty for the 1995/96 season. The previous season announced my emergence as a batsman, but 1995/96 well and truly consolidated it. In first-class games I scored 615 runs at 68.33 which included three centuries. It was enough to see me named as one of the *New Zealand Cricket Almanack*'s promising players. Myself, Paul Wiseman and Chris Nevin were the three chosen for that year. Even though I hadn't endeared myself overly much to New Zealand Cricket at the end of the previous season, my performances this season were startling enough to gain another run in an Emerging Players team and this time it was a tour of Australia. I'd racked up five first-class centuries now and New Zealand selection was in my sights. I'm glad it didn't come though, as looking back I really had no idea what I was doing. My batting processes were poor but I thought I was 'shit hot'.

Our coach for the Australian tour, in which we would play selections from Queensland, South Australia, ACT and NSW, was Mike Shrimpton. During our first practice session in the nets at 'the Gabba' cricket ground in Brisbane I was struggling a little and Shrimpo came down to talk to me. 'Great!' I thought, 'a bit of help.' I guess what Shrimpo said was 'help' but not the kind I wanted to hear. Shrimpo suggested that I didn't have a technique to succeed over here. Apparently I played too square too early, never got my weight forward, and didn't get in behind the ball. Well, what else do you expect from someone who's petrified of the quicks and has made runs in New Zealand because the quicks were dumb and just tried to hit him! I would stand on leg stump and cut, slash and back-foot drive my way to runs. Predictably, my response to Shrimpo was, 'So what! It's the way I play.'

That tour started on a low point and sunk lower and lower as it progressed. I wasn't having any fun and that was playing on my mind because I thought back to my summer of surfing and believed I needed to be having fun to perform. Unfortunately, the only place I could find to have fun while on this tour was off the field and in the pubs. As far as New Zealand Cricket was concerned my game was as disorganised off the field as it was on and I reckon my end-of-tour report was probably about as helpful to my future career prospects as an execution notice.

Higher honours were most definitely out of the question for now, but I was well and truly cemented in the Otago team and that made me satisfied, at least for the time being.

Chapter Five

So you think you know me now?

University was over now and on the completion of the 1995/96 season I faced my first real challenge to my new way of life as an Otago cricketer. Cricket and uni had mixed quite nicely. By first going to Waikato University I had been able to continue playing cricket in Auckland, as things were going okay there at the time. After losing my bowling I found myself in Dunedin, entirely due to the desire to regain my bowling (and because of the surf!) and, as Otago University was there, I thought I may as well finish my degree at the same time. Cricket paid a little money and I could also take out a student loan, so it was school in the winter and cricket in the summer.

After I graduated in 1995 with a Bachelor of Commerce degree I decided to take the opportunity to go back to Brighton and have another season in England. I didn't really have anything to do over the winter and I figured I might as well go back and catch up with Ray Bieber and the boys. I could get a good coaching job at the Sussex County Cricket Club doing individual coaching and helping to run kids' tournaments. Once again Biebs put me up in his house, so the odd couple were reunited, and with free board I was able to earn some tidy money to boot.

Second time round, this felt much more like being a professional cricketer.

With a reputation as a solid first-class player I got to play in some good-quality cricket matches, even getting a run-out against the touring West Indies — needless to say, I tried to avoid eye contact with Brian Lara. I'm no mug though, and while I've always wanted to be a fully professional cricketer and was enjoying my English summer this time, I began to realise that cricket at first-class level in New Zealand was not by itself going to make me enough to retire on. Thus going back to England again in the winter of 1996 was out of the question as I had already spent a fair bit on my education so I decided I needed to look beyond the cricket field.

I needed a job, but I also needed help in getting that job. You see, if you want to get work but also want to play first-class cricket you face a dilemma. While cricket is only played half the year round, for that half of the year it is a near full-time commitment. Four-day games are just that — four days — and throw in travel days either side and then a 10-game one-day schedule with travel and practice days either side of each one of those and during the summer your employer is not going to see much of you. Sure, you can play cricket in the summer and get a part-time job over the winter which should earn you enough to survive on — but savings? Yeah, right!

Even nowadays, with higher match fees and a contract scheme, the best first-class players who are on provincial contracts can still only expect to make enough to get by. As you get older the cost of playing cricket solely at the first-class level gets greater and greater. It is a lucky player who can find an employer prepared to give them work in a meaningful occupation with career prospects and see very little of them for half the year.

This is an area where the New Zealand Cricket Players Association can make a real difference in the years to come, but the NZCPA didn't exist in 1996 and I needed work. I hadn't spent a lot of money on a degree to do unskilled, part-time work, but how the hell was I going to find something that could lead into a long-term career but still keep playing cricket? Help needed to come from my own cricket association as they had contacts and could find employers sympathetic to my needs.

Warren Lees was the executive director of Otago Cricket and had always been helpful in giving me some work to do for the cricket association, but I got the feeling my needs were well and truly in the 'too hard basket'. This was the first time I flexed my cricketing muscle, as I wrote letters to a number of the other major cricket associations saying that if they could find me meaningful employment I would shift to their province. I then let this slip out to Otago. Two people came to my assistance. They were the guys who commentated on games held in Otago. Garth Gallaway was a lawyer and son of the great Ian Gallaway, and Steve Davies still commentates down in Dunedin. Work came in the form of radio sales for a Dunedin station called 93Rox. It was the start of a period in my life that taught me who I really was.

Motivator 3: Achievement

The sales manager at 93Rox employed me because he thought that given I was an Otago sportsman I must be an achiever and thus should be able to adapt to sales quite well. I had a good shot at getting my life on the financial up and up so was keen to achieve at this sales game too. Very quickly I realised what the job was all about and just as quickly I realised what type of achiever I was. I was rubbish at the sales game, but in my defence though, 93Rox was a station with a young and small listening share that was operating in a very competitive market. That said, I should still have been able to make a reasonable go of it, but to tell you the truth I saw no value in the effort required. I got sick of talking struggling retailers into pathetically small and ineffective advertising campaigns or taking crap from sad people who liked the fact they were in a position to be obnoxious to you.

The reality was that the chances of really making a go of this radio sales game were quite low and the company knew it. They knew they could get a little value out of you, probably would never have to pay you a commission above your base retainer, and then just get another sucker once you gave up the ghost. It was a dreadful time for me, I hated it and I reckon it was almost turning me into an alcoholic. I longed for the cricket season to come round so I could get the hell out of there. When it did I promptly walked.

But my six months with 93Rox taught me more than the fact that I was a crap salesman; it also taught me that I was prepared to work hard and strive to achieve in something that I could see a definite future in — or at least a tangible result worthy of the effort. I didn't see this in selling radio space, but in cricket I could still see the personal benefits of reaching the top. Selling an advertisement gave me very little self-respect, but scoring runs for Otago made me feel important and successful.

Looking back, I realise that I never really worked as hard as I could have at either school or university. I knew a degree would be handy and did have some value so I would put the hard yards in when required, but I never really desired to get the very best results — just enough to get the job done would do. However, from a very young age everything had been about cricket. My daydreaming was about cricket: I could see and hear the crowd roaring, I could feel the sense of achievement, I would revel in imaginary adulation and at times these dreams were strong enough to choke me up a little. If I hadn't taken that ghastly job I don't think I would have come to the realisation that I was one thing above all others, and that was a cricketer.

The minute I walked out the front door of the Radio Otago building I gained the clarity and direction in my life I needed. I had unfinished business on the cricket field and I was going to get the job done. I was lucky in that Sky TV had come to the party with its coverage of cricket, and players' match fees had received a well-needed shot in the arm. I knew I would get some reasonable money in the pocket over the summer, but I was still aware of the cost of choosing cricket at the provincial level over the development of a more lasting occupation. I was 25 years old going into the 1996/97 season and I decided that I had till I was 28 to make the New Zealand team or get a real job. So I sat down and drew up some goals.

It was my first experience with this sort of thing. I thought about where my game needed to improve and what changes I needed to make. I then wrote them down on a big bit of cardboard and pinned it to the wall above my bed. Not a great look if you managed to get any girls back to your room, but it meant I saw my goals every time I went to or got up from bed. Most of the things I put on this chart were outcome goals in terms of runs I wanted to score and changes required to my technique, but the big thing was that I had till the age of 28 to achieve them — which was three years. I was on the road towards completing that unfinished business.

I will define the difference between 'outcomes' and 'processes' later on, but for now I'll just explain that I believe 'outcome goals' to be important for motivation. They are things like 'I want to score three hundreds this season' or 'I will straighten my front foot out when playing forward'. My goals were headed with the desire to reach New Zealand selection by the end of the 1999/2000 season. I had a list of run-scoring achievements that I believed I needed to attain to gain selection and then beneath that a list of technical improvements I felt I needed to make. They were good goals in that they were challenging but achievable, and in achieving each little step on the road my motivation was maintained. The problem was that they were outcomes and thus did not outline what I really needed to do on a daily, game or season basis. Nevertheless, in looking at the chart daily it kept my desire burning.

1996/97 season

The 1996/97 season was an indifferent one. In the first-class games I had a challenging season, only managing 423 runs at 28.2 with no hundreds. I did reach 98 not out at Invercargill, but blew my chance of a century when I ran out my last three partners. The last chap to go was David Sewell who I called through for two and who was run out trying to complete the first. The season was a little like 'second-year syndrome' but happened in my third year. I think bowlers had realised that I could in fact bat a bit and that I thrived on the cut shot so they tended to hit the right line and length more often. All of a sudden I had to work hard for starts and learn to leave more regularly. I also think that because I now had a few goals and I was focusing on results more than fun I felt my anxiety a little more. However, it was heartening to know that even in a tough year I could still compete and contribute.

In the one-dayers I actually had a great season: 442 runs at 55.25 with two consecutive hundreds. It also indicated to me that I was beginning to understand my game a little more. I had had a poor start to the Shell Cup, batting in the middle order, but I believed that my game might be better suited to the top of the order. I tended to hang around on leg stump and give myself room to slash, cut and back-foot drive. Due to this trait I reckoned that I could be effective in hitting the hard white ball through the off side, so campaigned hard for the role. I finally got it and the results were instant.

It was during this season that I began going for my pilot licence. As a kid I'd had a fascination with planes and always wanted to learn to fly, but thought you needed to win Lotto to afford it. For a change though I had a few bucks

My first cricket team. I'm at the far right of the front row … perhaps an early sign that I was headed to the top of the batting order.

Demanding a wicket on my first-class debut, against India. Also appealing are Adam Parore (behind the stumps) and Ken Rutherford (left).

I'm on the left in the blue gear, but really I always wanted to be in the beige ...

I eventually did wear the beige ... but not as I'd expected.

The traditional 'end of series' 100 m sprint race . . .

. . . became the 110 m hurdles.

The Dream teams

The '80s:

BRUCE EDGAR Tests: 39, 1958 runs @ 30.59, 100s: 3
Had every shot in the book and exercised his right not to play them. Retired too soon and with numbers beside his name that don't truly reflect his value.

JOHN WRIGHT Tests: 82, 5334 runs @ 37.83, 100s: 12
Within the space of a test could be capable of playing the most dashing, then dull, innings. A gem who spent most of his time in the field collecting grass stains.

JOHN REID Tests: 19, 1296 runs @ 46.29, 100s: 6
Loved the spinners, but when the quicks came on was happier pursuing his teaching career. Like borer, once in, difficult to remove.

MARTIN CROWE Tests: 77, 5444 runs @ 45.37, 100s: 17, 14 wickets @ 48.29
Statistics tell only half the story of what it was like watching him in full flow. His 188 at Brisbane (1985) was the best televised innings played by a New Zealander. Almost convinced kids it was cool to play straight.

JEFF CROWE Tests: 39, 1601 runs @ 26.25, 100s: 3
Only after he retired did he show he could bat like Martin when freed from the shackles of the middle-order-stooge role. Apparently told good stories at first slip.

JEREMY CONEY (C) Tests: 52, 2668 runs @ 37.59, 100s: 3, 27 wickets @ 35.78
Perfected the rarely spotted leaping back-foot defence. The Windies hated bowling to him, which is a badge of honour. Great hands, decent captain, strangely effective bowler, self-styled raconteur.

RICHARD HADLEE Tests: 86, 3124 runs @ 27.17, 100s: 2, 431 wickets @ 22.30
The greatest. Very good on flat pitches and unplayable on pitches with a bit of grass. Realised late in his career that batting was easy too.

JOHN BRACEWELL Tests: 41, 1001 runs @ 20.43, 100s: 1, 102 wickets @ 35.81
Pugnacity personified. Could turn it on glass, but went for a few runs as well. Team-mates not always appreciative of his "motivational" lectures. Amazing transition to a temperate coach.

Today:

MARK RICHARDSON Tests: 26, 2024 runs @ 49.37, 100s: 3, 1 wicket @ 17
Untapped reserves of stamina and concentration. Doesn't always make for pretty viewing, but Fleming wouldn't swap him for anybody at the moment (except, maybe, Matt Hayden).

LOU VINCENT Tests: 13, 738 runs @ 33.55, 100s: 2
Great bookends to his brief career. Not a lot of reading in between though. Brilliant fieldsman all around the wicket.

STEPHEN FLEMING Tests: 77, 4710 runs @ 37.98, 100s: 5
Will soon become New Zealand's highest scorer in tests. Great to watch when he hits down the ground and is over his extended delightful-50-then-out phase. Fantastic slipper, very good skipper.

100s: 2, Dismissals: 176 (8 stumpings)
Brittle early on, became New Zealand's finest keeper and a fearsome batsman when on song. Only player in history who could late cut a ball from outside leg stump.

LANCE CAIRNS Tests: 43, 928 runs @ 16.28, 130 wickets @ 32.92
The myth sometimes over-rode the person. Was primary a bowler who chimed in with some handy wickets with huge in-swingers. Inspired a generation of schoolkids to slog over midwicket.

EWEN CHATFIELD Tests: 43 180 runs @ 8.57, 123 wickets @ 32.18
Unlikely hero, but hero nonetheless. Nathan Astle scored more test runs in a few hours than Chatfield did in 10 years of test cricket. A foil for Hadlee into the wind.

NATHAN ASTLE Tests: 59, 3592 runs @ 39.04, 100s: 9, 36 wickets @ 47.53
One of the few batsman in world cricket who is stronger on or outside off stump than off his legs. As long as knee holds out, will pass Wright's century count. Great hands, under-used bowler.

CRAIG McMILLAN Tests: 46, 2856 runs @ 42.63, 100s: 6, 27 wickets @ 44.26
All the talent in the world, but his brain got in the way for a couple of years. Now back to doing what he does best: watch the ball and hit it. Fast bowler's mentality in a short leg's body.

CHRIS CAIRNS Tests: 55, 2853 runs @ 32.57, 100s: 4, 197 wickets @ 28.81
If he knew then what he does now, he would be modern day Sobers. No exaggeration. Can hit the ball further than Tiger Woods and is a brilliant outfielder.

DANIEL VETTORI Tests: 48, 1048 runs @ 18.07, 147 wickets @ 35
When New Zealand plays near a desert he is treated like a camel, with all the work dumped on him. Will take 300 wickets if he gets to stop at the odd oasis. Has torn up the coaching manual when it comes to batting.

ROB HART Tests: 9, 231 runs @ 19.25, Dismissals: 21 (1 stumping)
Gutsy batsman, sound 'keeper and about 10 years older than he looks. Won't let the side down.

DARYL TUFFEY Tests: 16, 163 runs @ 10.19, 55 wickets @ 27.15
Come into his own of late. Looks like he bowls well within himself and when he realises he truly belongs in test cricket, could be lethal.

SHANE BOND Tests: 10, 53 runs @ 10.60, 43 wickets @ 24.30
Has there been more column inches devoted to a 10-test cricketer. Potentially our second greatest bowler ever – can the body match the mind's desire?

SUNDAY STAR-TIMES BEST COMBINED XI: John Wright, Mark Richardson, Stephen Fleming (c), Martin Crowe, Nathan Astle, Jeremy Coney, Chris Cairns, Richard Hadlee, Ian Smith, Daniel Vettori, Shane Bond.

It was my favourite time. The *Sunday Star-Times* compares our team with our idols of the 1980s. We were being 'Better Than Before' and it was great. Top right corner is the BTB card I carried with me. It shows our ideal (BTB), our poem for after test wins, and my inspiration — John Wright.

Umpire wrecks Lord's dream

Left: The *Christchurch Press* headline and my expression say it all . . .

Above: . . . one innings later, though, I achieved my dream and had my name on the Lord's honours board.

The addictive feeling of scoring a century and my enjoyment of talking cricket with Stephen Fleming kept me coming back for more . . .

. . . but the self-loathing at getting out, coupled with my lack of fielding ability eventually turned me away.

in the back pocket and a bit of time on hand so I thought why not go for it. While selling advertising I had been introduced to Mainland Air which was a small charter and training organisation operating out of Dunedin Airport. I hadn't been able to sell for shit but I was the king of contra, and by the end of my six months at 93Rox there were two planes with the station's logo flying in the ski over Dunedin. By summer's end I also had my Private Pilot Licence (PPL).

I enjoyed flying and found it challenging but also saw a worthwhile future in it. If I couldn't be a cricketer I'd be quite happy being a pilot. As a kid I thought pilots were cool so could perceive the self-esteem benefits in becoming one myself. The great thing about going for my Commercial Pilot Licence (CPL) was it fitting in as nicely with cricket as had my years of academic study. I was just going to need a bit of cash to do it.

However, at the end of the 1996/97 season I was unemployed again. I had saved some cricket money and sold my car, but with living costs and the plan to fly planes for a living I needed to find an income. I wasn't overly concerned about finding work with a future because cricket or flying were my future, so I just needed to finance that goal. I still kept hammering away at Otago Cricket to help out with finding a good job, but also registered with an employment agency who found me temping work while I searched.

My two main temping jobs were running along behind the rubbish truck and working in the Greggs coffee factory. I quite enjoyed being a 'dustman'. It was hard yakka but good for the fitness — great for the fitness actually — although very tough on an icy Dunedin morning. I didn't have a car so would get up at 5 a.m., have breakfast and walk an hour in the cold and dark down to the depot. The factory job was a bit less enjoyable as my main responsibilities were packing boxes or taking the underweight and overweight coffee sachets that the machine rejected, cutting them open and pouring them into a big drum. I would come home stinking of coffee with nostrils full of the stuff. Perhaps this is the reason I'm so addicted to it now. Most importantly, what these two jobs once again reinforced to me was that I was prepared to knuckle down in the pursuit of something I really wanted. I really wanted to fly and these jobs kept the dream alive. As an aside, I also developed a genuine respect for a few of the guys I worked with in the coffee factory. You often got people well into their forties, who had been made redundant from good-paying jobs but who were prepared to pack coffee to keep the food on the table — I see nothing but honour and no shame in that.

I was just making ends meet myself and was feeling the pinch a little. I was worried that I would run out of funds for the flying and that too much was riding on continuing to perform on the cricket field. Then I got a job that would prove to be hugely significant in allowing me to attain the coveted Black Cap selection.

The Dunedin City Council was placing some emphasis on its economic development strategies. Times were a little challenging in the southern city and it appeared to be good politics to be seen to be trying to aid local business. So the council invested in a new economic development tool called Businesslink. It was a scheme whereby local bodies would play their part in a national web of databases aiming to find local suppliers for local business, or if not, to use each other to source suppliers from around the country for their listed businesses. I was the Businesslink Otago coordinator. It was an interesting position and I got to learn about business in general and the things that help stimulate economic growth; but most importantly, if I wasn't there all the time, the thing wouldn't fall to bits. My bosses were more than happy to let me have as much time off in the summer as I liked. In fact, it was more like having a sponsor than an employer. Unexpectedly, I had a job that was relatively meaningful, looked good on the CV, let me play cricket, and was paying enough to allow me to pursue my goals. I was even able to buy a house. I was perfectly positioned.

1997/98 season

The 1997/98 season was steady. In the Shell Cup I continued to show promise as a one-day opener, scoring 369 runs at 36.9 with a century, and in the first-class games 494 runs at 38 with one century. That century, which was 162 not out against Central Districts at Carisbrook, was significant in that it was my first time opening the batting in first-class matches. We were struggling with our top order so made a change. I put my hand up and got the job. I got a duck in the first innings, but it was a duck that identified another one of the things that motivates me — proving others wrong.

Motivator 4: Proving Others Wrong

The century I scored in the Shell Cup game during this season was against Central Districts, and following that innings I made the comment in the media that I always got runs against Central. A short while later, Otago played Central Districts in a Shell Trophy game. In the first innings of this game I got bowled for a duck, so it was rather predictable perhaps when Lance Hamilton, one of the Central District's bowlers, came across to me as I trudged off the ground and said, 'Ha, ha, I see you always get runs against Central Districts!' Then in the dressing room Matthew Horne told me I got bowled because I didn't get in behind the ball — he was politely telling me I was a coward.

My response to both of these guys was to think, 'F**k you! I'll show you.' I managed 162 not out in the second innings and carried us to victory in chasing 317 to win. All I thought about that whole innings was getting in behind the ball. It was an innings I would draw from for many years to come. The motivation to prove others wrong in that game would become a big motivator for the future.

Like myself, I believe there have been a lot of sportspeople who have been motivated to prove others wrong over the years. When somebody says 'You can't' or 'You won't' it has an immediate effect on me. Perhaps it's natural competitiveness or simply that I don't like not being able to do something I would like to. But I'm not silly in this regard — I'd love to be able to run fast but know I can't, no matter how much work I put into it. So when Scott Styris says, 'You'll never beat me over a hundred', I can handle it; however, if I think I might just have the capacity to do something and someone says 'You'll never', by God it sets me to work!

For instance, I was teased when I was younger for being so skinny and having no muscles, and in response I've followed a weights programme with regularity. I can't say it's done much good but I've stuck at it. Then my physics teacher said I wouldn't become a professional cricketer but I showed him. And the 'fish-heads' at Cornwall Cricket Club told me I was a crap bowler in 1988 and wouldn't play me in the top team so I left the club and a year later played for Auckland. Simon Doull said I would never play for New Zealand as a batsman alone to which I politely agreed with him at the time, that yes I needed the bowling as a second string, but underneath I thought, 'We'll see' — and we did. Maybe the problem with regard to my bowling was that after I lost it no one ever said I couldn't get it back. Everyone had advice and encouragement instead.

I've even used this type of 'reverse' motivation on myself from time to time. Some people may have seen me as a negative person because of it, but usually I would be expressing my doubt as a way of motivating myself. If I was struggling with something I would often talk to coaches and team-mates in terms of 'I can't' or 'I'm crap at' and then go and get my arse into gear anyway. Maybe a lot of this can be put down to my aversion to 'expectation' but we'll deal with that particular bastard later.

Conference Cricket series

The start of the 1997/98 season was punctuated with the inaugural Conference Cricket series. It was an initiative to find a level of cricket between New Zealand first-class and international cricket and also provide extra games and extra match fees for first-class players in New Zealand. The six major associations were reduced to three teams which were Northern, Central and Southern, with Bangladesh invited to participate. Obviously, being an Otago player I was in the Southern team.

My performance was steady in the series, with a couple of fifties and solid contributions in all games. This series was an important one for me as memories of my failures for the Emerging Players teams in the recent past were playing on my mind. I was a lot more serious about moving forward with my batting now, was beginning to understand my game, and wanted to perform at the next level — which in this case was Conference Cricket. I played well and then backed it up with a solid season for Otago.

However, if I wanted to know where I was with New Zealand Cricket I found out with a jolt at the start of the following season.

1998/99 season

Pakistan 'A' was included in the 1998/99 Conference series and I did not get selected in a team. It was a kick in the pants and I must admit I was upset. Sure, I wasn't doing myself many favours with New Zealand Cricket, but I was still one of the better-performing first-class batsmen over the last three years. I was upset but I was pissed off too. However, I had a good job at the council to get absorbed in and decided to 'show the bastards' come the normal provincial season.

As luck would have it though, Chris Cairns was struggling with a back injury and I was placed on standby. As I waited to hear whether or not I would be going to play in the first game for Southern against Central I liked what I was feeling. I really wanted to play cricket. It was another chance and I really wanted it. I got the game and scored 40 in my only innings. It was also during this game that I realised I needed more than just a few runs to get back in the New Zealand Cricket scene and this was the start of my politicking.

I was pissed off that other players who were lesser performers than me were getting places in the Northern and Central teams. The Central team was rife with bits-and-pieces cricketers as New Zealand Cricket was desperate to find a batting all-rounder to play at No. 6 in the test team. I can understand why I may have missed out in the original Southern team as the make-up was heavily dominated by Canterbury players from the days when the New Zealand side was also dominated by Canterbury. It seemed unjust that I might miss out on being in this series because the South was so rich in cricketers and it was wrong that the country's best performers were not all involved.

So I pushed my case with passion and made sure after a good first game that I was transferred to the Northern team. From this point on I don't think I ever shut up again when it came to putting forward my merits. Having talked my way into the remainder of the series I can't say I had a blinder but I went okay.

This series coincided with a proactive period in New Zealand Cricket's history. It had come through a torrid time with trouble between players and management, poor performances and an even worse culture, but things seemed to be on the up and up. Chief executive Chris Doig seemed to be doing some good things, especially in generating money; new coach Steve Rixon was hitting all the right chords with the team; and there appeared to be a progressive management forming.

I was hearing a lot about all these new initiatives and protocols from Paul Wiseman, the Otago off-spinner who was beginning to make more regular appearances in the Black Caps set-up. I liked what I was hearing and was desperate to be involved, but knew I had a reputation I needed to break and that it would take a hell of a lot of runs and actions to demonstrate that I had the makings of an international player and was serious about proving it.

There was a New Zealand 'A' side selected from the series, but I didn't make it. I wasn't overly surprised or disappointed, and although my performances may have given me an outside shot I was just happy to have got in the faces of the selectors once again.

I finished off the 1998/99 season having scored 391 runs at 48.87 in the Shell Cup and 468 runs at 33.42 in the Shell Trophy, including another first-class century. It was another solid year, nothing startling, but solid. However, it was during this year that I found a very important ally in the media. Richard Boock, who is now the country's premier cricket writer, was beginning to make a name for himself. He had come through the ranks with the *Otago Daily Times* and was obviously full of ambition. I reckon every journo at some time in their career wants to test the power of their own press and he knew I was simmering away down south and not getting much recognition at the national level so began to push my case in his writing. Over the next two years Boocky's persuasive prose would increase the capital of my run-scoring no end.

1999/2000 season

The New Zealand team was in India at the start of the 1999/2000 year, which of course would weaken the Conference teams, so it was decided to cut the three New Zealand teams down to two — North Island and South Island. The overseas team was the strongest yet by way of England 'A'. I was a little concerned about my chances of selection in the Southern team, especially given what had happened a year earlier, but I was rewarded appropriately for my solid previous season. Another of those career-defining moments was to come during this series.

It seemed that every year there would be some statistic or other that the New Zealand Cricket management and selectors would get all wound up over. This year it was ratios of first-class hundreds to innings played. This time the powers that be had got their feathers all ruffled up over the poor ratio of hundreds scored per games by New Zealand first-class players. Ashley Ross had been appointed by NZC a year or so earlier to a 'technical advisory' role, and as a result these types of statistical investigations have become commonplace from that day till the present.

Anyway, the 'fish-heads' had got all worked up over these apparent poor results, which I thought were easily explained by the fact we only seldom played on surfaces that you could truly 'get in' on. Nevertheless, before the first games of the series everyone was given a stern lecture on how they were expected to score hundreds. So I went out and got one.

It was bullshit really because everyone wants to get a hundred, most times, if not every time, they go out to bat. I got 108 in the second innings of the game between the South Island and the North Island at Hagley Park in Christchurch. It was an important innings because it directly followed the unnecessary lecture from the selectors and gave them what they had asked for. Things could have gone so differently though, because I top-edged a hook shot when only on 11 which presented a very easy catching opportunity for North Island wicketkeeper Chris Nevin. Somehow he dropped the catch. If he had taken it, as he should have, I would have only scored 6 and 11 and very much doubt I would have received the opportunities that followed.

At the conclusion of the two-match Conference series, one against the North Island and the other against England 'A' in which I scored 27 and 45, there was a New Zealand 'A' team selected to play a series against England 'A'. Myself and our opening bowler Warren Wisneski had been two of the more consistent performers during the series, but it was rumoured that we wouldn't be selected in the 'A' team as we were too old and not a good investment for the future. Hell, I had only just turned 28, and yes this was going to be my last year of cricket; Warren was about the same age, maybe a year older. From a cricketing performance point of view we were both still very much young enough as far as I was concerned.

It has always pissed me off how selectors are continually looking to the future and overlooking mature cricketers at their prime (that philosophy has changed a little these days and thank God for that). You can easily select a guy at the peak of his powers at the age of 30 and expect three to four good years out of him. Meanwhile a young pretender has the extra time to mature and become consistent. I'm a believer that if you pick the best team for the present, the future will look after itself, so long as the level below is strong enough, as the current team sets an appropriate benchmark for others to aspire to. Anyway, in spite of the rumour-mongering, Warren and I both got selected for the 'A' team thanks to our South Island coach, Denis Aberhart, who pushed our case. We then went on to become the most consistent performers in that series as well.

A key turning point — getting to the top

Going into the 'A' series against England 'A' I figured I had three games in which to make my mark. There were two first-class games and three one-day games against England 'A' and a three-day game against the touring West Indies. I was beginning to become more recognised for my longer game and thus believed I would not play in the one-day side.

Thinking back to the Emerging teams that played Sri Lanka, South Africa and the tour of Australia, I promised myself that I would not blow this chance to showcase my wares. This is the series that I look back on and pinpoint where things began to happen for me — and they needed to, because if they didn't I was gone for good.

In the first game at Lincoln I scored 74 and 67 not out followed up by 17 against the West Indies at Taupo and then 30 and 43 in two low-scoring innings in the final first-class game at the Basin Reserve. It wasn't fantastic but it wasn't the disaster of previous years and it was the most runs from any of our batsmen. So that was okay, but there were three very important things that happened during this series that were significant in my development.

Firstly, I had my first real exposure to Ashley Ross. A large part of Ash's time appeared to be spent analysing the game and its techniques. He didn't have a playing pedigree of any real note, but could be described as an academic of the game. He was assigned to coach the 'A' Team, and while I found his approaches to discipline and man-management a little over the top I was extremely interested in some of the training methods and batting principles he presented. A few of his theories on such things as defence and execution of shots, training and accountability I found value in exploring further — they gave me some focus and definite things to work on.

Secondly, and most extraordinarily, I was made captain. I had had my problems with New Zealand Cricket — or more accurately perhaps, my image with New Zealand Cricket — and was trying hard to turn this around, but to be seen as a captain was a quite unexpected turnaround. I must admit, I'm not overly fussed with captaincy — I have enough trouble trying to organise myself out in the middle let alone worry about anyone else. But I was awarded the task for the second first-class game and then for the one-dayers. I lost them all, which wasn't really surprising — most of the time I was just trying to keep everyone happy. I also reckon that it is difficult to make your own mark on things in this type of 'one-off' cricket where the team is brought together for only one or two matches.

However, the circumstances which lead to my being picked as captain also lead to what proved to be the most significant of these three things — being asked to consider filling a possible hole at the top of the batting order. The incumbent opening batsmen for the Black Caps at this time were Matthew Horne and Gary Stead. Gary was captain of our side in this 'A' series but hopelessly out of sorts. Yet for the sake of consistency and continuity the selectors decided to stick with him for the upcoming test series against the West Indies. Taking Gary out of our team so he could join the Black Caps in training camp meant that we would have a hole at the top of the order.

I was having breakfast during the West Indies game with our manager Ross Dykes, who was also a New Zealand selector, when he asked me if I would be interested in becoming an opening batsman. Obviously New Zealand Cricket wasn't happy with who was currently out there at provincial level and was considering manufacturing one. I thought back to the 162 I had made a couple of seasons back when I opened for Otago and immediately put up my hand, saying that I'd love to have a more consolidated crack at the role. It was the truth, because I always quite liked the idea of being an opening batsman. As it turned out, they decided that Gary would remain with us and open in the upcoming game as a means of trying to regain some form, but that they would take the captaincy off him so he could concentrate solely on his batting. So I stayed in the No. 5 position for the time being — as it turned out, for too bloody long actually!

The important thing though was that the selectors had given me a definite indication that they were interested in me — but not as a middle-order player. Fair enough, as the current middle order read something like Fleming, Astle, McMillan and Cairns, all of whom were playing well. It excited me on two fronts as all of a sudden I had renewed hope and an incentive to continue playing, but also because I had wanted to become an opening batsman for quite some time.

Turns for the worse?

At the completion of the 'A' series I was returning to play for Otago and was excited about the prospect of opening the batting and pushing on to national selection, but then I hit a huge hurdle in the form of Glenn Turner. Now, I believe Turns to be a fantastic cricket technician and judge of a batsman. But I also consider him to be extremely headstrong. If Turns has made up his mind, hell will freeze over before anybody can convince him otherwise. And he had made up his mind over where I would be batting for Otago and it certainly wasn't in the opening slot.

It seemed that Turns didn't really like my style of batting as it had developed over the previous few years. It was getting slower and more patient and now that I knew which side my bread was buttered on with New Zealand Cricket it was headed in an even slower and more patient direction. Turns was in favour of a more aggressive approach and had had me removed from the opening spot in the one-day games because he felt I was too slow. Fair enough, as he wanted an all-out assault in the first 15 overs, a strategy that was not suited to my style which was to occupy the crease and bat out the overs looking to be 90–100 not out at the end. My view was that when consistent scores of 230 would get you through to finals in New Zealand it was important to have an 'anchor man'. Turns disagreed and so I perished.

It frustrated me as I was back in a one-day role in the middle order which I was very uncomfortable with. At the end of the day that didn't overly matter — what really mattered was getting to the top of the order in the first-class games and Turns had made it very clear that that wasn't going to happen.

So I sat in my office space at the council and worried. I was worried that Turns' assessment was going to cost me a shot at the big time. I was still determined to be true to my plan of packing it all in at the end of the year if I hadn't broken into the Black Caps. It was frustrating because I knew how close I was — yet if I couldn't get to the opening spot I might as well be a mile away. Then I thought back to the Conference series when I replaced Chris Cairns for Southern and then talked my way into the Northern team and it hit me what to do. 'Get on the phone, Rig,' I thought to myself, 'get on the phone and start talking!'

So I rang up Ross Dykes and explained the situation to him. I knew they were picking an 'A' team to tour England over the winter and I also knew that to have any chance to break through I had to get on that tour. I told Ross that I wouldn't be opening for Otago that summer but wanted to; that I was still extremely keen on the role and would like to be considered for the 'A' tour of England as an opener. It was a good opening move, but I still needed a few other things to fall my way and thankfully they did.

The domestic season began and it was business as usual. There was one change made to the Black Caps for the Boxing Day test against the West Indies. Matthew Horne had been injured in the first test and thus a gap opened up for a top-order player. Matthew 'Skippy' Sinclair who had been playing pretty well in the No. 3 position for the 'A' Team got the call-up. There had been speculation that I might get the nod, but it did make sense to give the spot to Skippy. Craig Spearman had been batting at No. 3 but could move up to opening as he was accustomed to that role, which meant Skippy could come in and bat in his usual position — 214 runs from his first-up effort would suggest that on this occasion the selectors got it right. It was a special innings and those sorts of heroics give everyone a buzz, although I must admit I found it tough to watch as I saw my own dream being taking from me with every run Skippy belted.

When he regained fitness, Horne would take his place back in the team and I believed Spearman to be a superior player to myself. Skippy, well it seemed he was there for life and so all gaps in the Black Caps' line-up were well and truly filled. Needless to say, I wasn't overly confident at this point of the Richardson name appearing on scorecards for very much longer. Then the Aussies arrived.

It's fair to say that Australia played a strong hand in ending my career, but I have no doubt they also had a good hand in creating it. The combined quality of Brett Lee and Glen McGrath destroyed our top order and sparked off the Radio Sport witch-hunt to find replacement new openers. Myself and Gary Stead appeared to be the people's favourite, but you can imagine my frustration when presenter Brendon Telfer commented I wasn't doing myself any favours by not opening for Otago. I wanted the job desperately, but my hands were tied. Talk about feeling helpless.

But there was hope in the form of an 'A' tour, as an opener, and a Black Caps tour of Africa at winter's end. The press and public were both on my side.

I had a job to do that summer and it was simply to score no matter what spot I was doing it from: 299 runs at 37.37 in the Shell Cup and then 638 first-class runs at 42.53 was a job well and rather timely done. At the end of the season I was off to England with the 'A' Team and the dream was alive again.

England 2000

The 'A' tour to the UK had a high interest factor for New Zealand Cricket. The Black Caps had the winter off before a four-month tour of Africa. There were tour spots up for grabs and the 'A' tour would provide a perfect vehicle for the selection team to assess the merits of the next crop of hopefuls. It was to be an extensive tour that would include games against Holland, county teams, Zimbabwe and the West Indies who would be touring while we were over there. I was relieved to be in the squad and when I looked at the make-up of the team I realised that I was also a little lucky. As far as I was concerned it was full of kids, not a genuine 'A' team. It was more a development team with myself and off-spinner Glen Salzberger the only two grizzly old buggers. A young-looking team that included greying old me at 29 years hammered home the reason I was there — it was a trial in the opening role and I had this chance and this chance alone to make or break my international career. The challenge was daunting but exciting at the same time.

To underline even further the critical importance of this tour the management would be that of the current Black Caps — David Trist as coach and Jeff 'Chopper' Crowe as manager. Tristy had decided that before the tour left New Zealand shores he would get round and interview all the participants. He wanted to stress its importance and get a preliminary idea of the characters he would be developing and assessing. When I met with Tristy I went through what I had been doing over the last couple of years and I think it would be fair to say that it put a glimmer in his eye.

David Trist: My last interview for the 2000 NZ 'A' Team's tour of England was in the coffee shop at the Southern Cross Hotel in Dunedin with Mark Richardson. It turned out to be both stimulating and rewarding. After exchanging pleasantries, Mark drew out a folder which contained data on his progress over the last two years, and how it was being used in his quest to be the best he could be. I will allow Mark to elaborate on this process but I remember thinking, 'This guy is just what we want: thoughtful, clinical and focused. All he needs to do is concentrate on opening the batting in all the four-day games to be played in England, score plenty of runs, and a Black Cap will be his. The rest is history. Without a doubt the greatest contributor to Mark's progress to this point was Mark himself.

He achieved everything he set out to and it could all be put down to hard work, discipline and single-mindedness. Old-fashioned traits not seen as much as coaches would like in the modern-day cricketer.

There were three elements on the 'A' tour that I feel were beneficial to my success. Firstly, there was Tristy. Tristy is a man who oozes personality, and while some might see him as a little eccentric I prefer the word 'enthusiastic'. He was widely travelled and his tales of places visited and people met were quite captivating, but it was his passion for cricket that really captured my imagination. He used terms like 'arousal' and 'efficiency' when describing the game and he had a way of seeing things in players that were not immediately apparent to the naked eye. Most importantly, his views on how the game should be played were in line with the conclusions I had arrived at over the last year or so. He also left you in no doubt of where you stood and what he expected from you. I learnt this after we arrived in London early in the tour.

We had played two one-day games in Amsterdam prior to the tour proper in England and in both I had batted in the lower order. I was a bit worried about why Tristy had played me so low down, especially since I had had success opening the one-day batting for Otago before Turns had me removed. So I approached him in the lobby of our London hotel and asked straight out, 'Why did I bat in the lower order in the last game when I have the best provincial one-day record of anyone here?' To his credit, Tristy answered back so directly it left me in no doubt whatsoever about why I was there.

He said, 'I don't give a shit about your past record, I only care about your future record for the Black Caps and it sure as hell won't be a one-day record. You don't have the skills we want for ODIs and you won't play another one-day game on this tour, but you *will* open the batting in all the first-class games.' With that he left to entertain his dinner companions while I walked off with real focus.

Secondly, there was Martin Crowe. He was on this tour to help with the batting coaching and he was outstanding. I've always enjoyed Martin's coaching when I've been able to get it. As well as being New Zealand's most outstanding batsman with tremendous natural skills, he also appears to have a real passion for the game and it shows in his coaching style. Most of the time his advice is very simple. He is a massive advocate of having a dominant head position, which for the most part means forward and still, and of looking to play straight. He also has an ability to read an individual player's game and coach accordingly.

When I went to Martin for advice his enthusiasm would rub off on me and I would leave wanting to go out and bat, which was a very rare phenomenon in my career indeed. He really worked hard on that tour and gave me a ton of throw-downs. I thoroughly enjoyed our quite competitive sessions in the nets on the mornings of games and believe he really helped with my psychological wellbeing on the tour.

The third major contributor to my successful tour was the Black Cap protocols. In the mid '90s, by all accounts the national team was running amuck. There were all sorts of misdemeanours being reported and the team's public image was one of 'designer-stubbled party boys'. To sort it out, former All Black and Auckland Boys Grammar headmaster John Graham was appointed as manager. He introduced a number of protocols designed to instil some discipline and team ethics into the unruly mob. Curfews, physical appearance and dressing-room rules were put in place and did the trick in uniting and redirecting the team.

The management on our tour decided that the same protocols would apply to us as well and I liked it. I felt part of a larger Black Caps environment and I think I responded to it quite well. Of course, I was a little older than the others and theoretically less likely to stray from the correct path, and I found that watching some of the younger members of the touring party who were trying to buck the system, opened my eyes up to some of my own past mistakes. Call me a nerd — and I don't mind admitting that I was placed into a tour clique called the 'arse-lickers' — but I loved the very controlled environment and felt it gave me excellent focus and direction.

True to Tristy's word, I did open in all the first-class games and went bloody well. I started off with scores of 47 and 57 not out against Lancashire and then

39 and 74 against the West Indies, but it was my innings against Sussex at Hove that was without doubt the highlight — and the critical one for Black Caps selection.

A basic rule for selection: If you are going to make a score, pick the game that the chairman of selectors and the CEO of the team you are aiming for turn up to watch.

Which was precisely what I did when I scored 212 not out. It was the third longest innings played by a New Zealander and the longest outside of test cricket. But what really sticks in my mind is what I had said to Martin Crowe a couple of days beforehand. After the game against the West Indies, Martin asked me what goals I had. I told him that I didn't really have any specific run-scoring goals, just goals for the way I wanted to play. 'You really should have some outcome goals because they help keep you motivated,' he said. 'OK,' I replied, 'in that case I want to score a double hundred — I've scored hundreds but never gone on to the double.' And I went and did it, in the very next innings.

I remember going back to my hotel room when I was 100 not out overnight, dropping my bag, looking in the mirror and yelling out, 'Yes!!!'

While I was keen to add to the score the next day, I knew how important the innings already was to achieving my Black Caps goal. I went on to accumulate 642 runs at 71.33 on the trial tour and left nobody in any doubt about where I would be playing next — Zimbabwe.

Chapter Six

I've done it — finally!

Getting selected for the Black Caps' tour of Zimbabwe and South Africa was in the end a bit of an anticlimax. National selection was what I'd worked for all my cricketing life and it had finally come. I'd visualised the moment many, many times and the euphoria that it would bring, but sitting there on the boundary at The Parks ground at Oxford in England it was a very matter-of-fact occasion. The news that chairman of selectors Sir Richard Hadlee brought to me that day came as no surprise because I had simply demanded it.

While it was a very satisfying moment because I had aimed for it and achieved it, what was most important to me was that I had *earned* it. Most sportspeople say they never forget the moment they heard of their selection to the national team and I agree, but I particularly remember mine for the words spoken to me by Sir Richard and my reply.

Sir Richard asked me to join him in a stroll around the boundary. A stroll around the boundary is coach and selectors' speak for, 'Come into my office.' I knew exactly what the subject of the conversation would be and I remember thinking, 'This is it.' It was 'it' but it was the way 'it' was put to me that still amuses the cynic in me to this day.

'As you know Rig, we are very concerned about our opening partnership in tests at the moment,' Sir Richard began. 'Craig Spearman just isn't scoring enough runs and while Matthew Horne has a few test hundreds he gets too many low scores in between times. We want an opener who is going to score runs *all the time*. We took you on this tour to see how you would go as an opening batsman and you've gone well. Can you do the job for us? We want consistency.'

My reply just came out, 'Yeah, I can do that.'

It was probably the first and only time I ever made an unrealistically optimistic estimation of my abilities. I remember walking away with a wry smile on my face and thinking, 'Shit, I can't score them *all* the time, cricket just doesn't work like that; and I think Matthew Horne is going okay actually.' A simple 'You're in!' was all I really wanted to hear. Nevertheless, as it turned out, in my 38-game test-match career consistency was to prove what I was most appreciated for — well, that and a bit of stupidity from time to time. Fancy that!

Prepared, willing and able — to graft!

I believe wholeheartedly that when I was selected for New Zealand I was peaking as a batsman technically, tactically and mentally. I had a good balance between attack and defence, but more importantly, mentally I was ready for it. I say 'ready for it' because I'd been around long enough and played enough cricket to have a sound understanding of where I was as a player and an appreciation of the challenges that lay ahead. While the thought of walking out to bat against the world's best bowlers and being under the microscope of media and public attention while I represented my country was daunting, I wasn't at all overawed by it. I would have been had it happened three seasons earlier but not now. I knew I had earned the right, appreciated it would be a real struggle given my defensive-style game, and was absolutely determined to ensure that when I walked out to the crease for New Zealand I would be prepared for the difficult graft I would face in each and every innings.

In some respects I must admit I actually felt a bit cheated that my first bat in a test would likely be against Zimbabwe. I say likely because I still had to perform in warm-up games to ensure a test spot. Even though Zimbabwe was a lot stronger back in 2000, they were mainly a batting side and their bowling was only really a first-class attack. Heath Streak was a good bowler and Paul Strang the leg-spinner was every bit test quality when he had his rhythm, but there was little class in the rest. Your first test is a milestone to remember and I always envisioned mine would involve taking on the Australians or some other cricketing superpower. I'd wanted it to be cricket at its best, not a low-key affair against an average attack in Bulawayo.

On arriving in Zimbabwe, while it was rumoured in the press that I had the inside running for one of the openers' spots I still had to score runs in the warm-up encounters. Like I said, you always imagine your first game for your country taking place on a major ground like Eden Park, Lord's or the SCG but mine was on a little ground barely worthy of a club venue in New Zealand, with a concrete toilet block for changing-rooms, a raging bushfire crackling away on one side of the boundary and Mozambique on the other, in a place called Mutare. It was a nondescript match in which I scored 47 in the second innings, but the most memorable feature was the bushfire which at one stage seemed quite out of control.

The next warm-up game was quite the opposite though. It was another one of those moments in life where a twist of fate pays amazing dividends. I was keen to prove to the players around me that I had something to offer. I'd never really scored many runs in front of the Black Caps incumbents and I really wanted their approval. But I almost didn't get the chance to earn it because by rights I should have been run out without even facing a ball. Matthew Horne hit the ball to mid-off and called me through for a single then sent me back but not before I was stranded mid-pitch. I will never know why the fielder didn't just pick the ball up and sprint to the wickets and run me out by yards, but for some unfathomable reason he threw the ball at the stumps from about three metres and missed. I had given up the ghost, but upon the throw missing I went on to play the longest ever innings by a New Zealander in scoring 306.

A few people have asked me since how I managed to keep focused for so long and I tell them in all honesty that it was because I wanted to bat with all the guys I admired so badly. I had tremendous respect for the Black Caps batting line-up. I had watched and adulated them from afar for so long, but I finally had the chance to bat alongside them and I was loving the experience.

I would be partnering Stephen Fleming and my whole thinking was that if I could outlast him then I could bat with Nathan Astle, Craig McMillan and Chris Cairns. It was quite a thrill. This was the privilege that went with my test cap.

Aside from the fact that my test debut was against a minnow it was a very disappointing experience from a performance perspective. I let myself down mentally and that was the most disappointing part. I was in great form and the Zimbabwe attack held no real terrors on a very flat Bulawayo pitch. The only real threat would come from within and I regret to say that I let that bastard win. In the first innings I lost control in hitting a long hop straight to point and in the second ran out of patience and tried to pull a ball that wasn't there to hit when on 14.

Patience and control were the twin cornerstones of my success to date and so my first test effort made me extremely irate with myself. For some reason though, that made the second test a little easier. I simply wasn't going to let myself down like that again and my focus at Harare was exceptional. I was out in the last over of the day having batted 89 overs for 99. One run short of a maiden test century in only my second test and you would expect me to be devastated, but in truth I had to work hard to keep a straight face that evening. Sure I missed the magical three figures, but I had won the battle within and that pleased me no end. It also meant I had booked a place in the side for what I considered my first real test: South Africa.

Confronting Allan Donald and Shaun Pollock felt a lot more like test cricket than taking on Heath Streak and Mluleki Nkala. It was daunting but it was the yardstick I knew I needed. The first test was in Bloemfontein and we lost, but in the second innings I scored 77. It was a patient and controlled knock and one of the true highlights of my career. It was a highlight both because it signalled to me that I could have success at this level and also because it kick-started possibly the healthiest form of motivation one could have and the one that for the most part drove my test career from then on — BTB (Better Than Before).

Motivator 5: BTB (Better Than Before)

I was now playing cricket at the highest level, I had achieved my lifelong ambition, and now I wanted to see just how good I could get. BTB was an ideology of the Black Caps and one which I bought into 100 per cent. This motivation allowed me to achieve some important goals and even surpass my own expectations.

I've said from the start that I would work hard for something which held value for me. Applying my game, batting with control and patience, and scoring runs against world-class bowling held real value for me. I guess I was getting some enjoyment out of the game, but it only came when I took off my pads, sweaty and exhausted after having batted for a good length of time. It was hard work and nervous work, but doing my stuff well gave me a terrific sense of self-worth and achievement.

Although I believe I was at my best as a batsman in 2000, my drive to improve my effectiveness at the top level allowed me to maintain my consistency for the next three years. The ethos of 'never-ending improvement' is an ideology required to not only get better but maintain form. My strong belief is that once you cease trying to improve you very quickly begin to slide backwards.

At this stage I didn't really have any confirmed outcome goals apart from scoring a test century. However, there were little milestones that came along as a result of maintaining my consistency. They weren't targets as such, but when they came along they were like little pats on the back from myself. For example, I was first equal to a thousand test runs by a New Zealander and then first to 2000 and that sort of made me feel as if maybe I was a reasonable sort of player.

When I played at the Bert Sutcliffe Oval at the New Zealand Cricket Academy I would walk around the pavilion looking at the records of previously successful New Zealand players. These were my idols and to be on the path to a similar record as these past greats gave me a huge sense of achievement. I haven't been back to the Academy since retiring, but I can tell you that if my record is now on the wall I will really feel as if I achieved something special in playing my part in the history of New Zealand Cricket.

I also remember the moment I learned that I had broken into the top 10 test batsmen in the world according to the official rankings. Early on in my test career I had earned a ranking in the mid-teens and had thought that was quite cool. At the time, I remember thinking how great it would be to break into the top 10 one day but didn't think of it too much again as, let's face it, I was a very limited opening batsman. But when it came over the radio as I was driving back from Raglan after a morning's surfing that I had made the top 10 I punched the steering wheel and yelled out 'Yes!!!'

The world rankings try to put some objectivity into a very subjective process of rating teams and players, but they have become quite recognised and accepted now and it was wonderful to earn the placing. In all honesty I didn't expect to stay in the list for long, but in fact did for a while and even moved up as high as No. 6 in December 2003. I was rated above Adam Gilchrist and Sachin Tendulkar at one stage and that still makes me smile. I wonder if the ranking administrators reassessed the scoring system after seeing that . . .

These were all outcomes that gave me a kick but the bottom line is that they were essentially side-effects of a desire to get better and better — better technically, better mentally — and Better Than Before.

More BTB, than before

From November 2001 to the end of 2003 this motivation to be BTB grew even stronger. Once I had been tried out in one-day cricket and failed miserably I was free afterwards to concentrate and specialise my efforts into becoming as controlled and tight as I could in my test game. I was providing the Black Caps with much-needed consistency in the opening role and was determined to maintain the record I had established thus far.

My life was getting BTB as well. I was back playing my provincial cricket in Auckland, which was most satisfying given that I had been dropped from Auckland 10 years earlier and was now returning on my own terms. In fact, I scored a hundred for Auckland soon after moving there, and it was on my old club ground at University St Heliers against my old province Otago. It was one of the most emotionally enjoyable events of my life.

I met my wife around this time too. She was my flatmate and very quickly became my girlfriend. Mary was a flight attendant and that was perfect. We understood and could handle the time we spent apart and we both understood that the reality of a life staying in hotels was not all about holidaying. My cricket was going well, I loved returning home to Mary, and I felt that my life was finally going in the right direction. The Black Caps were becoming collectively BTB too, and I loved the team dynamic at the time. Denis Aberhart was coach at this time. As coach, 'Abo' was more like a father to the guys than a harsh dictator.

He was good at assessing the wellbeing of players and derived outward pleasure from the success of his charges; he was always good to talk with and to express your feelings to as well. However, the real direction of the team was coming from Stephen Fleming. His role as captain seemed to stretch way beyond placing the fields and ringing the bowling changes; he was moulding the team into one that was doing better and better things and it was great to be a part of it.

We had a good team and had real balance to our side. Shane Bond gave our bowling attack some real bite for a change and the team was operating as an effective unit. New selections were rarer than they had been for a while and those who came in, like Scott Styris, made an immediate impact. We were making history, doing things that the teams that had gone before us had not, and were now being compared with the victorious side of the 1980s. Those guys were our idols, they were the players who we were in awe of as little kids and now we were being viewed as their equals. It was truly a good time and also one of the few times in which I felt there was something greater to this game than just my personal performance.

Like I said, Stephen Fleming was becoming BTB, and it was Flemo I was feeding off. It was like he had his band of merry men — we were touring the world getting stronger and stronger as a unit and he was leading from the front. It was his most successful period as a cricketer. His average was going up and he was shaking off the stupid monkey the press had put on his back over not converting 50s to 100s.

At first I was a little in awe of Flemo, but after I became established in the team his position as captain became less intimidating and his desire to talk cricket theory was a lure I found very hard to resist. I hated getting out and was a very poor watcher, but if I had to sit and watch others bat it might as well be Flemo. He's a very attractive shot maker, but it wasn't his style I appreciated — it was his ability to back up his words with actions. The ability to formulate a plan and carry it out with precision is true batsmanship, and as far as I'm concerned Flemo's a true batsman. I could never time the ball or play through the covers like he could, but that didn't concern me greatly. What I did want to emulate was his ability to formulate a game plan and stick to it. I hated making mistakes and playing shots I hadn't trained or prepared for, and as such I admired the control he had over his game.

Actually, batting with Flemo was the best though — he helped me through a number of times when I thought I might do something silly and would often talk to me quite authoritatively mid-pitch to ensure I kept on task. We put on a record 172-run partnership together against Sri Lanka at Colombo and it was Flemo who ensured I didn't get out cheaply. He was on his way to 274, which says a lot anyway, but it was the way he played Sri Lanka's only real bowling threat of freakish off-spinner Muttiah Muralitharan that was a true inspiration.

Murali came on early as always on the grassless, spinner-friendly Sri Lankan pitches and I had a plan for him. I was going to play with the bat out in front of the pad, hitting the ball before it could really turn too much. I played and missed at the first five balls, the Sri Lankans were all jabbering away with amusement and I was panicking. With sheer luck I survived his first over and went to see Flemo in mid-pitch. 'What the hell are you doing?' he said. 'I thought I knew, but I don't,' I answered him. He then practically ordered me to change my plan immediately and kick the pad at everything that wasn't a straight ball. The theory was that the ball was turning so much that if you were hit in the pads by one of Murali's normal off-spinners or 'doosra'-type deliveries the umpires couldn't give you out LBW because they just couldn't be sure the ball would have hit the stumps. 'Look, watch me,' instructed Flemo.

In the next over he got himself down to Murali's end and proceeded to back up his words with a very 'educated' front pad. It was a technique I had never trained for and was uncomfortable with, but it was the only way to go on this day. We batted for hours, kicking and thrusting the pads at more balls than we played. If I got it a bit wrong all it took was a questioning look from my captain at the other end and I'd be quickly back on task. I was eventually out to the second new ball for 85 and Flemo went on to make headlines with 274, but for me it was an innings I'll always treasure for its partnership value and the way I planned something on the spot and carried it out — it was a genuine BTB experience.

Captain Flemo

My most enjoyable period as a Black Cap also coincided with that of Stephen Fleming's most influential tenure of the captaincy. It began in Perth in 2002. Flemo was one of the four guys to score a century in helping us build a massive first innings total of 534, but it was what he was doing with his field settings and bowlers that was really being noticed.

In Australia we began to get very precise in the way we planned for the opposition. No stone was left unturned and game plans for certain bowlers were established, but it was where the whole team could operate as one against a particular batsman that we were achieving better than anticipated success. We had plans for each batsman that covered an initial assault and then modified to different methods of attack if Plan A didn't work. The skill of the Australians meant we had to work hard at it, but then in the final test of the series a lot of the plans came to fruition and we were only robbed of a win by some poor umpiring. It may have wound up in a draw, but that test match was our catalyst for success over the next year or so.

Planning for the opposition became very formalised after that and Flemo led the way with the strategy. The one crucial part of the system was that Flemo had trust in the plans and trust in his team to carry them out. It meant we showed patience, application and belief. While my part of the puzzle was very small — go out and blunt the attack, hold an end up and set the middle order up to whack the older ball and tiring bowlers around — I could appreciate my role in the bigger picture. I developed the media nickname of 'The Rock' and I felt that I was achieving personally as well as helping the team achieve.

However, this golden period of test-match success ended when Flemo lost belief in his men. Perhaps he never really said it but I believed you could see it. We lost some key men to injury, Shane Bond being possibly the biggest loss, and some others lost a little form. The wobbles first appeared in the form of batting collapses in the second innings of test matches. We lost a test against Pakistan at Wellington seemingly from a situation where we were comfortably placed for a win. The 2004 series against South Africa in New Zealand was a well-fought one, but we floundered a little in the last and deciding test and lost; and England was frustrating as hell for all concerned, not the least Flemo.

Memories of the previous tour in 1999, when the Black Caps won the series, were strong enough to provoke real emotion in our captain and there was a massive desire to back that success up with another victory. We had Bond back and were being touted as the finest cricket team to leave the shores of New Zealand. But we lost Bond again to a stress fracture, Dan Vettori was struggling for form, and so was key bowler Daryl Tuffey. In the end, we went down three-zip in the series. Three losses from three tests doesn't really tell the story. In all three tests we batted well in the first innings and got ourselves into winning positions. However, the English batsmen matched us and with plenty of time left in the game we crumbled in our second innings.

The next tour was of Bangladesh and Australia. Bangladesh was pretty much a waste of time except for allowing Dan Vettori the volume of overs he required to regain his best; and in Australia we got thumped.

The batting was copping a lot of the blame for the poor showing in the second innings of games, but I feel that the bowling had to shoulder a lot of the responsibility as well. We posted good totals in the first innings of many games that you simply should not lose from. For one, it should take the opposition too long to draw parity to place you back under pressure and thus if you can't take all 20 wickets you still won't lose. However, without Bond we had lost our spearhead and were not operating as a bowling unit. We were essentially trying to bowl sides out with three third seamers and a spinner — a world-class spinner sure, but one who needed to be part of a bowling unit. So we could not get the 20 wickets needed to win test matches.

There had been some warning signs a little earlier in Sri Lanka and India, where we had massive first innings totals but were simply unable to bowl the opposition out. The main problem, however, was that we were haemorrhaging runs. Our bowlers were being pasted and not just by the opposition's top-order batsmen. Our first innings totals were being reined in far too quickly with far too much time left in the game, meaning we found ourselves under pressure. There was a time when 300 in the first innings was a score you didn't lose from, but now we were scoring 450 and still losing! Cricket is a game about momentum and when you go to the middle with the opposition having gained the momentum, even if you are still in a position of strength, the game can take on a very different aspect indeed. We were still planning meticulously, but the trust and belief in the plans had evaporated. As a result, we were developing a slight batter/bowler split as the batsmen were throwing blame the bowlers' way and the bowlers were critical of the batting performance in the second innings.

In Australia I saw Flemo's shoulders slump. You could see he must have felt that it didn't matter what he planned, his bowlers couldn't effect it for him, and he became quite introverted. His contribution to meetings became less and less enthusiastic and the situation was quickly turning into an 'every man for himself' scenario.

The change in management structure and coaching regime probably didn't help matters either, as the power had been removed somewhat from Flemo to new coach John Bracewell. Braces is an enthusiastic coach, a good coach, and to his credit he turned the flagging fortunes of the Black Caps' ODI team around dramatically; but in test matches, and that was *my* life, we were nosediving. Flemo maintained his high standards of batting — he is, after all, a world-class batsman — but he was far from his inspirational best. He always referred to test-match cricket as the 'pure form of the game' and the lack of success was bugging him. My observation was that without the steering role and the belief in his bowlers to effect his plans he lost some of his spark as a batsman. Some people need more than a few runs to be happy and I reckon Flemo is one of them.

Even though we were getting thumped in the test matches I still wanted to be a part of the team, but in doing my thing I no longer had a feeling of contributing to a greater cause, nor was I gaining a sense of self-achievement or BTB, just a sense of relief. I was scoring runs solely for my own purpose of protecting my record and keeping my batting average high. It became a very lonely time. The game had become simply a means of making a living and my motivation became just that — doing my job.

Motivator 6: Just doing my job

When I was first selected for the Black Caps I had a steady job in Dunedin, but all my life I had wanted to be a professional cricketer. Upon being selected I decided it was my time. It was time to take my chance to make it at international level and, if I could, then I would finally claim cricket as my occupation and get paid well — it all seemed very attractive. I'm a one-task guy (I am, after all, a man) and so it was a case of all or nothing. I made the decision to resign my job and throw everything into preparing for my debut tour.

I had about six weeks between returning from England and going to Zimbabwe, and during this time I began my full-time cricket occupation with two net sessions a day and a fitness session. A couple of young Otago prospects would come along and bowl to me during the day, and Lochie Weir, Otago Cricket's greatest supporter and expert throw-down giver, was always on hand. Lochie was on a 'team-issue clothing for throw-downs' deal and worked tirelessly with me. It was all I'd ever wanted and I loved committing to being a fully-fledged professional cricketer. It got even better after I played well, established myself in the team and earned my first New Zealand Cricket contract. It was $15,000 a year but throw in match fees for New Zealand and Otago and I was making over $40,000 per annum.

With each year of solid performance my income grew — and quite dramatically following the players' dispute over contracts in October 2002. However, after I became a test specialist I often bitched and moaned about the lack of opportunity to earn anywhere near what the one-day boys were getting. They played in tournaments for huge prize money and took part in so many games that they earned substantial match fees. So it probably appeared to some that all I was motivated by was my pay cheque — and to tell you the truth, it seemed that way to me, at times. But while money was a nice consequence of performance, its value was really only superficial when it came to inspiring me — it was more my pursuit of BTB that kept me motivated. Once I lost that overriding ideology and was playing solely for the pay cheque I quickly realised it wasn't enough. I needed other motivators and when they became harder to find it became very apparent that my days of professional cricket were numbered.

Financial planning

During my early to mid-twenties, while established in the Otago team, I was always aware of the need not only to earn enough money on which to survive, but also to take steps towards financial security in the future, whether that be by building up my savings, paying for an education, or finding meaningful employment. I also felt that as you reached your later twenties the opportunity cost of playing at the first-class level increased every year. Even when Sky TV came to the party with an extremely healthy payment to New Zealand Cricket in 1996, which came about as a result of the televising of the revolutionary Cricket Max, and player payments increased dramatically, it was always only enough to get by on. You needed more strings to your bow than first-class cricket if you wanted financial security.

However, as I said earlier, cricket at this level was a six-months-a-year commitment and it was tough finding employment with career prospects to fit around that timetable. I reckoned I needed and would have been happy with around $30,000 a year to allow me to become a professional cricketer at the first-class level. It frustrated me that the only professionals we had in the country were the incumbent Black Caps, making it tougher for me to improve my game at the same rate as they were able to improve theirs and so be in a position to be able to challenge for someone's spot. Not surprisingly, I often found myself verbalising these frustrations to anyone who would listen or to anyone I reckoned needed to hear it. Then in 2001 came the birth of the New Zealand Cricket Players Association and the solution to the problem.

Getting the correct share of the pot was, amongst other things, a key goal of the negotiations between the NZCPA and New Zealand Cricket. If the players could get a reasonable percentage of the total revenue of New Zealand Cricket then payments would improve and players, especially those at first-class level, could become more professional. There were plenty of other things being negotiated as part of the contract schedules, but it was the payments that I was primarily interested in.

On a personal level I was ticking along okay and making some good coin, but I really did want to see more financial security for your average provincial cricketer. I believed that many players — successful, experienced players, but players unlikely ever to play at international level — were being forced out of the game at far too early an age. As a result, our first-class game was being dominated by younger, less accomplished players and weakening our cricket overall. New Zealand Cricket simply couldn't afford to lose experienced and proven performers at this level if it wanted to have a strong domestic base.

It is commonly accepted that Australia's dominance at international level is because of their outstanding strength at domestic level, which also allows players to be thoroughly professional through adequate payments. It is my belief, however, that the NZCPA's desire to follow the Australian system, while fine in theory, in the end perverted the course of negotiations.

Once an appropriate percentage of the money pool was designated for player payments — in the late 20th percentile seemed the desired goal, and boy was that a point of contention between the two parties — it was to be divvied up in a way that in my opinion simply hasn't been successful in truly helping the group of players that really needed it. Sixty per cent was to go to the 20 players given national contracts, the Black Caps, and 40 per cent to the players contracted at the domestic level. The parties settled on 23 per cent as the percentage of the money pool that would go to player payments — but the problem was that 40 per cent of 23 per cent of the total revenue of New Zealand Cricket divided by 66 (11 cricketers contracted in each of the six provinces) simply wasn't enough to turn the domestic game in New Zealand professional or provide enough incentive for an ageing performer to stay in the game.

Maybe this sort of system works in Australia where the pool of money is substantially larger but it doesn't here in New Zealand. I'm not saying the top cricketers shouldn't get paid a lot more money than your second-tier players — after all, they are the shop window and generate the majority of the income — but the way the system works here in practice hasn't fixed the problem I believe we were trying to fix in the first place. The other part of the player payment system based on the Australian model was the ranking of players and contracts. Players were ranked according to their expected worth to New Zealand Cricket, or their provinces, based on their past and expected future performances. Retainers offered within contracts corresponded to players' rankings and because of this I considered the negotiation process to be tainted by ego and greed. In other words, there was an underlying drive to see who would be the top few New Zealand-ranked players and how much they would be paid. In the end, my team, Auckland, of which I was the middleman between the negotiation team and the players, was the last to say yes to the final deal and did so begrudgingly.

My own financial situation was fine under the scheme. I had a good ranking in the New Zealand contracts, which was a bit of a coup given I was only playing one form of the game. Perhaps this was because I've always been one to do my own politicking and the powers that be realised I'd probably blow my top if players I believed were lesser performers were getting paid more.

So while financially I felt I was moving forward, by the end of 2003 I had lost that crucial BTB motivation. I decided that if my contract position slipped dramatically I would look at moving on. Cricket had become simply a day job, with performance at the crease the prerequisite for being paid to my satisfaction.

Chapter Seven

And then it was over — finally!

The 2003/04 season was a tough one. It began with practice games for the New Zealand Cricket Academy in which my form got worse with every game. I got frustrated and worried and although I managed a couple of reasonable scores against Pakistan in the December test matches they were scratchy, drawn-out affairs that left me questioning my style of play.

Looking back now, I was probably showing the first signs of staleness, but I was still motivated by the desire to protect my record, mainly because not doing so would probably mean a pay cut. So I gritted my teeth and got on with it. My enjoyment levels were very low and I was constantly asking myself why I wanted to keep playing. My bank balance was moving forward and that was about it. However, every time I played a test I was confronted with the words:

RIG
Be more composed; be more controlled
Take a step forward; take up the challenge
BTB

I couldn't avoid them as I had inscribed them in permanent marker on the inside of my black cap. With my motivation waning I took heart in these words and decided that if I was to continue I had to recommit to the BTB ethos. Unfortunately, I think I got it wrong this time.

Confused and frustrated days

I had got out for 82 at the Basin Reserve in the Boxing Day test after batting for over seven hours. While it was satisfying to have taken on Shoaib Akhtar, one of the fastest ever bowlers, and got through, my tired shot to relinquish my wicket only 18 runs short of a century left me feeling frustrated and scratching for answers to my poor conversion rate of 50s to 100s.

My main job had always been to provide consistency of resistance at the top of the order for New Zealand in test matches. We had a powerful middle order and they were expected to be the engine room when it came to churning out the runs. I was there to protect and lay a foundation for the engine room, and while my average of just shy of 50 suggested I was doing this job to good effect, my century tally of only three at this stage made me feel I was missing out on the glory. My reputation with the media and public meant my poor record of turning starts into big scores for the most part went unnoticed, but not with me.

Stephen Fleming, for instance, took a ton of unwarranted criticism over his poor record of converting half centuries into centuries. At one stage Flemo had one of the worst, if not the worst, conversion rates in world cricket and did he take some crap over that! Yet Flemo's healthy average in the high 30s suggests to me that he would have played his part in many great partnerships, and it is partnerships that win matches because you don't ever bat on your own. I, on the other hand, managed to escape a lot of this criticism, perhaps because the opening spot had been a problem for quite some time and I was probably achieving above expectation anyway. However, I wanted more hundreds in my century column and it was frustrating the hell out of me.

Eventually I came to the conclusion that my slow rate of scoring was costing me centuries. It was taking me 100-plus overs to pass the 100 mark and thus I was facing a lot of balls in the process. In the course of an innings you will receive many good deliveries and also make a few mistakes — you just hope that the mistake that gets you out comes after hours at the crease and not minutes. I felt that I wasn't maximising my returns before that fatal ball or mistake occurred. In the time it took others to get to 100 I could only expect 60-odd at best. I also believed that because bowlers knew I was particularly defensive in my approach and would not look to pressure them or take them on they could run in with more confidence, and as such were less likely to deliver up rubbish that I could take control of. It appeared that I was handicapping myself in more ways than one.

Becoming preoccupied with this dilemma, I took a very cluttered mind into the post-Christmas series against South Africa. My application was as good as always,but the level of satisfaction I drew from what I was doing at the crease was correspondingly low. I lost focus on the things that were important to my success; they were never pretty things, but they were my prerequisites, and to the outsider at this point my game probably looked disorganised and my demeanour perturbed.

'Braces'

It was at the start of this season that John Bracewell took over the reins as Black Caps coach. Braces had had a lot to do with me when I was a young up-and-coming spin bowler many years before. He knew my personality well, and while I had matured and achieved success at a different discipline I bet he would have recognised the same compulsive and analytical mind he had watched self-destruct over 10 years earlier the minute we were reacquainted. He must have been shaking his head in bemusement when he was confronted with this uptight, grey-haired, crusty old man whose response to burning out was to hold the bat ever tighter and scrabble for answers that were far too complicated. 'Shit!' he must have thought, 'that left-arm spinner's back.'

I rate John Bracewell as a very good coach. He has an extremely extensive knowledge of coaching principles and the techniques of the game and is totally enthusiastic when it comes to applying them. His record, especially in test matches, has come under fire in the past couple of years, but I feel a lot of the problems have been out of his control. The major issue has been the plague of injuries that struck the team around the time of his induction, with probably the most significant being the loss of Shane Bond. When Bondy went, so did the effectiveness of the bowling unit in general.

I don't think the dramatic change in the Black Caps management structure that accompanied Braces' appointment helped either. It was a big shift that saw the power of direction further taken away from Stephen Fleming — who up till then had operated with a back-seat style of coach and a manager whose job was mostly to organise the team while assembled — and given to a very business-orientated manager, and to a coach who took the major role in the team's selection, strategy and direction and who was held mostly responsible for on-field performance. Basically, Braces became the boss.

However, when our performances went sour I think this led to Braces turning defensive. The more Fleming let go, the more Braces tightened his grip on the team. Perhaps he tried to do too much himself. There were opportunities to enlist specialist help along the way but he didn't take them, possibly because this might have been construed as a sign of weakness — and possibly because he has a seemingly unconquerable belief in his own knowledge and ability. This was never more apparent than when our batting philosophy was challenged in Australia: the Aussie bowlers had a stranglehold on us and Greg Chappell let it be known that he was interested in working with our batsmen.

Greg Chappell was one of the game's greatest batsmen, but in recent years he has built up an equally impressive reputation as a wonderful batting coach. Myself and a few of my batting colleagues were dead keen on hearing what he had to say: at the very least, a new voice can be quite motivating, even if saying the same old things. Chappell's approach was made via the morning newspaper — the same one Braces had under his arm as he approached the breakfast table that day. The consensus was that we would assess Braces' reaction to the article and take it from there. He sat down, opened the paper and grunted something like, 'This happens every tour, the arrogant wankers', and then dived into his breakfast as if the approach had never been made, completely oblivious to the four Kiwi top-order batsmen who'd been staring across the table with bated breath. That was that then — there would be no contribution from Greg Chappell.

For all that though, I retain plenty of faith in John Bracewell as a coach and believe that with time, and if New Zealand Cricket do something about the appalling standard of conditions in our domestic game, the Black Caps will become a strong test team again. Looking back, Braces definitely identified what was needed in my own case and was endeavouring to move my game forward in the right direction. His main problem was that he was dealing with a very old dog indeed.

A new pair of eyes

At the conclusion of the South African series and the 2003/04 season, contracts came up for renewal. I took a bit of a dip in the rankings and found myself very much mid-table. While it was a pay cut, given my stuttering form it was a good result and I was still drawing a healthy retainer. Besides, I had considered packing it all in after the South African series or not taking a contract but still making myself available to tour England. I was unhappy and wasn't really sure I wanted to be obliged to play cricket when my confidence was low. Also if I got dropped, which was more and more on the cards now, it would have killed me to be forced into carrying on at the provincial level.

It was Chris Cairns and his wife Carin who turned me round. Over a beer in Wellington I made Cairnsy aware of my feelings. He said he had been feeling a little the same a year or so ago, and got Carin down to join the discussion as she had made good sense to him when he was near to throwing in the towel himself. We came to the conclusion that cricket had just got too big for me. It was all I had financially and I had no other outlet once the game or training was over to take my mind off it or put it into the right perspective. It worried me that I was taking my frustration home, and while Mary was hugely understanding of how important cricket was to me it was bound to wear her down eventually too. A plan was formulated that I would accept a contract, whatever my ranking, which would set me up financially for the next year, but spend my time off the field working on something to do after cricket. The idea was to add something else to my life and reduce cricket's impact on my wellbeing. A good plan, if only my psyche would allow it to work.

At my end-of-year appraisal with the fish-heads I made clear my frustrations to Braces. He was well aware of them anyway and had observed how I had become very insular, even describing me as a 'caveman'. By that he was referring to my behaviour of going from the ground to my hotel room and only reappearing when the bus left for training or the game. He felt I needed to find a way of enjoying myself more and decided that his role over the next year would be to find ways in which I could enjoy my training and playing. So he devised some training methods aimed at lightening things up a little and providing some mental relief. It was an astute move as he could easily have focused on the technical faults that had crept into my game or simply given me a hurry-up for my lack of form, but he knew the only thing that could address both problems was finding a way to get me to 'lighten up!'

The single most influential thing to come out of my appraisal, however, actually came from fitness advisor Warren Frost. Frosty had tried in vain for quite some time to make me faster and more agile, but it was when he handed me a phone number that he made the biggest impact on my cricket. Giving me the number of optometrist Brett Howes, he told me to go and have a sports vision eye examination. I did — and walked out wearing contact lenses. My left eye was knackered. I'd known from the time I'd applied for the air force years earlier that I had a dodgy left eye, but it was now discovered that I had astigmatisms in both eyes and my left eye, which was my dominant eye, was now really quite bad. So that was it — I was blind! Well, at least that explained the poor form!

I don't really know if my eyes were quite that bad when it came to cricket vision and if the improvement the lenses made to my eyesight made any real impact on my hand-eye coordination, but what I do know is they had a massive impact on my mental game. New eyes gave me new belief that I could turn my form around, but more importantly drew my attention back to the most vital priority in cricket — watching the ball. When I got to England all I concentrated on was how closely I could track the ball and I left behind a lot of the theory I had dragged around behind me uselessly in New Zealand.

England 2004

My tour of England in 2004 was the highlight of my career. It was also the tour that essentially finished my career. I believe there to be three big tours for a New Zealand cricketer in the current era: India, Australia and England.

India has a mystique all of its own. It is hot, the change of diet can be challenging, but the enthusiasm of the Indian people gives it a certain chaotic charm. Not much is in your favour when you tour India, but the importance of the game in that region makes it a cricketing fortress that every cricketer must try to conquer at least once in their career. I got a test century in India, despite the fact that not much was in my favour leading up to the innings, having had 'the squirts' for four days and not being able to eat anything solid for 24 hours. In fact, my extreme level of dehydration led to a severe and rather comical bout of cramps a few runs short of a 100, which I will probably never be allowed to live down. I was unable to run between the wickets for fear of cramping up in mid-pitch and the only shot I had to score boundaries with against their accurate spinners was the sweep, except every time I played it I would be left writhing around on the ground in agony. *You* try to stop playing the only shot you have to score runs with when only six runs shy of a century that would mean so much to you! I got there in the end though and will forever treasure my Indian ton.

Australia is sort of the other way round to India. Everything is in your favour to perform. Facilities and playing surfaces are excellent, and hotels and hospitality outstanding; the only problem is that the opposition are the best players in the world. Australia is the proving ground. In New Zealand you are often judged on how you fare against our traditional foe, and as an individual you want to measure yourself at the highest level. Any success you have against Australia is highly valued success indeed. I've always been ashamed of my personal record against Australia.

England, however, is the big one. England has both tradition and history and English tours are the ones that tend to go down in history. We often get reminded of the 1949 tour and the respect the ''49ers' earned for New Zealand cricket; Bevan Congdon's 1973 team were highly competitive; and the celebratory photo from the first test victory in England at Headingley by the 1983 team is an unforgettable image in the history of New Zealand Cricket. The run-scoring exploits in England of Kiwi players like Bert Sutcliffe in 1949, and then Glenn Turner — whose county cricket record is outstanding — are still celebrated.

Perhaps it all stems from the days when the boat was the only way to get there and so you would stay for the entire English summer. A tour became a season and unforgettable. Plane travel has brought the UK closer and tours are shorter, but success in England still provokes real feeling. Stephen Fleming has been moved to tears when he reminisces over the series win in 1999 and

Chris Cairns labels the Lord's test win of the same tour his most memorable.

It's hard to explain precisely why it is still such a big deal, but I reckon it has something to do with the relationship we share with the Poms. They started the game and introduced it to the world. It's the 'motherland' and returning home to take on the master is a special occasion.

England is also often the first place a New Zealander will experience professional cricket. We have a long tradition of our best talent playing county cricket, and a county placement is well respected even though the strength of the English domestic game is always a topic for debate. Many younger players will experience cricket in the English leagues as they develop their games, and all up over the years we have developed a strong familiarity with English cricket.

The English also know how to stage a cricket match. From village greens to test-match venues there is invariable charm. From the wives and girlfriends who supply the tea at the local club, to the fine wines and three-course meals in the hospitality marquees at first-class games and test matches, it's about more than just the game. From the guy in the cheese-cutter cap and his dog that walk round the boundary every Saturday to the members in the pavilion who have watched the greats of the past, it's the quality of the cricket that takes precedence over the final score for them. While the fortunes of their national team ebb and flow one thing never changes — England does cricket *well*.

The other thing that England has — and it is rather a big thing — is Lord's. Playing a test at Lord's is like exchanging vows at a wedding — there is a lot else of importance happening in and around it but it's a defining moment — one you look forward to and hope you don't fluff. If England is the motherland, then Lord's is its womb, and for many touring players, playing a test at Lord's is quite a spiritual experience. It is little wonder that England's record is poor at Lord's, as touring players are aware they may only get one shot on the hallowed turf and are all desperate to rise to the occasion. I have to admit that it was never a major thing for me, and I remember Jeff Crowe got quite upset when I said I'd rather smash a century in a one-dayer at the 'G' (Melbourne Cricket Ground), but the closer it got to the date and the minute I walked on the ground on the first day of practice the significance of the environment took hold of me well and truly.

While some say the playing arena itself is not the greatest, I disagree. True, it has this quite unbelievable slope running across the ground, but that is part of its uniqueness and charm. I like the white bucket seating — it's traditional cricket white. There's both new and old at each end, with the almost space-age-looking media centre that encapsulates the scribes and commentators in one gigantic, all-seeing, 'Cycloptic' enclosure mounted intimidatingly at the 'nursery' end, and then at the other end, the iconic and quite beautiful old Members Stand. It is when you enter the Members Stand, which houses the dressing-rooms, that the Lord's experience really takes hold. There's memorabilia and fantastic artwork everywhere and one could lose hours taking a jaunt through cricket's history.

The staircase that ascends through three levels is regal and takes you from ground floor to the dressing-room, the centrepiece of which is the honours board. That's the target for all concerned. It's the board you want *your* name on and to record your place in the history of the game. To get your name on the honours board at Lord's by taking five wickets in an innings or scoring a hundred is an ambition of most if not all international cricketers. Other grounds around the world have taken up this practice of recording past successes on that particular ground for the players of the future, but just as Lord's is at the heart of the cricketing universe, so is the honours board, the centrepiece of Lord's.

The Lord's test was the first test of our tour and since I had just re-signed and committed to cricket for another year I wanted my turn at the historic venue. First, however, I had a few problems to sort out, with the major one being my flagging form.

Fighting for my place in history

From the moment I'd first walked out to open the batting for New Zealand at Bulawayo back in 2000 my place had never come under pressure, but going into this tour I was starting to feel a little insecure. Michael Papps had come into the team during the home summer and looked promising. Braces obviously rated him, and he was very much in favour. Stephen Fleming had also made noises about moving to the opening role, and as he is our best player and captain he can basically do what he wants. All of a sudden I was playing off with Pappsy for the one remaining opening berth.

I was feeling the heat, but in the back of my mind I knew I had worked extremely hard in the months between the end of the New Zealand summer and this tour, and anyway, I had a new set of eyes to rely upon. I simply had to score runs in the warm-up games. They were crucially important as I needed to regain form, but also because it has always been important to me to know that when I walk out to bat for New Zealand I do so by right of performance.

I didn't play the first game of the tour against an English Players Association selection. It was a one-day game and a little Mickey Mouse but I wasn't asked to play and I probably read a little too much into that. Pappsy got plenty while I watched and fretted. My first innings was a small start against British Universities on a wet wicket, but the technical work I'd done at home felt like it was kicking in and I took a little more confidence but also a bundle of nerves into the first really important build-up game against Worcestershire; 48 and a very scratchy 20 not out in that game was okay but not enough to relax me, and the first innings of the next match (and final warm-up match) was quite a spectacle.

Well, it wasn't quite such a spectacle for the small crew of Kentish faithful who turned up to be entertained by attractive cricket, but for those in the know, and there were bugger all of them, it was a gripping display of stubborn determination and a grim war of attrition between two opening batsmen desperately trying to win a place in a Lord's test match. Neither myself nor Michael Papps was prepared to be first one out, and from a team perspective it was great as we went on to post a first wicket partnership of 244.

You have to feel for Pappsy a little as he did everything that could have been asked of him with a century, but my 92 backed with a couple of starts in the previous game and the thought of a media outcry if I was left out earned me the prized Lord's spot. Truth be told, it was more exhausting than preparatory cricket as far as I was concerned, but to know I would experience cricket's Mecca was exhilarating.

I'd got amongst the runs in the lead-up games, but, most importantly, the pressure I had placed upon myself meant I had forgotten all the theory and frustration of the New Zealand summer and focused on the things that were key to my success: watching the ball as closely as possible and keeping each one out, with runs becoming a consequence of this watchfulness. This determination didn't vary for 971 balls and 1316 minutes of batting throughout the English series.

Walking through the Longroom at Lord's on the way out to bat in the first innings of the test series was an uplifting experience and it is one of cricket's great traditions. The dressing-rooms at Lord's are three stories up at each end of the pavilion and so you must descend the staircase and walk through to the centre of the Longroom, which is a regal old chamber full of memorabilia and ancient members almost as old and significant as the pieces hanging on the wall, before heading out onto the ground. What I loved about Lord's was that it wasn't at all a stuffy environment full of self-important dignitaries, but rather a venue where the players were celebrated and appreciated by true cricket enthusiasts who know what the game is all about. As you progress through the Longroom the applause grows and you feel like you have arrived to play out your role in cricket's annals. Of course, you don't want that to turn into a trudge back through a hushed room, out for a duck.

I did trudge back, out for 93 — devastatingly close to a century in my Lord's debut. It had been an ugly knock, but it was a much-needed score in the context of my recent test form. I was cruelly denied my hundred by an umpiring mistake after edging the ball onto my pad and being adjudged LBW, and the applause as I returned was tinged with sympathy. I tried to look disappointed as I wandered off, but really I was trying hard to hide a broad smile — I was back in business once again.

I always placed a lot of importance on the innings directly after one in which I had made a good score. I hated following up a good score with a low one. If I failed I felt it showed complacency and looked bad. My goal going into the second innings at Lord's was to place all my mental energy into getting through the new ball and not giving my wicket away with a poor shot or piece of sloppy judgement. Brendon McCullum came out to bat at No. 3 and his enthusiastic and positive play dragged me along quite nicely, and before I knew it I had a few runs on the board overnight.

Getting out early the next morning after taking a score to stumps always annoyed me too, so the goal was to fight my way through the first session. I managed that and all of a sudden I had a century in my sights again. When I got to 100 late in the second session it was an amazing feeling. I'll never forget the noise of the 30,000 people who celebrated with me as I jumped up and punched the air. After being given out unfairly in the first innings it was as if even the locals were on my side in the second.

Not out 101 at tea, it was the walk back through the Longroom that brought the emotion out of me. I walked through to rapturous applause and felt that I had at last achieved something truly great. When I arrived in the dressing-room my name had already been put up on the sacred honours board. All this, combined with the congratulations of my team-mates, drained all my emotional resolve. I was exhausted and it was no surprise I got out quickly after the tea interval without adding to my score. I still rue giving my wicket away as it exposed our tail to pressure and we fell short of batting England out of the game by about 50 runs. If I had batted another hour we could have been in total control of the game, but emotionally I was spent.

We lost the game as England chased down a reasonable total on a wearing wicket thanks to a century from Nasser Hussain. Hussain had come under selection pressure leading into the game; he no longer had the captaincy and had been forced to field in the undesirable short leg position. However, he fielded outstandingly and batted even better in the final innings run chase, but it was his retirement announcement at the end of the match that left me in awe and a little bit jealous. That's the way to go out — on top.

Playing out for a draw

I don't believe I ever really recovered from my Lord's experience. It all sounds a bit melodramatic, but it was a peak I knew I was never likely to reach again and it was also utterly draining emotionally. The test loss tempered my delight a little; however, I had reversed my form slump and you would have thought I would have been excited about the next two tests to come. But to tell you the truth, if I could have driven out the Lord's front gates straight to Heathrow airport and onto the first flight home I would have. I just had this feeling deep down inside that my career was complete.

I had never really thought I'd have a long career as a Black Cap in the first place. My role model was John Wright, but 82 tests was never really on the cards. I'd started late and thought anywhere between 30 and 40 would be a good result. I actually remember signing up for the New Zealand Cricket superannuation scheme which required me to play around 30 tests to get the necessary points for the payout at the end and thinking how unlikely it would be to achieve them. As it stood now, I had played 32 tests, had a batting average of just under 50 and a century at Lord's to my credit. There really wasn't that much more I wanted to achieve.

Braces could see the fatigue in me and told me to have a few days off, do a bit of sightseeing and make my own way to Leicestershire. I only had to be there on the morning of the game to do the twelfth man duties for the practice game between the first and second tests. 'Freshen up' was the call, which was a good idea, but what really happened was that I found that I enjoyed *not* playing far too much. I loved it in fact!

Thus, for the remainder of the tour my goal was not to ruin my personally excellent first test by failing in the next couple. I would scratch and fight as best I could and value my wicket as if it was my life. My focus was brilliant. It was ball by ball and runs were inconsequential, I simply wanted to last at the wicket as long as possible. By the time I was dismissed in the first innings of the third and final test at Trent Bridge, which by the way is a beautiful test venue, for one of the scratchiest and most grafted-out 73s you will ever see, I was mentally debilitated and I had bugger all concentration left in the tank. I finally surrendered my wicket in that innings meekly in a lazy attempt to loft the spin bowler, but I had really just got sick of defending. I'd had enough of batting and as I walked out to bat in the second innings I just didn't care any longer. I had had a good tour regardless of my final innings and really couldn't care less if I got out first ball. And for the next hour or so I struck the ball the best I ever had in my entire test career — my God it was liberating — but then on 49 I started trying again, got scratchy, and got out.

I'd had enough

Now reading this you might be thinking, 'You selfish prick'. Well, you might be right. I was a selfish player, but in a way that is what was expected of me. I had a very defined role in the Black Caps unit and it revolved around playing tight and holding up my end for as long as possible. The guys around me knew I struggled to up my pace but they appreciated the platform I could lay down for the team. There were certainly times when I needed to up the ante and of those times there were only a few occasions on which I held up proceedings — most of the time I would get out trying to score faster and open the way for Nathan Astle, Craig McMillan or Cairnsy to come in and pick up the rate. In England we were losing, and while I didn't want to play any more I still gave it everything I had to stay in when out in the middle, except for the last innings when I just wasn't strong enough any longer. Ironically, in the next four test matches — my last four test matches — I was selfish because I wasn't selfish enough.

I had four months off before the tour of Bangladesh and Australia began. I'd had many periods like this before and usually I would surf, freshen up, train, set new goals and look forward to getting back with the team. This time it was different. I surfed and trained all right but I certainly didn't freshen up, and when it came to writing down new goals I would end up with an empty sheet of paper. I was making all the right noises about looking forward to getting into it again and what a challenge the Australians would be, but it was all bullshit.

In Bangladesh I turned up swinging from the hip. All I wanted to do was smash quick runs. My batting lacked all control, it wasn't me at all, and I certainly wasn't doing my job. Problem was, I couldn't be arsed either. In Australia, because of the environment, I got a little more focused but not for long enough. I was back to my pokey, proddy self again, but not really by choice, and I only had the mental resolve to keep it up for about an hour tops. Midway through the second test I realised what was happening. I was distraught with my form and frustrated as hell. All I could talk about was Langer and Gilchrist and the way they played so positively. I had become agitated and destructive in team meetings and found myself throwing tantrums. I simply didn't want to be me, 'The Rock', the grafter at the top of the order, any more. I'd completely lost my desire and my focus, but I knew that if I was going to get my form back — which I'd realised wasn't really form at all but just a decent score after hours at the crease — I would have to get back to my gritty, determined and restricted style of play, but by choice and for hours on end, and nothing at that point could have looked less attractive to me.

I had proven in my short career to date that I could be reliable, apply myself and show courage and determination. I now wanted it to be time to express myself, show people how good I could be and expand the game I had tried so hard to contract. It was the only way I could see myself staying with the game. The problem was that I knew I couldn't make these changes at test level, mainly because in such a highly accountable environment I was never going to be able to fully commit to the thing that was the most crucial element of all — letting go. I had had my time as a grafter, but to have my time as a stroke player would take a couple of years of development at lower grades of cricket. I reckon I could have done it, but two years was two too many as far as I was concerned.

As I walked out to bat in my last test innings I didn't have a care in the world. I drank in the beautiful and historic surroundings of the Adelaide Oval, marvelled at Glen McGrath's bowling, at last silently chuckled with a sense of pity at Shane Warne's ridiculous, incessant rambling. I poked, prodded, got all tied up, got out to a dreadful shot and walked off the test field for the final time with a feeling of a massive burden lifted from my shoulders and thinking, 'Thank God it's all over.'

A few months after my retirement I played for an invitation team in South Africa. The team consisted of many international players whom I had played against and they all queried me on my perceived premature retirement. Some couldn't quite understand my reasons; however, it was Jimmy Adams (the former West Indian batsman who played a little like myself, on the defensive side), who defined it perfectly. After watching me get out after seven balls of pathetically constrained attacking batting, Jimmy sat down beside me once I had sheepishly rejoined my team-mates, patted me on the shoulder and said, 'I know son, I know. You can only play like Geoff Boycott [the notoriously methodical and slow-scoring English batsman] for so long before the mind finally rejects it.' He was so right.

My satisfaction from the game of cricket had become defined by the number of runs I could score, not by the process I went through to generate them. In the next chapter I describe that very process. It is the process that took me from an average batsman at the first-class level to a successful test-match opener. It is the process I trusted and believed in, and it is also the process that eventually drove me from the game. I have no doubt that if you are aiming to achieve something in your life you will gain value from the next section of this book, but remember — this was the way I did it; parts may suit you, and others might not.

Alex McKenzie: Within the first few pages of this book Mark asked an important question of himself: 'How could a mere game have such a profound effect on a person? It hadn't started out that way, and if I could have foreseen what it would do to me as an adult perhaps I would never have picked up a bat as a kid, but I did — so why?'

Good question! He then went on to explain and describe in some detail all the various factors that contributed to this situation for him, and within this section we read about a number of these — factors that sports psychology people call 'participation motives'. There was a myriad of them, ranging from fame and fortune, and proving others wrong about his ability, to overcoming fear, or simply enjoying the sensations of batting (or even bowling in his earlier years — and at least once in test-match cricket, judging by the subsequent celebration after taking Yousif Youhana's wicket against Pakistan in 2002!). However, while I enjoyed reading about all of these things, and how they manifested themselves throughout the various points in Mark's career, the simplest answer to Mark's original question came in the first chapter. He said that he was a 'true cricketer' because he had 'a natural aptitude for the game and an indescribable desire to succeed'. This was his core motivation, and even though various other things motivated him as well, these weren't as powerful as that overwhelming desire to succeed. If this weren't so powerful, why else would he have persevered with the game when he so freely admits that he didn't really enjoy the actual act of playing cricket at senior level?

Motivation is quite a complex issue. Sportspeople are no different from anyone else in that they are motivated by all sorts of things, but generally speaking these can be divided into two overall types of motivation: intrinsic and extrinsic. Intrinsic motivation comprises those things that drive the individual from within, such as enjoyment, a feeling of satisfaction and achievement in overcoming adversity, a feeling of competence and control over the situation, or simply the physical sensations of participating in sport. Extrinsic motivation, on the other hand, can perhaps best be described as the motivation to obtain an external reward such as winning a competition, making a particular team, getting paid, public recognition and so on. It is motivation that is controlled by other people or other things, rather than something that is within the individual. In this section, Mark talked at length about the extrinsic and intrinsic forms of motivation that were meaningful for him. I've actually listed the ones that I identified from this section in the following table (most are direct quotes from Mark), and they are listed in the order in which they appeared throughout this section.

What is interesting to note is that towards the end of Mark's career, it seemed that the intrinsic motives were becoming less and less important to him, and that the extrinsic ones became correspondingly more powerful. It's a common saying in most sports that the best form of motivation 'has to come from within' in order for it to have the greatest effect on performance, and once that intrinsic motivation disappears, enjoyment and satisfaction follow closely, and performance starts to decline.

Mark also stated that:

Even though we were getting thumped in the test matches I still wanted to be a part of the team, but in doing my thing I no longer had a feeling of contributing to a greater cause, nor was I gaining a sense of self-achievement or BTB, just a sense of relief. I was scoring runs solely for my own purpose of protecting my record and keeping my batting average high. It became a very lonely time. The game had become simply a means of making a living and my motivation became just that — doing my job.

He then went on to say that: 'Cricket was simply a day job and performance at the crease became the prerequisite for being paid to my satisfaction.'

So what does all this mean? Basically, Mark's main motives for playing the game had changed in their importance to him. His burning desire to succeed, because of the intrinsic benefits that it gave him (a sense of achievement and elation from playing well), was being replaced by the desire to protect his average and to get paid, both of which are purely extrinsic motives. Mark felt that these latter motives, which had become more important to him, were the wrong reasons to be playing the game, and this realisation fuelled his decision to retire.

He was no longer acting like the 'true cricketer' that he felt he was deep down. In other words, extrinsic motives were replacing his intrinsic ones as the most powerful reasons for playing the game, and he didn't like it!

Intrinsic motives

- Indescribable desire to succeed
- An innate belief that I was good at the game
- Cricket was fun . . . because I was good at it
- I loved the act of bowling
- If there have been two little words someone could say to motivate me into action they would be 'you can't'
- I enjoyed how cricket made me feel following a success
- I loved the camaraderie and dressing-room banter
- Success with the bat began to make me feel great
- I loved playing good shots
- I was happy to bowl for my club because I wanted my club to win
- It was the first time I experienced that magnificent feeling of relief mixed with elation that you achieve when you get to a hundred and I definitely wanted more of it
- The chance of facing the West Indies quickies was an experience that had a masochistic appeal
- One thing I enjoyed was a bit of on-field banter
- Scoring runs for Otago made me feel important and successful
- I was now playing cricket at the highest level. I had achieved my lifelong ambition and now I wanted to see how good I could get
- Applying my game, batting with control and patience and scoring runs against world-class bowling had real value to me. It gave me a sense of achievement
- Doing my stuff well gave me a terrific sense of self-worth and achievement
- From a cricket perspective it was the Black Caps team dynamic that I loved
- I developed the media nickname of 'The Rock' and I genuinely felt I was achieving and helping the team achieve

Extrinsic motives

- To show the world that I was good at the game
- I loved the kudos I got from being singled out at school assembly following a triumphant Saturday
- For fame and fortune
- Recognition
- Bit of cash
- Picking up chicks
- The motivation to prove others wrong would be a big motivator for the future
- As my cricket career began to flourish and my profile began to build it became a reward for success that I loved and needed more and more
- I've always read my own press and get a buzz out of compliments I receive
- I was excited about playing against and seeing in person Brian Lara
- I love it when people in the street congratulate me on a good performance and I welcome it
- Generating profile from something that I was not renowned for [end-of-series sprint races]
- I quite enjoyed being the centre of attention
- I enjoyed the things that success provided: staying in hotels; seeing interesting places around the world
- I would revel in imaginary adulation
- My goals were headed with the desire to reach New Zealand selection by the end of the 1999/2000 season . . . It kept my desire burning
- I wanted to bat with all the guys I admired so much
- I was still motivated by the desire to protect my record, although on reflection, I was probably showing the first signs of staleness
- To get your name on the honours board at Lord's by taking five wickets in an innings or scoring a hundred is an ambition of most if not all international cricketers

The good old days of bang, crash, wallop became ...

the leave ...

the push for one ...

the forward defence ...

the back-foot defence ...

the work to leg ...

the sweep ...

the cut ...

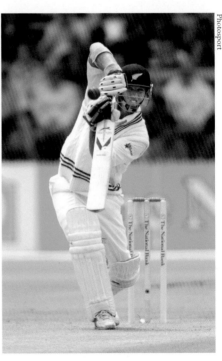

the straight drive ... on the whole a little boring, but they were effective.

And getting away with the odd 'cock-up' was always kind of fun.

The role models

John Wright, who possessed the game plan I endeavoured to copy.

Martin Crowe — next to perfect technically, tactically and mentally.

Matthew Hayden — a batting machine when in form.

Adam Gilchrist — the body position at the point of bowler release that I thought perfect and a game I'd die for.

Justin Langer, who did what I couldn't . . . took his restrictive game and expanded it.

My Process

FRONTAL LOBE
Skilled muscle movement, problem-
solving, planning, goal setting and
decision-making

PARIETAL LOBE
Processes sensory information

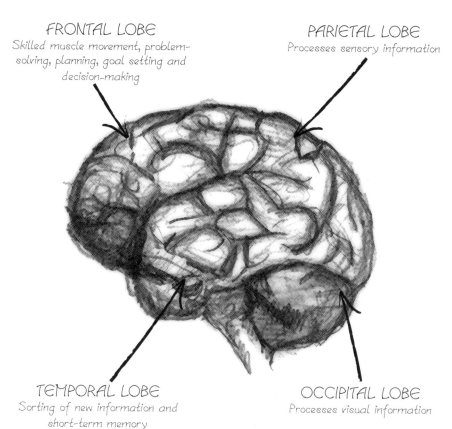

TEMPORAL LOBE
Sorting of new information and
short-term memory

OCCIPITAL LOBE
Processes visual information

Left hemisphere cerebrum — sequential analysis, systematic logical interpretation
Right hemisphere cerebrum — holistic processing of multi-sensory input

Chapter Eight

Introduction — a decision had to be made

In late December 2004 I walked off the first-class cricket field for the final time. I had earned a reputation as one of New Zealand's most successful opening batsmen, had achieved more goals than I would have thought possible, but most importantly I was personally satisfied with what I had accomplished over a first-class career spanning 15 years. Retirement is a time for reflection, and as I look back on my career — the highs, the lows, bowling and batting — I find that I cannot value highly enough the decision I made leading into the 1997/98 season.

As I went into that season I had begun to realise that if I was going to achieve the goal I had set myself of making the national side by the age of 28 I needed to do something about my game. I felt I had reached the grade in terms of being a useful first-class batsman but I was well short of the mark needed to be a test or ODI player. I was an average performer and thus needed to break out of my cycle of mediocrity.

There was no question that I had the necessary motivation and drive to put in the work to succeed, but in the back of my mind I knew I could do more — yet what that more could be was a mystery. When I turned 28 and quit I didn't want to look back and say 'I could have done more'. In my view, 'could have' people are sad individuals and lacking in excuses when it comes to failure, and I had no intention of becoming one of them, so what could I do *now* to get the results I desired?

The particular game that finally made me decide that I had to do something was the 1996/97 Shell Trophy Final. Otago played Canterbury at Lancaster Park (now Jade Stadium) in Christchurch on an extremely batsman-friendly surface. Canterbury batted first and made 777 and in Otago's reply I made 14 and 0. It was an important game, a final, and I failed; but what really hit home to me was that the national incumbents and a young Craig McMillan, who was on a non-stop run-scoring ride to the national team, all scored big in this game. Harris (198), Astle (160), Horne (98), McMillan (94), Fleming (66) and Cairns (57) all looked streets ahead of everyone else in the match. My failure hurt and it left me smarting. All of a sudden I had begun to make comparisons between myself and international-quality players and I didn't like what I was seeing one bit.

Quite simply, I had failed every time I had played in an Emerging Players side and the comment had been passed in response to those who rated my skills that I didn't score runs when it really mattered. My persona and actions had led to me being regarded by those that mattered as a 'head case'. Admittedly, I had always been a little eccentric when it came to handling pressure both on and off the field — it was just my way — but it was counting against me heavily if I couldn't score enough runs to render my reputation irrelevant. Change had to be made and that change had to come in the way of sheer volume of runs. I determined that the best way to achieve this goal was to target my mental approach to batting. This decision and the choice of the person to assist in this process would prove the most influential decision I made in my cricket career.

Alex McKenzie

Alex McKenzie worked in the field of sports psychology. He was a lecturer at the University of Otago and part of the faculty of Physical Education. He worked with sportspeople as a consultant and he was the man I contacted to help me. I worked with Alex each week and he charged me $50 for an hour of consulting. On a modest income this was quite an expense, and to Alex's credit after a while he dropped the fee as he was quite enjoying the sessions himself and felt he was gaining from them as well.

Under Alex's guidance we embarked together on a journey of discovery — and his style was very much about self-discovery. He would give me readings on various topics and introduce me to sports psychology principles, but it was mainly about me discovering how these ideas related to my own game. He never tried to force things on me and it was always about my own experience and travelling my own path.

Alex McKenzie guided me down a path that saw me go from an untouchable 'head case' in the eyes of the cricket fraternity to a player who was regarded as having one of the strongest mental games in the country and worthy of being used as a role model for the New Zealand Cricket Academy. Scoring runs was great, but earning the respect of my peers, past and present coaches, and New Zealand Cricket in general was, to say the least, immensely satisfying.

Which is not to say that when I took my gear off for the last time in first-class cricket I didn't feel that I could have done more. I certainly could have done more to improve my stroke play and my one-day cricket; I could have put in more work on my fielding, my speed and my agility; I could have relaxed and 'turned off' more to lengthen my career. However, when it comes to the path I decided on — that of the tight and disciplined opening batsman I believe I did all I could at that pursuit. Sure, I could have done things *differently*, and as the saying goes, there's more than one way to skin a cat, but with Alex's help I discovered a *process*, it was *my* process and it produced results that, at the end of the day, I was satisfied with. My hope is that reading about what I did will help you find your way to some satisfying results as well.

Alex McKenzie: There is no doubt in my mind that Mark was enormously successful in developing his mental game because (a) he believed in the process that we went through, and (b) he worked hard at it and contributed at least as much as I did to that process. He has been the athlete with whom I have enjoyed working the most for these and a number of other reasons. Firstly, he bought into the idea that the relationship had to be a two-way street, in that we worked together on everything that we did. I may have introduced him to some concepts and ideas, but it was Mark who tried them, gave me feedback on how they worked (or didn't work), and together we refined them to suit his needs and purposes. He didn't expect me to be the one with all the answers (which of course I wasn't!), and his input into the work that we did was the key to its success. To my mind he was a tremendous student of the game with regard to the mental side of cricket, and it has been tremendously satisfying for me to know that he continued to develop this aspect of his game long after we had finished working together.

Essentially, Mark became his own mental skills consultant! He would occasionally contact me after he had left Dunedin to discuss an aspect of his mental game, but generally these conversations were very one-sided, in that I would simply affirm that what he had thought about was the right thing to do. He was also prepared to pick the brains of other players (past and present), coaches and sports psych people to get their ideas, and to read widely and formulate his own ideas about how to approach the game. Like many cricket fans, I too was disappointed to hear that he was retiring from the game, but understood his reasons once I had spoken to him. In the back of my mind I felt that I might have been able to help him get through some of those dark days, but I soon realised that this was the fan in me talking, and that if Mark felt I could have assisted in any way, he would have consulted me.

The other reason that I believe our work together paid dividends for Mark, was that he didn't treat the work as a reaction to a specific problem. In other words, he bought into the notion that developing his mental game was a process that was going to take time, and would change and evolve as we progressed. We weren't 'fixing a problem' so much as 'developing some skills', just as if he were developing a new shot technique. I strongly believe that this approach was a key element of his success in this aspect of his game. In contrast, too many coaches and athletes are still under the misconception that all people who work in sports psychology are 'shrinks' who fix psychological problems that an athlete might have. While this can be the case, developing 'mental toughness', as many people like to call it, is often more about learning skills than it is about quick-fix solutions to 'psychological' or emotional concerns.

Mark was regarded as one of the most mentally tough cricketers that this country has ever produced, and all of the work that we did together was about developing the mental skills required to cope with the technical, tactical and psychological demands of the game. We never once talked about any deep-seated personal 'problems' that Mark might have had from a psychological perspective (even if he had any!).

Chapter Nine

Finding *my* techniques, *my* tactics, *my* thoughts . . . *my* game

Step 1: Peak Performance Profile (PPP)

Before I could move my game forward I had to understand my game. The first principle Alex introduced me to was that of 'peak performance'. I needed to find out what I did when I performed at my peak. We needed a starting point from which to move and so my first Peak Performance Profile (PPP) would be an estimate.

To begin with, I broke my game down into three main categories: technical, tactical and mental. You will notice that there is also a category for 'physical' in the chart opposite but I found this category less important to my development as a batsman than the other three. I figured that time in the middle was good enough to keep me cricket-fit, and besides, I have always kept fit as a matter of habit; furthermore, in latter years this aspect of my cricket was taken care of pretty comprehensively by Warren Frost, the Black Caps' fitness advisor.

What follows is an explanation of my first PPP — essentially an estimate made from memory of past games in which I felt I had batted particularly well. Note that while I've identified key indicators for my good performance when I did perform well, that does not mean that I did all these things perfectly.

Current ○ Best ●	Poor			Average					Excellent		
	0	1	2	3	4	5	6	7	8	9	10
Technical											
Weight on delivery (Head still — forward — upright)							◑				
Up & over top of shot				○			●				
Bat v pad technique						◑					
Opening up front foot						◑					
Tactical											
Starting (play straight/let ball come)							○	●			
Percentage hits						○		●			
Working the ball around (making ones from good balls)							○			●	
Physical											
Flexibility	○		●								
Endurance							○				●
Speed/Power					○	●					
Strength							○		●		
Psychological											
Present moment focus				○				●			
Confidence/Positivity			○							●	
Relaxation				○				●			
Imagery					○			●			
Mental toughness (Boon/Border/Taylor)						○					●

Explanation of first PPP

Technical

Weight on delivery

At a very early stage I realised that you needed a still head and no lateral movement across the crease at the time of delivery. It was crucial for picking the line and length of the ball clearly and then not overbalancing to the off side as you aim to play — which is a very common problem even for test players. I had always worked hard on my stance and my balance, and at this stage it was one of the stronger parts of my batting and a good starting point from which to improve.

Up & over top of shot

This really means getting your weight through the ball. I was up on my toes on the back foot and not leaning back when playing off either front or back foot. This was a poor part of my game at this stage and I believed it was getting me out a lot.

When I did it well I felt in control of my shots and dominant at the crease (think Matthew Hayden in full cry!). I struggled with this as I was a bit dodgy against the quicks and they forced my weight back, which led to leaning away from my shots and nicking out.

Bat v pad technique

I was a middle-order player and often started against spinners. I tended to lunge at the ball and get pad onto bat caught-in-close types of dismissals. I knew when I had confidence in my technique against slows I was more selective in my play and not hurried or panicky.

Opening up front foot

Often left-handers have the habit of closing their front foot off and pointing it towards cover when playing forward. This leads to playing either around your front pad, which is a batting sin, or not playing straight balls back straight. I got out LBW a lot and I felt this habit was to blame. In reality it was a symptom of the first two technical points on this list but I didn't yet know that.

Tactical

Starting — playing straight and letting the ball come

This simply cannot be overstated when starting an innings. While I lived by the cut shot, I had learnt from previous failures that I needed to be watchful early on and at least look to provide a full face and straight bat to the ball.

Percentage hits

When under pressure and bogged down it was handy to have some boundary options from good balls. At this stage in my career I was playing good one-day cricket for Otago, and playing for New Zealand in the limited-over stuff was not out of the question.

Working the ball around

It's amazing how when I played well in the late '90s I did this so well. Perhaps it was because I was playing in the middle order for Otago in one-dayers. This skill left me in a hurry as my test game progressed — I wish it hadn't.

Physical

I have always been aerobically fit and relatively strong but also stiff and slow. Being fit helps you handle stress and it is vital that after running between wickets you are not huffing and puffing trying to focus on the next ball and thus you need to recover very quickly. I wasn't overly concerned with this part of my PPP as fitness was a way of life for me then — however, in retrospect I wish I had placed a higher priority on flexibility and speed (in defiance of my 'Rigor Mortis' moniker).

Psychological

Present moment focus

It's vitally important to stay present. You cannot change the past and you can't let it impact on your ability to play the next ball. This is a very tough skill to acquire indeed and one which I had no idea how to apply regularly.

Confidence/Positivity

For most of the time confidence and positivity were non-existent in me except once I was in and going well — and then I was generally a cocky shit.

Relaxation

Anxiety leads to tension and mistakes. I had a ton of anxiety and it affected me hugely, especially when starting an innings. Generally it took till I got to a score of 30 before I relaxed at all.

Imagery

I had heard a lot about this technique and thought it was important. I thought back to some good innings and had to concede that I *had* thought about them beforehand and envisaged success before it happened — so in it went to my PPP.

Mental toughness

At this stage I didn't have much of a handle on what this concept actually entailed, but in the end I had a pretty good grasp of it, and I believe now that mental toughness is the outcome of the whole mental management process, not simply a part of it. But in 1997 I looked at Australians David Boon, Allan Border and Mark Taylor and thought they had mental toughness. That was mainly because they appeared to be no-nonsense types of players who simply gritted their teeth and got on with it. Thinking back on my own success I could see that mental toughness often came when I got stuck in and was determined to give the opposition bowlers nothing — such as when we needed to get through to a score in a tight game and my whole focus was about denying the bastards my wicket.

So when you really look at it, this initial PPP uncovers pretty well the person I really am — a little negative. The list is full of things I felt I *didn't* have but *needed*. I guess my cup has always been half-empty and that is what drove me in pursuit of the things I didn't possess. I don't really see a problem with this. I was still aware there was a good quantity of water in my glass but I wasn't happy with either a half-empty glass — or a half-full glass for that matter — I wanted a full bloody glass goddamit!

The other most noticeable feature of this initial document is that it reveals that the skills that I had and was executing relatively well were regarded more as one-day cricket skills. I thought I could work singles quite well and hit boundaries when required. These were the things that you had to do early on in a one-day game, or that I could do when established in a first-class innings, not skills you associate with *starting* an innings in first-class games. Getting more starts was of course a major goal in the development of this process. It was time to start working!

Step 2: Analysis

My initial PPP provided a starting point on the path to self-discovery. It was now time to play and discover. So in 1997 I began to log my thoughts and observations on each innings I played.

At this point I realised that I had entered into a process — if I was going to improve my batting there was simply no quick-fix. Immediately I realised the error of my ways when I'd been trying to regain my bowling. In those days all I'd wanted was a quick-fix — a tip, a technique, or anything that would instantly fix my problem. I had been to see sports psych people during this time but always wanted them to send me home with a wonder cure. Alex opened my eyes and I realised that the only healer was time, and time well spent. If I was to improve my mental approach to batting and achieve my goals I now knew I had to make a commitment to the process and that I had to be patient. I had a path to travel down, and it would take some time and a lot of training and games of cricket before I would find any answers.

It began in club cricket and at the time I was playing for Albion in Dunedin. Over the course of the 1997/98 season I religiously documented my day at cricket. I logged everything, from information on the opposition, the pitch conditions, my mode of dismissal, how I was playing to basically anything else that I thought had relevance.

While I tried to be as comprehensive as possible, I realised that the most important element was honesty. When you put an innings down on paper it is so easy to fall into the trap of allowing your appraisal to fall victim to subjectivity. So often if someone makes a big score we simply say that they played well, and if they got out for not many then we say they played badly. 'Read it in the scorebook' is one of cricket's great clichés, and simply put means history will record your *result*, and the *way* it occurred means nothing. Believe it or not, I know of selectors and reporters who have picked teams and written match appraisals based on what they read in the scorebook — yet the scorebook records the most inaccurate account of a day's cricket.

It was crucial to my process that I manage to look beyond the superficial outcome of how many runs I scored and was as objective as humanly possible in analysing my last innings; in fact, the whole process depended on it — *honesty* and *objectivity* were pivotal components in my batting development.

Gradually, as the years and seasons ticked by, my analysis moved from a case of self-discovery — whereby everything and anything was recorded — to become more targeted and self-appraising in assessing my performance against an increasingly accurate list of key performance indicators. This appraisal process was the cornerstone of my cricketing development and it became somewhat more of a religion than a routine in the end.

At the time I was breaking into the Black Caps, the management was introducing a 'workbook' system for the players and encouraging this very form of self-planning, organisation and appraisal. We would be issued with tour workbooks to use and fill out as we pleased. Needless to say, I used mine diligently. Between tours I would use a school exercise book and eventually got to design my own workbook for the tour of India in 2003. I simply couldn't operate without them.

Step 3: A changing PPP
= a developing understanding of my game

Like I said, over the first couple of years I was logging masses of information — which was fine but useless without every so often taking a step back and assessing it. I wanted to find key correlations between the things I was recording and my on-field performance. When I did discover a correlation it became part of my PPP. Consequently, I found that over the years my PPP became not only more accurate but a hell of a lot simpler and abbreviated. Shown below is the very last PPP I completed in the winter of 2004 just before the England tour in May.

Current ○	Poor			Average					Excellent		
Best ●	0	1	2	3	4	5	6	7	8	9	10
Technical											
Head forward – hands back						○	●				
Playing under eyes						○			●		
Tactical											
Remain within game plan											
seamers										○	●
spinners			○								●
Bat v pad technique								○	●		
Mental											
Absorbed in pre-balls								○			●
Score first — defend second						○			●		

This PPP did not really change over the last three years of my career. At times my attention would be drawn to the parts of it I was failing to achieve, but for the most part it stayed constant, which served to prove I had a good handle on my game. That did not mean I stopped analysing my game, however, it just meant that my analysis had something to benchmark against.

Explanation of final PPP

Technical

Head forward — hands back

This was the position I wanted to be in at delivery. 'Head forward' suggested a forward intent, and getting my 'hands back' meant they were in a good position to strike the ball. It was a position I struggled with and worked hard on. In test cricket I faced a lot of fast bowlers who would try to intimidate and force me into poor defensive positions. I would counter by trying to keep my weight forward at all costs. Most of the time I would keep my head forward but also push my hands forward. From this position I lost all my shoulder preparation and had no back-lift. This meant I often got into trouble if I wanted to play an aggressive shot because I had to quickly lift the bat back to generate any power and thus would end up very rushed and go hard at the shot. It was the reason why, for a strongish guy, I couldn't hit the ball very far.

Playing under eyes

This was how I ensured I played the ball late, letting it come to me and getting in behind it. If I couldn't defend it under my eyes then I could most probably leave it. It was also very important from an attacking point of view because it meant I used the pace of the ball and timed my shots. Mistiming is often a symptom of going early at the ball and getting way out in front of yourself. By waiting a little longer you ensure you track the ball with your eyes for longer, stay on top of the shot, and are more likely to play the shot with control.

Tactical

Remain within game plan

It was this ability that defined me as a cricketer. Many players who scored fewer runs than I did had better body positions at delivery, played the ball later and had more shots in their repertoire and more time to play them, but my advantage was a knowledge of what I could and couldn't do from a stroke-play perspective and the ability to stick to my game plan for long periods of time.

Early on in my batting career, and even when I was a bowler, I could hook, cover drive and back-foot drive. However, these shots got me out, especially early on in my innings, far more times than they got me big runs. They simply had to go. The cover drive, for instance, is the bane of left-handed batsmen in New Zealand. On good surfaces, if you play the ball late and under your eyes you can hit the angle of the right-arm bowler on the front foot through backward point — very much like Australia's Justin Langer does — but on our seaming wickets the cover drive is deadly. I've seen some promising left-handed batsmen here ruined by their inability to put the cover drive away.

Half volleys are even worse as they're the ones you get closer to and are likely to nick, and they have been the scourge of New Zealand cricket over the last few years. Too many bowlers at first-class level lob up half volleys just outside off stump at medium pace, let the track do its work, and get the edge. In response, the batsman who wants to be successful in this country is hesitant to drive with authority and becomes negative.

However, to make the Black Caps I had to score runs in New Zealand before I could even think about scoring them overseas, so out went the two shots you need true wickets for — the pull/hook and the cover drive. The back-foot drive — which was one of my favourite shots because not many could play it, and a well-played drive in front of point played on your toes from your back foot is a beautiful thing indeed — was discarded after a year of test cricket. I realised that against quality new-ball bowlers who got a little extra bounce and pace it was a nicking shot, so it went too.

When I understood that my chance of Black Caps selection was as a test opener the crunching-down period began in earnest. I wanted to eliminate all risk from my play. I knew you also needed to score runs, but I would only score runs from shots I felt were low-risk options. Many players spend countless hours trying to develop a full array of shots, but I really concentrated hard on developing the skills to *not* play certain shots. Not possessing the ability to play an expansive game, I focused my attention instead on having a small selection of shots that I was totally confident with and putting aside those I believed were just not worth the risk.

On the front foot I waited till the ball was full and very straight, at the stumps in fact, and looked to drive as straight as possible. This was safe, as my eyes would be over the ball and I had more control over the shot. By leaving as many as I could outside off stump and being patient I could encourage the bowlers to bowl straighter, and when they did I could work the ball into the on side from both back and front foot, which again was safe because the ball was under my eyes.

The cut was my 'queen' — it was my big attacking piece. You simply cannot let bowlers get away with short, wide crap, and at test level you must have a back-foot option. I felt the cut was safe as you were hitting the ball after it seamed and had time to adjust — also, the width and bounce meant that edges were likely to go over the slips and not to hand.

I worried a lot about getting out after playing outside of my tight game plan. Getting out playing expansive shots I saw as a lack of control and as throwing my wicket away. As a younger player I was criticised regularly for 'giving my wicket away' and it is another one of those clichés you hear bandied about when players get out or teams get rolled for very little. I hated being accused of giving my wicket away with a passion, because it was something I never *ever* wanted to do

You can see from my PPP on page 124 that I was struggling to play within my game plan to spinners. About this time I had started to rebel against my defensive ways and it manifested itself in some pretty reckless batsmanship against them.

Bat v pad technique

This refers to my defensive technique against the spin bowlers. Simply put, it means if I can kick the ball away with my pad and not risk LBW, then how effectively am I doing it? Conversely, if I must hit the ball, am I effecting that technique properly as well? Use of the pad in defence to the sharply spinning ball is essential, especially when it is turning back from off to leg. Good use of the pad can encourage the bowlers to bowl a more defensive, straighter line, thus not using the footmarks out wide; and with a straighter line you can use the bat out in front of the pad and generate singles close in on the off and leg sides.

Having a well-organised defensive technique to spinners was paramount to my overall batting approach. If I was confident in defence then I could 'sit on the bowler', defending away happily and waiting for the bad ball — which comes along at all levels eventually — and put it away. If my defence was threatened, then I would be forced to take some risk to put pressure back on the bowler and play more adventurous shots — and as you should well know by now, I was risk-averse. I did actually develop the sweep and slog sweep for such occasions, but later on tended to want to play them all the time without laying a solid defensive foundation first, or I ended up using them unnecessarily in situations where I didn't need to employ them to score at a good enough rate — that is, against poorer spinners.

Mental

Absorbed in pre-balls

In the upcoming chapter entitled 'Routines' I outline and explain the conception and importance of my pre-ball routine, so for now I just want to say that the effect my pre-ball routine had on my game was massive. In fact, when it comes to the relationship between the mental, technical and tactical components of my play, the mental side was without doubt the dominant force. If I couldn't get my mental game into line, it would have major repercussions on my ability to effect my technical skills and tactical objectives with any success. I also always felt that even if technically and tactically I was lagging a little, if I could get my mental game right I could at the very least soldier on and graft out a score.

Score first — defend second

Sounds a bit strange doesn't it? How could someone who batted so slowly and was lauded for his stoic resistance say he went out to score runs first before looking to defend? Well, it's true, I did — in theory anyway.

The more I analysed the game the more I decided that a score-first mentality was the ideal mental outlook for batting. It means that every time a bowler runs in your mentality should be to score runs. Actually, let me rephrase that a little: *you should be prepared to score from every ball*. This doesn't mean you *are* going to score from every ball, just that you should be *prepared*. The trick is to be prepared to play the shots you play to those balls when they come along and if the ball isn't right — like perhaps a good-length ball at off stump or one that is too wide to reach — then either defend it or let it go. If you are looking to score then you are more likely to actually score with authority when the opportunity arises. If, however, your mentality is defend first when the ball is there to hit, your attack is more of an afterthought and you will probably be in a less than ideal technical position to strike with timing, be rushed with the stroke, and generally cock up a prime opportunity.

I freely admit that I struggled to fully grasp this concept. I agreed with it wholeheartedly, but putting it into practice, especially in latter years, was always a challenge. My inability to think this way definitely hindered my technical desire to get my 'hands back'. Often I got out to balls that should have been put away through poor shot execution and mistiming. Missing out on scoring opportunities was also frustrating and often put me under pressure, leading to my downfall once established at the crease.

When I began the process I had little understanding of how I achieved positive results, but over time I developed a growing awareness of my technique, tactics and mental realities. Awareness is all-important for making improvement and my Peak Performance Profiling and analysis provided a sound base of understanding to work from.

The identified key criteria to my game were all interrelated and it was rare that they were at their best all at the same time. Sometimes I could be fine technically, but tactically I was loose or vice versa, and if one element was out it could definitely affect the other two. If I was struggling with my technique I might get frustrated and lose it mentally, or if I just couldn't get my mind right, and plenty of things can cause that, then remaining within my game plan could be near-impossible. When they did all fall into place and were peaking, then batting *almost* became fun.

Chapter Ten

The 'Zone'

Many people have talked about this magical thing called 'the zone'. When you can get there it's a place where everything seems to come perfectly naturally; your performance is accurate and effortless and you achieve things that you previously thought you couldn't with ease. Some have even described their experiences within 'the zone' as like being in a state of brainlessness, almost as if operating on autopilot. It is a state where you just 'push play' and let everything unfold.

There have definitely been one or two occasions in my own cricket career when I was in 'the zone' and I would describe it as 'like being in a state of total clarity'. It is an experience where between balls I would almost say to myself something like, 'If you bowl it *there*, I'll hit it there,' or 'If you bowl it there, I'll hit it *there*' — and then I would. Basically, it felt like I had every scenario rehearsed, had a clear plan for each ball, and then would carry it out with precision. The game seemed to become so simple, so clear, and I almost felt as though I was in total control of each delivery, almost to the point of knowing what it would be.

When I was younger, however, and was a bowler, I found 'the zone' to be slightly different. I did get into it quite often — in fact, more often than when I was batting — but it was not quite as conscious a place. As a bowler it was very much a state of 'autopilot'. It was a total rhythmical experience in that I had rhythm with my action, but also there was a sense of timing and rhythm in the whole operation. I would almost feel as if after bowling a perfectly pitched delivery I would then get the ball back in my hand at the same time and place, the walk back to my mark would be constant, I would turn, run in and then bowl again and it all felt like some well-choreographed dance. It was trancelike and it had a flow which lasted balls, overs, whole spells.

Batting rhythm

While we often hear the term 'rhythm' used in relation to bowling and bowlers, and it is such an important element of success in that discipline, it is not so often used in relation to batting although I believe it to be equally as important to effective batsmanship. Batting rhythm may be different for various batsmen, but when a batsman finds his rhythm he plays at his best.

Many batsmen operate at certain tempos and perhaps a batting rhythm is more closely associated with that. My own tempo was fairly slow — about one run an over in test cricket when at my best. For someone like Australia's Adam Gilchrist, however, it would be a lot faster. When I looked up at the board after 10, 20, 30 or however many overs of good-quality bowling I was relatively happy to see my score roughly equal to the indicated overs. Your tempo is something you feel happy with. When you are within your usual tempo range you generally feel comfortable and experience less pressure. In my final year of cricket I tried to raise this tempo to about one-and-a-half runs per over but just couldn't do it. However, tempo is only a *part* of batting rhythm, and if the bowling is so tight that you can't get it away or so loose you are able to score more quickly, what then?

Some batsmen are able to raise and lower their tempos regardless of the nature of the bowling and still remain quite comfortable. Stephen Fleming can do this well, so can Australian captain Ricky Ponting, and these are the players that appear to adjust quite nicely between the requirements of ODI and test cricket. But it is not an easy skill and one which I never really mastered. Even when batting in the middle order for Otago and a lot more attacking in nature, my tempo in each form of cricket was very similar — about two runs an over.

Obviously tempo is heavily influenced by the bowler and the field placings. If the bowling is all over the show you can score more quickly or more slowly if it is tight. My tempo of one run an over was geared for test-match bowling, provided a guideline from which to assess my progress, and was an outcome I felt comfortable with. However, it is the combination of tempo and the manner in which you are achieving that tempo that defines batting rhythm.

When you are in rhythm your tempo becomes a function of the bowling quality, shot selection and shot execution. I would achieve rhythm in my own batting when, against quality bowling, I would be going along at an average of one run an over — achieving it through the use of my main scoring methods and playing my strokes with accuracy. But if I was batting at my tempo but forced by good bowling to look outside my usual scoring areas, those I felt comfortable with, then I would not be in rhythm because my scoring was very much a forced process.

Much like a bowler who usually operates in the 130–135 kph range but because of a lack of coordination on the day is having to 'muscle' the ball down to achieve those speeds, if I am scoring at a rate way above my tempo but doing it with shots outside those of my usual game, then I am not in my batting rhythm. On the other hand, if I am way below my tempo because I'm tied down by good bowling, then I might feel under pressure, lose my rhythm and be forced into a silly shot — Australia's bowlers are expert at taking your rhythm from you in this manner.

It was in the year 2000 that I really began to become aware of my tempo and increasingly interested in this concept of 'batting rhythm'. I never shared this concept with my team-mates or coach because I was always getting accused of overcomplicating things at the best of times anyway — perhaps they were right. Nevertheless, it began to dawn on me that to bat well and for long periods of time I needed to find my rhythm as quickly as possible and maintain it. It was also apparent to me that finding my rhythm was not a forced process but had to occur naturally — almost as if I was striking an equilibrium, or balance, between my own game and that which the bowlers were confronting me with.

When it all fell into place it was a feeling of being totally immersed in the competition between bat and ball. It was reactive in that my actions were dictated by the nature of the delivery bowled at me and they would be those I trusted and was totally comfortable with. My scoring would be at a pace I felt appropriate for the situation, and I would be quite happy ticking along at *my* pace. I realised that when I had this rhythm and a feeling of total clarity in what I was doing, then I was in 'the zone'.

> I now had an understanding of what 'the zone' was to me. It was that point at which my technical, tactical and mental games were in complete harmony.

My state of mind would be as it should be for peak performance — tactically I was playing the type and pace of game I trusted and was comfortable with, and my shot selection and execution of them was technically sound and thus accurate —and at this point I was as close to a *reactive* batting machine as I could be.

Zone shift

Interestingly, as my game developed so too did my 'zone' shift and change its nature. When I was first making my way as a batsman and as a middle-order player my 'zone' was very much a brain-dead but also quite an attacking and aggressive place. I tended to find I would begin to bat with authority around the 40–60 run mark and it was a time when I would really take it to the bowlers. My batting would be punctuated with flowing cover drives, punchy back-foot drives, and I would almost play a shot to every ball. It was a great place to be and when I got there I really relished batting.

When I made my hundred against the West Indies in 1994 I got into 'the zone' from about 30 on and really took it to the bowling. I was almost reckless but everything just kept hitting the middle of the bat. Likewise when I struck the 33 off the over at Geraldine — I had been playing positively leading up to the final over, and when I think back now it was almost like I knew Hamish Kember was going to bowl a good length on off stump and it seemed so natural to just run down the wicket and bash it over mid-on and off. I also recall another memorable innings against Northern Districts in the 1995/96 season when on about 60 I just couldn't wait for the bowlers to bowl so I could whack it.

However, when my focus began to shift from attacking middle-order player to more defensive-minded opening batman my 'zone' became a more patient state. It was a feeling of ball-by-ball focus, control and total immersion in the art of 'staying in'. Rather than a sensation of attacking dominance over the bowler, I felt more as if I couldn't be removed from the middle and that I had total control over my actions and methods of scoring. There were times in test matches when I felt as if time and deliveries just passed me by. Hours felt like mere minutes and I knew I was 'in the zone' when I would start a session and then after what felt like about 10–20 minutes I would ask the umpire the time till the break and he would say, 'About 15 minutes'. Thus, although at test match level I very seldom dominated the bowling — it was always just too good — I certainly did experience periods in which I felt totally immersed in the task of batting.

It was during the period covering the 'A' tour to the UK in 2000 and the end of the 2001/02 season that I attained this state more frequently than at any other time in my cricketing life. I posted some big scores and had some marathon stays at the crease — for instance, my 212 against Sussex at Hove and my 306 in Zimbabwe. It was a period in which I gained massive satisfaction from batting error-free for hours on end, no matter who the opposition was. It was when I batted for the sole purpose of spending time at the wicket, 'time' literally flew of the middle of my bat.

'The zone' is a fickle mistress

'The zone' is a fickle place. You play many innings, even large innings, when you never attain it. You can still score runs when you feel dreadfully out of form but you graft and survive; or you can have times when you are totally out of control but you continue swinging with abandon, unable to pull in the reins, and somehow you still survive. There are also times when you do get into 'the zone' but just for a fleeting moment and then it is gone again.

In fact, what frequently happened with me was that I would get into 'the zone' and then pull myself out of it. This would occur the most if I was batting at a fast pace, especially post 1999. I had been celebrated for my patient, solid, slow but reliable method of play and knew that this was what was expected of me. But there were times when the bowlers just bowled rubbish and I would be scoring with freedom and regularity. I would be miles above my usual and expected tempo, but fail to realise that I *was* in fact in the correct tempo and had my rhythm for the particular bowling display I was facing. I would then purposefully slow down, not realising that my run rate was actually being achieved through my usual and trusted methods.

In retrospect, these were my chances to dominate — rare chances — and I didn't take them. For example, I'll never forgive myself for the day I was in 'the zone' against Canterbury. I had about 70 runs from nearly a run a ball and was playing superbly. Their bowling had struggled to find the right line and length. They had been pitching too short and I was cutting and back-foot driving with ease, scoring at a great rate but in total control. Then I questioned myself. I pulled back when a century was probable only half an hour away, if that, lost my timing, went outside my game plan in frustration and was caught and bowled trying to pull Chris Martin. I never scored a century against Canterbury and the memory of that day still haunts me.

The last time this occurred was also my last innings of any real note. It was the second innings of the third and final test against England at Trent Bridge, Nottingham. I had had a huge series and occupied the crease for record amounts of time. However, while it could be said that I played well in this series I never really found any sort of timing and indeed never felt comfortable at the crease in any innings until that last one. Through to about 45 my batting was unreal — I was timing the ball the best I had for ages and hitting straight and cover drives with ease, and my scoring rate was ridiculously fast — well, for me, anyway. Then I thought to myself, 'Bloody hell, you're going okay here. This could be one of your great hundreds. Head down, nice and steady now.' Then I stalled, shuffled across my stumps to an average ball from Ashley Giles, played a weak shot and got out LBW!

Combatting 'the zone'

When an opposing player gets into 'the zone', watch out, as they become a clear and present danger to your own team's chance of success. As I became more and more interested in the concepts of batting rhythm and 'the zone' I began to ponder how this concept could be utilised from a team perspective. Most players tend to be preoccupied with finding their own 'zone' as individuals and remain oblivious to its application in respect of their opponent. But if you stop and think about it for a moment, while it is important to your team's chances of success to attain your own 'zone' as often as possible, so too is it vital to restrict your opponents from attaining theirs.

I've always thought that if you can understand the particular rhythm and tempo that your opposition like to play, then you can employ appropriate methods to break this up. In other words, if you can make your opponent uncomfortable and force them to play a less preferred style of cricket, you limit their opportunities to find 'the zone'. For instance, someone like Brian Lara likes to score in boundaries, so in response some teams have had success by putting boundary fielders out very early in his innings so that his boundary shots only yield a single. He would get his 'four ball' but only end up hitting it to the boundary rider, take one and lose the strike. When this tactic was employed well he has been known to get agitated, impatient and lose control.

And take the Australians, who are very adept at assessing where you like to score your runs and then blocking those areas off. Although we associate the Australian seamers with being great fast bowlers, they actually operate in a very defensive mindset — they are masters at stalling your progress and frustrating you into playing poor shots. Glen McGrath, for example, is a bowler of theirs who appears to get into 'the zone' often. He will bowl incredibly accurately for ball after ball and appears in total control. The players who have had success against McGrath have been able to break up his rhythm. I always rue the fact that I let him bowl as he pleased at me and never tried something like changing my guard from middle to off or off to leg as a means of knocking him out of his 'zone' and generating scoring opportunities.

'The zone' and my PPP

From my analysis and development of my Peak Performance Profile I had a blueprint for successful personal performance. I believed in the things I had identified on my PPP chart and knew I must implement them to perform, but what I also surmised was that when they were in total harmony together I was in 'the zone'.

However, while it was all well and good to have such an in-depth and developing understanding of my game, it was at this stage a retrospective process. It told me what I did when I played well, but it did not yet tell me how to ensure I did it on a regular basis now and into the future. It came time for Alex and I to take my process to the next level.

For the 1998/99 season I had set a goal of getting more 'starts'. As I mentioned earlier, I would attain 'the zone' around the 40–60 run mark of an innings, but I was getting there and going on to a big score only once or twice a year. In between times I was getting a lot of low scores and this was what I believed was holding me back. I wanted to find a means of ensuring I could get into 'the zone' much earlier in an innings — even, if possible, *before* an innings — and then remain in it for as long as possible. So we began to explore my *routines*.

Chapter Eleven

Routines

I remember the conversation, although I'm a little foggy on the date, but it must have been early in the 1996/97 season. I was sitting with Paul Wiseman outside the changing-rooms at Hagley Park in Christchurch smarting about getting out cheaply. I was thinking about players like Stephen Fleming, Chris Cairns and Matthew Horne — they were all playing pretty well and it frustrated me that they didn't seem to make nearly as many elementary mistakes as I did, especially early in their innings.

I was getting out in all sorts of silly ways and it was mystifying and angering me. Paul had been around these guys a bit as he was making his way into the Black Caps set-up. He asked me if I had any routines. My answer was that I didn't. He said that a lot of the best batsmen had quite distinct routines they went through before batting and that perhaps I should think about finding something that worked for me.

At this stage of my career the time before I batted was spent in all manner of ways. I was always nervous, but some days I would sit quietly with my legs swinging and banging together using up nervous energy, others I would be charging around joking and laughing with team-mates, and I'm buggered if I took any notice of the things I was doing the night and morning before play. There was nothing constant in my preparation. I recalled how on the Emerging Players tour to Australia, Mike Shrimpton, who was the coach, had got annoyed with the way I didn't tend to pay any attention to what was going on in the middle before I went in. But at the time I didn't really heed Paul's advice. It all seemed just too flowery. However, as my work with Alex progressed it became very clear that I needed to find some routines as a means to maximise the value of the results uncovered from my analysis.

As I began to pay more attention to and understand my own game I also began to understand the game of cricket in general a little more clearly. I realised that there was only one thing that could ever be constant and that you had any real control over — *yourself.* A game that had so many participants, a moving ball, differing venues and so on provided for so many different variables. I realised I had very little, if any, control over these variables but they were affecting me nonetheless.

There is a great cricket cliché that goes 'Control the controllables' — in other words, control yourself and your own performance and don't let it be affected by things that are out of your hands. Things like poor umpiring, substandard playing surfaces, other players, the weather and so on are all things you have little control over so don't waste energy trying to control them. (That said, though, there are one or two players in world cricket who do control the umpiring quite nicely, but for us mere mortals it is very much a case of 'put up and shut up'!)

On the flip side of the coin, you *can* choose the style of your play, your preparation and your behaviour, and in so doing make the best of a given situation. Personally, I don't believe there to be a more important or truer concept in cricket — or even life for that matter.

So there I was, playing my cricket in various towns, on various grounds, in differing situations, and against ever-changing and diverse opposition. I was also producing vastly differing results and getting out in all sorts of fashions. There were very few constants about my game and I was getting frustrated with my results and wanted answers, but was struggling to find them. Until it dawned on me — even if nothing else around me could be, I would ensure that *I* was constant. My PPP was telling me what I needed to do to succeed — now I would set about finding out what I needed to do to ensure I played that way more often and especially earlier in my innings.

I was a poor starter but knew that when I got in I was a good and effective player. My rationale was that if I could get more starts I would not only get more big scores but I would boost my runs aggregate and average. If I wanted to make a play for the big time I knew I had to make more runs, simple as that. It was at this point that things really began to happen for me.

It was during the 1999/2000 season that I finally developed a pre-innings preparation process that would give me the best chance of effecting the key elements of my PPP from the very first ball. It had been hard to find a starting point for this process, but possibly the fact that I had been thinking about and working on understanding and developing my game over the preceding couple of years subconsciously provided the basic framework. From then on my pre-batting routine never really altered from the point I formalised it to the day I left the game, barring some minor refinements along the way — oh, and the odd tantrum when I tried to reject it altogether, of course. Here's how it went.

Pre-batting routine

Step 1: Analysis

If I could sum up in a nutshell how I transformed myself from a tail-end batsman to a test-match opener in one statement it would be this: *I thought about it.* From the minute I put my mind to batting it began to improve. The more I thought about it the better it became, and the more accurate and appropriate that thought, the faster the improvement and better the results. So when first I sat down to develop my pre-batting routine it quickly became very clear that an understanding of what I had just done, what I was doing in general, and what I needed to do in the future was the logical first step in preparing for my next innings.

My pre-batting routine therefore began at the point of being dismissed from my last innings (albeit I did allow myself the luxury of a few hours, sometimes 24 hours, of sulking, of course). Had I achieved my PPP? If so, why? If not, why not? What was I doing technically, tactically and mentally? Were the things I was doing and thinking appropriate for the situation? How did I get out and why? These were all questions for which I needed to find answers. But because I wanted the *right* answers it was critical that my self-appraisal was objective.

However, it is hard to be objective in an emotional state, and believe me, I was particularly emotionally unstable following a dismissal. Some players could walk off, correct their mistake in their heads as they departed the ground, take their pads off and then be reasonably relaxed and civil, but not me! Once the disbelief surrounding my dismissal subsided the anger would set in about a second or two after I left the crease. Then about halfway off in would kick the self-pity and I would enter the dressing-room in a cloud of doom and gloom. Quite often the first words I would say to myself would be, 'Well, that's it then, you've scored your last run, your career is over.' I would then take my gloves and helmet off, sit down, put my head in my hands and stay there for anywhere between half an hour and an hour.

Every so often I would raise my head and pour out my soul to any passing team-mates. After a while the analysis would finally start. Not the good stuff, no way, it was the 'I'm ready for an argument stuff'. I would ask a team-mate for his appraisal of the situation, but was really asking them to say what I wanted to hear or God help them! Objectivity was not a welcome participant in the early hours following a Mark Richardson dismissal.

When finally my world regained some semblance of perspective I could begin to objectively analyse my current batting situation. This was the beginning of my pre-batting routine and without doubt the most important step in the process because it put the wheels in *motion*; and if it was an objective and accurate analysis that reflected the true situation, then I could set those wheels off in the right *direction*. In short, my analysis determined my training goals which led me to the next step in the pre-batting routine process.

Step 2: Set training goals

My analysis would have determined the areas I needed to train in when building up for my next innings. Up till now most of my reference to analysis had been very much about *self*-analysis. What do I do well? What do I do badly? Where am I struggling? It was all about *my* game. In developing my PPPs and improving my game this inward approach was still necessary, but analysis of the opposition and their strengths and weaknesses in relation to my game now also became important in setting my training goals. This part of the process gave me focus. It meant that my time at training would not be wasted.

And boy was I a massive trainer. As far as I'm concerned there's no substitute for honest hard work when it comes to training. I believe wholeheartedly in the cliché *practice makes perfect*. Training was far more to me than just skill development. It had enormous mental benefits and helped me deal with some of the 'demons' that haunted me throughout my career. But we'll deal with those demons later.

Mark O'Donnell, Auckland Aces Coach: After returning to New Zealand from the South African circuit I had the privilege of working with Mark for three seasons — my throwing arm will never be the same again! 'Attention to detail', 'work ethic', 'determination' and 'obsessive compulsive' are all phrases that describe Richie.

He reminds me very much of former South African and Eastern Province captain Kepler Wessels, whom I worked with as coach of Eastern Province. The same single-mindedness, preparation, style, similar test record and speed — although in Wessels' defence he did have a dodgy knee.

Richie was a challenging individual for a coach with his practice requirements, often going through entire team practices batting, padded up or waiting to bat again. You could not fault his desire to maximise every ounce of his ability and talent. Essential to the New Zealand and Auckland teams' dynamic. Did he add value — absolutely!

My cricketing memory of Richie — the lycra? No, rather a blinding one-handed catch at third slip with a sore back and after not wanting to be in the slip cordon.

I wish him good luck for the next chapter of his life and presume it will be handled just as thoroughly.

Outcome goals and process goals

It's fine to set goals such as 'I want to play for New Zealand'; 'I want 20 first-class centuries'; 'I want to be the player of the year' and so on. These are *outcome* goals and they are great for keeping you motivated — even better when you start marking them off. For the record, once I got selected for New Zealand I wanted to play 30 tests, score three hundreds and average 30. This ambition was based on the record of one of my idols and role models and the player I was most often compared to — Bruce Edgar. Then, after I'd played about 20 tests I upped my expectations to 40 tests, six hundreds and an average of above 40.

I achieved the majority of my goals and actually surpassed my expectations at times. It was very satisfying but I didn't achieve them simply because I set them.

> I achieved my goals because I identified what I actually needed to do to make them a reality and set about doing it — I set *process* goals.

Process goals are the tasks that you believe you must accomplish to achieve an outcome. When I learnt to set process goals and then work away at them I achieved desired outcomes, but more importantly learnt *how* to achieve.

Cricket is a game full of clichés and I've already brought a few out so far. My belief is that something usually becomes a cliché because it works. Here's another: 'Focus on the process and the result will look after itself.' For it to work though, you must first know what the process is. Which is why I analysed and evaluated my game, compared it to that of other cricketers, and sought out information and coaching advice. Once I settled on a process that I believed was the way forward it became a goal, a series of goals, and ultimately a road map to success. Thus, beginning with my PPP, my cricket training life became a series of daily, achievable goals all planned out in detail.

Training timeframes

It is also important at this point to distinguish between my training timeframes. I've described my game in terms of technical, tactical and mental elements and thus my goals for improvement were always categorised under these main groupings.

Technical changes and thus technical goals need plenty of time to work on and need to be gradually introduced. It takes time to groove a body movement and in a game like cricket when it has to happen very quickly it *must* be grooved. You simply do not have the time to tell some body part to move in a certain way and move it consciously. Likewise, tactical changes are all well and good, but you still need the skill to effect them and that can take time. It takes time to learn a new shot and then have the ability to bring it in and out of your game at will.

Therefore if I was going to set specific goals for the improvement of both technique and tactics I would need to ensure I had plenty of time up my sleeve. For this reason technical and tactical improvements were often pre-season or pre-series goals and any work done on them within a series or a season was very much of a maintenance nature — although I will admit here that I possibly could have been more proactive when it came to modifying my tactics during an innings or for a particular innings. I was found out in my last trip to Australia because I didn't take a more positive approach to my batting. In a way, that is a valid assessment, but I also felt I hadn't developed the right tools to *be* more positive against the Aussie attack.

Because I considered pre-season and pre-series work as a legitimate part of my pre-batting routine my analysis work therefore followed not only individual innings but also series and seasons. As I came closer to competition time my focus would turn more to my mental management and associated improvements. Believing at this stage that little more could be done to integrate techniques and tactics into my game, I now had to ensure I could achieve the necessary mental states of mind to allow the changes to flow and achieve my peak performance. Thus, during a series with little time between games most of my daily goals were about preparing my mind for the upcoming challenge. Which is all quite wordy, so below is an example of exactly how I went about this process.

What follows was my winter training programme and goals in 2003, leading up to the Indian tour. It was developed in response to my desire to convert my starts in test-match cricket into more hundreds. My analysis from the previous summer and recent tours had shown me that I was stagnating through the middle of my innings, and losing both patience and concentration. Twice I had been dismissed in the 80s in the first over of the second new ball to weak shots and even worse concentration. The end result of this plan was not a lift in scoring rate but it did allow me to achieve another test century.

Operation 'Rigor-rate'

Aim

- Approach each innings in a way that gives me the best chance of staying in for 90+ overs while still allowing me to accumulate runs fluently with a minimum of risk.
- Maintain defensive effectiveness.
- Lift average scoring rate to 100 runs in 70 overs.
- Improve 50 to 100 conversion rate.

Method

Overs 1–20 New ball/Getting in

- Threats — new ball, movement, not 'in' yet, fast bowling, excessive nerves.
- Requirements — arousal control, courage, restricted game plan, quality leaving, in behind defence.
- Game plan:

  > Look to play — late
  > Leave balls not threatening stumps
  > Defend within body lines
  > Scoring: work off hip
  >   onside drives
  >   cut

- Outcomes — get 'in' and get a feel, defend solidly, leave as much as possible, score when bowlers get too straight or short and wide, 15–30 runs.

Overs 20–60 Accumulation/Adaptation

- Threats — defensive bowling, scoreboard pressure, spin.
- Requirements — patience, sticking to GP, ability to tick score over, precision, process focus, quick adaptation to new bowlers, adaptation to situation.
- Game plan seamers:

  > Play first/leave second
  > Looking to find gaps
  > Scoring: driving straight and on side
  >   single in front and angled to gap
  >   cut
  >   work off hip

- Game plan spinners:

  > Organise defence (2–3 overs)
  > Assess quality — sit or proactive
  > Scoring: cut
  >   pull
  >   work square for single
  >   sweep *
  >   slog sweep
  >   hitting over top
  >   use of feet *

* Depending on type and quality of spinner; proactive option

- Outcomes — scoring within GP options, score at a steady rate, score with control, remain process focused, manipulate GP with control, 60 runs

Overs 60–80 Getting through
- Threats — fatigue, scoreboard distraction, reverse swing, new ball distraction.
- Requirements — process focus, control, and accuracy.
- Game plan seamers:
  play late
  scoring within GP
  restriction options according to reverse swing
- Game plan spinners: as above
- Outcome — 20–30 runs

Where am I at the moment?

Phase 1 — New ball/Getting in — 8/10
  Leaving well
  Ball-by-ball focus good
  Control nerves well

Improvements needed
- Defending within body lines, not following ball
- Getting forward with better shape, not squaring
- More control on back foot

Phase 2 — Accumulation/Adaptation — 6/10
- Good control
- Defence to spinners good
- Scoring focus to spinners OK

Improvements needed
- Positive mindset
- Gapping
- Controlled scoring on front foot
- Control on short ball and bouncer

Phase 3 — Getting through — 4/10
Improvements needed
- Losing process thinking, getting out of the now
- Searching for runs
- ✦Negative thinking
- Not where I want to be on scoreboard

Key training focuses for winter

Phase 1 (Technical improvement)
- Shoulders and hands in line
- Solid footwork in defence and attack
- Defending within body line

Phase 2 (Tactical improvement)
· Control over stroke play (execution and manipulation)
· Develop sweep shot/use of feet
· Gapping

Phase 3 (Mental improvement)
· Process thinking

The schedule

July   Technical focus, drills and throw-downs (T-D):
- Hands and shoulders in line
- Still, forward head
- Timing of front shoulder, foot, hands to ball (strike)
- Sweeping drills/use of feet drills
  5 T-D sessions per week.

August
- Increase speed to T-Ds and begin facing medium bowling/spin bowling
- Late August begin bouncer training — incrediballs
- Late August begin focusing on gapping
  5 T-D sessions, 3 bowling nets p/w

September
- Face faster bowling and incrediball pressure
- Focus on manipulating game plans and working through game phases
- Net in game simulation
- Go through pre-ball routines
  4 bowling nets, 4 T-D sessions p/w

India   Game ready
- Solid defence/simple technique
- Control over GP
- Gapping
- Organised method of scoring against spinners
- Short ball not a factor
- Only mindset is on the next ball and job at hand

I have many other such plans from my playing days. They begin from the analysis of the previous period of play and then address concerns arising from that analysis via the setting of achievable goals. Goals range from general, long-term and outcome-orientated ones such as those under '*Aim*', to specific, process-orientated, daily goals like the ones outlined in the '*Schedule*'. You can also observe how at the start of the Schedule my goals were very technically focused and that as I got closer to competition I began to put myself under more and more pressure and began working on mental preparation.

This analysis and training goal-setting process prepared me for tours and seasons and helped develop my game in preparation for my next innings. If that innings was four months away, as in the previous example, then I could work on many things, but if that innings was only a day or two away I still went through the process, but obviously on a micro scale. It was just as important though.

The following is my analysis of my first innings from the test match versus England at Lord's in May 2004 and subsequent training focus for the second innings.

Result: 93 LBW Harmisson — Caught on the crease, still on the move

Technical: Squaring up with shoulders but feet closing off (crossed up)
Pushing at the ball

Tactical: Very expansive on the front foot
Searching for runs

Mental: Good fight
(Good) Focus excellent
Positive intent

Work on between innings: Maintaining focus
Letting the ball come, playing late

I went on to score a century in the second innings which was the highlight of my career. Yet you can see from this example that I only had time to work on a couple of things. Even though my mental game was good I chose to focus on maintaining that and also worked on one technical skill. While I accepted that with the very short time I had between innings I was unlikely to make any improvement on this technical point, it was a way of focusing the mind on one small skill — but one very important to my success, and a way of keeping my mind less cluttered.

When the training had been done — and hopefully it was *perfect practice* — then the focus of my routine turned mainly towards preparing my mind for the challenge ahead.

Step 3: The night before — programming time

Pack bag

The first thing I did before going to bed was to pack my cricket bag. I would take my cricket gear from the ground and back to the hotel. Most people would take their gear to the venue and set it up in the dressing-room upon first arriving at the ground a few days prior to the start date. I would leave mine overnight if the next day was a training day, but on the eve of the first day of a test or first-class game I would uplift it and take it back to the hotel. I did this because the act of packing my bag and filling it with the essentials and possibly required items — and doing it in a precise and consistent manner — was important for my mental preparation. It was all about consistency, accuracy and control. It also allowed me to free my mind a little before bed knowing that everything I might possibly need for the next day was accounted for and packed accordingly.

Commit game plan to paper

The things I would be aiming to do in the innings to come would have been worked out days and sometimes months prior. Some I had been working on for years and some never changed. Many things can influence your game plan. The nature of the wicket, the game situation, the style of bowlers you may face, your current form and so on are all factors that may determine how you plan to go out and play. Some of these facets you have time to prepare for, others arise during the course of a game and then you must adjust quickly. I found that as my game progressed my game plan became more and more set in stone. I found a way that worked for me, and it worked against most types of test-quality bowling. That was my strength but also, as I've said more than once, at times my lack of flexibility let me down — as in my final test series against Australia when I stuck to my tried and proven, patient approach, but in retrospect needed to find a way of placing more pressure on the bowlers.

I 'trained' the things I wanted to do in my game plan, and while it was generally the same things, I just wanted to get better and better at applying *my* game. In later years I had a great knowledge of my game, but by sitting down and committing it to paper the night before it was like signing it off.

The work had been done and now I was just formalising it to myself and committing to the plan. My game plan was essentially the goals for the next day, the *process* goals, and it is commonly accepted that you are more likely to commit to your goals if you write them down.

The following is the game plan I wrote down before my second-innings hundred at Lord's:

Outcome: Get 100, bat 3 sessions
Process: Play late
Play ball under eyes
Focus, relax and trust

This was a very simple game plan. The English attack was based around seam and my game was consistent for seam. I was also happy with the shots I was playing and the way I was sticking to them. Therefore it was all about getting my mind into a state to play with patience and control, letting the ball come to me and then trusting my processes.

Playing against India could be different. The Indian attack revolved around their two spinners, Singh and Kumble. The following game plan came from my first-innings hundred in Mohali:

Seamers: Get forward
Play late and straight

Singh: Get forward
Bat v pad (lines)
Punch, work square, sweep when on leg

Kumble: Get forward
Leave outside off
Use deflections

Show composure, control, ball by ball

I tried at this stage to keep things as simple as possible. You don't want to overcomplicate your job so concentrate on just a few things you feel are important and that you want to reinforce.

Imagery

I've packed my bag, signed off on my game plan and organised my mind; now the last thing I do before bed is programme my game plan into my mind and I do this by means of imagery.

When it comes to sports psychology skills you hear a lot about the importance of imagery. In fact, many people who know very little about sports psych think it is all about imagery and warm-fuzzy hippy stuff. Imagery is certainly a large part of sports psych but it's still only one element. Some place great emphasis on imagery in their mental preparation, but for me it was generally a smaller contributor — important, yes, but not overstated. I wasn't one to sit down and spend half an hour in a trance-like state seeing myself playing like God; rather, I tended to daydream about batting intermittently throughout the day. There were a couple of specific times though in my preparation where I paid a little more attention to imagery. And the night before an innings was one of these times.

As I got more and more interested in sports psych and the whole mental game I began to read books on the subject. Chris Cairns recommended *The Inner Game of Tennis* by Tim Galway as a good read and quite transferable to cricket. Cairnsy was right; it was a book that I referred to often and I incorporated Galway's principles into my batting development plan on many occasions. One of Galway's 'Inner Game' principles is that you cannot tell your body what to do, you must rather show it and feel it. You achieve this through the use of imagery by using your inner mind to effect the changes in technique you desire. It's all about the mind and body connection. I used it in and around the practice nets and in general daily life as well. I imagined and felt myself doing the things I wanted to do out in the middle.

Thus I used imagery the night before an innings to try to programme my game plan into my mind. After committing it to paper I would then see myself carrying it out. I would visualise myself defending the ball how *I* wanted and also see myself scoring runs using only the shots *I* decided to use. If I was having trouble with a rogue shot, like the hook perhaps, I would envisage myself leaving that ball alone and gaining self-control. It was never an extensive session but just a quick run-through in my mind. Then it was time for bed.

Step 4: The morning — emotion control

Get up earlier

The morning of the game/innings is when the nerves kick in. The minute I woke up I would feel under pressure. In response to this my morning was all about getting my emotions under control and gaining control over my thoughts. I would get up at least two hours before we were due to leave for the ground as I liked plenty of time to get up, wake up, have breakfast and prepare for the day. Most of the time, for an 11 a.m. start we'd leave at around 9 a.m. so this meant getting up at seven.

This generally posed no real problems unless we got rain during the day. If you lose any time during the day's play then that must be made up over the remainder of the match. You can make up an hour a day and that is usually made up by adding half an hour onto the first and last sessions of the day's play. Sometimes test matches played in the subcontinent start early due to fading light — often as early as 10 a.m. Throw in the standard afternoon torrential downpour in a place like Colombo and you're on the field at 9.30 a.m.

With the notable exception of a dawn surf I'm not a morning person at all, so 5.30 a.m. get-ups weren't my favourite but they had to be done. The point behind getting up early with plenty of time is simply that I didn't want to be rushed. When you are under pressure and nervous it is easy to do things in a hurried manner or for things to appear to happen very quickly around you. Given that my game was all about being deliberate and patient, being rushed was not part of it so I wasn't about to contribute to the problem myself.

Tai chi

Once out of bed I did my tai chi. Tai chi became a part of my routine during the England series in 2004. I took it up mainly for the physical benefits as I was getting increasingly slower, stiffer and more inflexible. I thought about yoga but the Black Caps' fitness advisor reckoned that I wouldn't be able to get into the poses and that tai chi would be a little easier to do. I definitely recommend it as it combines flexibility with strength and helps with balance, which are all important physical attributes for a cricketer. I liked the way it got my body moving in the morning, but also that it was done in a very relaxed but focused manner which was exactly what I was after.

So before I left for England I had a crash course in it from a personal instructor. I made my wife leave the house while I was learning because it looked a bit silly. Then when we were in England I had to make her get up early and go for a walk because her laughing did nothing for my focus. She did, however, walk to Starbucks and bring me back a coffee which was also great in trying to wake me up for a day at the office.

Accurate everything

My game revolved around control, discipline and accuracy. I hated making a mental mistake and surrendering my wicket through ill-discipline. My pre-batting routine was all about minimising the times I let myself down in that fashion. Consequently, I talked to many players about the things they did as part of their routines and how they managed themselves at the crease. Gilbert Enoka was the sports psych professional who worked with the Black Caps while I was involved, and he believed that if you desire excellence on the sports field you must develop a general culture of excellence in yourself. In other words, you must *live and breathe excellence in every part of your life*. It's a good concept. Chopper Crowe also suggested that if I wanted to be controlled and accurate when I got to the crease, then I should be controlled and accurate in everything else I did. Perhaps he was just trying to make his job of manager a little easier but I liked the suggestion, and in 2001 my teeth-brushing and breakfast-eating ritual was born.

It was all about control. In an effort to become a controlled person as soon as possible, on the morning of an innings I decided to do everything with control and accuracy. Breakfast could vary in terms of the menu but it had to be eaten in a precise and controlled manner. I would chew each mouthful a certain number of times and it was a very orderly operation. After breakfast I would then brush my teeth with similar control and accuracy. Each tooth had to be cleaned individually and precisely and the job had to be done properly.

Early bus

Once all the morning rituals had been completed I could then plonk myself on the bus and head to the ground. One of the innovations I brought to the team while I was a Black Cap was the introduction of an early bus. If you wanted some extra work at the ground or a net when available the early bus was a good way to get more practice time in the morning. It also provided the non-playing members of the team a chance to have a practice before concentrating on the needs of the playing XI.

My team-mates always knew if I was due to bat that day because I would be quiet, focused and controlled, but if not required I'd be noisy, inquisitive and generally a pain in the arse. If I was due to bat I liked to play my music. When you are an international cricketer you go through duty-free regularly and accumulate a good array of the latest gadgetry. I had a great little Sony MP3 player and had programmed in music arranged in specific play lists. I like '70s and '80s music and had a selection of songs organised into groups for relaxation, focus, motivation and even celebration.

Step 5: At the ground

Organise gear

The first thing I had to do once at the ground was set up my gear. It was a very organised process. Everything had a place and there was a place for everything. The most important thing was to have my little space in the dressing-room as ergonomically arranged as possible. All the important gear like pads, bats and gloves had to be within reach and all extras like spare shirts, socks and hats had to be accessible but out from under my feet. I detested small dressing-rooms that meant gear was always under your feet and in the way.

A nicely arranged area is not only good for your own organisation but helps the twelfth man no end. There is nothing worse than when you're 'the bitch' and your team-mate out in the middle who wants some fresh gloves is getting stroppy because you can't find them in his unruly pile of pads, shirts, hats, socks, bats and mismatched gloves.

My little area would start out spotlessly but as the game went on it tended to lose a little shape. Although it would get messed up a little it was always an organised mess though. I could never maintain the pristine appearance of Nathan Astle's area. His was always a model of spotless organisation and I liked to taunt him for being a poof because of it. However, I can assure you that his fastidious behaviour was limited only to the arrangement of his cricket gear . . .

Warm-ups

Warm-ups were for me a chance to run out some tension. If I got to the ground early for a net, and I loved touring because other countries were good at providing an off-ground net facility, well that was great. I believe there is no better way to prepare the body for batting and wake the mind than to have a bat. New Zealand does not have a culture of providing nets for warm-ups and it is poor. Unfortunately, it's just another example of how we just do not 'do' cricket that well in this country.

However, whether I was having a bat in the nets or the usual runaround and field it was important to make the distinction between a warm-up and a practice. The morning before you are due to perform is not the time for a practice; it is the time to get everything moving and prepare the mind and body for action. If I was batting in the nets all I wanted to do was get my hand/eye going, get the reflexes tuned, get the feeling of playing the ball late and whack out a bit of tension.

If I couldn't bat in the nets and we did a fielding routine, for me it had nothing to do with fielding it was still about getting ready for batting. Running around and taking a few high catches or getting some reflex catches off the face of the bat was still all about expelling nervous energy and gearing my mind and body for the task ahead at the crease.

We used to do these complicated fielding routines with people charging and balls flying everywhere. I was crap at them and used to stuff them up constantly. It was good though because it would firstly get my mind trying to work fast, and then after stuffing the drill up I would get yelled at by those team-mates who liked to prey on the weak. In response I would 'spit the dummy' and throw a tantrum. This was great for shedding excess nerves and got me into a combative frame of mind. There's really nothing better than a good yell for that kind of thing.

Half-hour to go

With half an hour to go I would head out to the pitch, stand behind the stumps and do some imagery and shadow batting. It was great if I could actually stand on the crease and do it from where I would be batting, but apparently according to the International Cricket Council (ICC) that was illegal — illegal for the 'plebs' anyway. It appeared to be okay for the likes of Justin Langer and Matthew Hayden, but if ever I got anywhere near the pitch it would almost certainly bring on an opportunity for the nearest official to flex his muscle. On one occasion, when an official in Bangladesh tried to collar me for shadow batting on the pitch, I had not yet thrown my usual nervous tantrum and I'll admit I was a little lucky not to lose some match fees on that occasion.

Anyway, given the chance, I would stand at both ends and try to imagine the first ball I was going to face and see myself playing it solidly. I would also act out a few cuts, forward defences, works off the hip and bouncer evasions, doing it all with control and composure. This would only take a few minutes and then I would head back into the dressing-room.

20–30 minutes until first ball

I liked to have plenty of time back in the shed before going out to bat. This little period became a lot more important when I was opening the batting, because obviously I had more time waiting to bat when I batted in the middle order and so more time to get my mind right. It was also a time to get very inward. I would be very nervous and I wanted to control these nerves — not eradicate them altogether, because you never could, but rather calm the mind and get focused on the job to come.

I would get padded up very quickly then sit down quietly and try to slow everything down. At the five-minute bell I would then get up, do a few quick stretches and get on my balance board. Standing on a balance board was something I did in my last year of cricket. The optometrist I'd gone to see who'd sorted me out with contact lenses as the astigmatism in my left eye had become worse believed that if you can fire up your balance muscles it tends to warm up your eyes and you can process more information quicker. This could be a help when it came to getting a head start into my innings. So I did it. I also liked how balanced and solid on my feet it made me feel once I got off.

While I was on the board I would also do a little more imagery. Then I would hit the ground running. As soon as I crossed the boundary line I would do some high knee running, heel to butt kicks and energetic forward defences. The nerves would make my legs feel heavy so this was a way of getting some blood pumping and trying to get them moving.

Once I got out to the wicket my next routine —my pre-ball routine — would take over.

It was all very well going out to the middle in the ideal personal state for batting, but all that work to get you there would be utterly wasted if after just a few minutes of batting it all turned to custard up top. It takes time to score runs and therefore you need to attain and maintain your ideal mental state for batting for substantial lengths of time. My pre-ball routine, which I outline below, was all about keeping myself focused and within my PPP for long periods of time. I reached a couple of pinnacles in my career. The first was in 2000/01 in England and Africa and the second time back in England in 2004. These were times when I was batting vast lengths of time without making too many mistakes, and I put it down to getting absorbed in my pre-ball routine — which was born out of the development of a 'coping stategy'.

Pre-ball routine

Introduction — coping strategies

Early on in my dealings with Alex he brought up the concept of a 'coping strategy'. A coping strategy is a document that tells you what you must do and think when things are not going to plan. This takes time to work out because first of all things have to go wrong, then you have to turn things back in your favour, and it is also important that you identify *what* it is you did to regain your form. And, as long as you actually learn from it, there is no substitute for experience.

The mere fact that you are working on a coping strategy means that you are likely to be taking more notice of the things that are happening to you, especially when they are not going well. It is a great concept because it has the capacity to transform negative days or negative experiences into positives. When things are going along well that's great, but when they turn sour if you understand what is happening and have a strategy to get things back on track quickly you will become a far more consistent player. The troughs of bad form should then become less deep and last for less time. Which is why I believe that provincial cricket needs to be of a very high standard. At the international level you are tested and placed under pressure in so many ways, and to survive and succeed you must have an understanding of your basics and the things that work for you — this must be learnt either at the provincial level or the level just below the one that you are trying to become established in. Which is why the international arena is no place for the young, inexperienced player. When someone is running hot that's fine, but I believe you will never gain consistency from a player until they have been through some hard times and sorted them out. It's amazing how many of the world's greatest batmen have been dropped early in their careers, learnt from their mistakes, and returned as more consistent performers. When I approached Alex I'd already had eight years of provincial experience and it was time to make that experience pay off.

My initial coping strategy was very much a working document. As my analysis and Peak Performing Profiling developed I also began to think more about the differing situations I found myself in, especially when I felt I hadn't performed so well. I would think about what I could have done differently and then would develop a theory for the next time I found myself in a similar situation. It was also important to draw reference from the times I felt under pressure in an innings but pulled through. I developed theories on what I should do in such situations as: batting after a few low scores; starting an innings; batting too loosely; getting bogged down; becoming intimidated by fast bowling; losing wickets at the other end, and so on.

After a while I realised that all my strategies for dealing with these situations were very similar in technique and tactics and that the biggest influence could come through getting my head right. They all pointed towards playing the ball late, knowing where my runs would be scored, looking to get forward, and most importantly, using breathing and imagery to control my mental arousal level at the crease.

For the uninitiated, 'arousal' is a term used in sports psych to describe how 'psyched up' you are, not how much you want to 'get your leg over'. Alex stressed very early on the importance of 'arousal control' and I also talked a lot about this concept with my first Black Caps coach, David Trist. Tristy used the term 'over-aroused' in an interview once and boy did that draw some ridicule from a few brainless sports followers.

Step 1: Analysis

Just as my pre-batting routine began with analysis so too did my pre-ball routine, but on a very micro scale. It was a technique I took from golfers actually: f**k it — fix it — forget it. If I made a mistake or played a poor shot, 'f**k it' meant a quick acknowledgement of the mistake, just to clear the air. Then I would 'fix it' by quickly telling/showing/thinking to myself what I should have done; then 'forget it' and move on — that ball has gone so get ready for the next one. I also backed up the 'forget it' part with a scratching of my guard. That was my way of signing off on that delivery, of saying to myself 'I'm still here at the crease' and getting ready for the next ball. I also liked this scratching act because taking guard is the first thing you do when you get to the middle and I always thought my focus was at its best for the first ball I faced. Perhaps that explains why I only got one duck in my entire test career.

Some people believe that you should be non-judgemental between balls. In other words, there is nothing you can do about it now so why even think about it? I can see their point, but I liked the feedback I could get from the way I played the last ball. The awareness of it could tell me things about what mental state I was in.

Step 2: Situational awareness

Once I'd signed off on the last ball I would walk away towards square leg or walk down the pitch and tap down various spots with my bat and start my preparation for the next ball, which began with situational awareness. Situational awareness is an interesting concept and a good topic for debate: should the situation dictate how you should play, or should you play the same way, the way you bat best, regardless of the situation?

The way I see it, for example, a short wide ball or long half volley is a short wide ball or half volley whether you are three down for bugger all or three for 300 and should be put away. Sometimes I'll concede that the situation dictates how you must play, but there are really very few players around who can drastically alter their games with total effectiveness — most of the time you must operate within your own parameters. I know former batsman, coach, and legend of New Zealand cricket Glenn Turner would argue in favour of the latter argument of playing your way regardless of the situation.

Regardless of the outcome of such a debate, I was lucky in the way that my career developed that I was only ever expected to play the one way, only really developed the one way, and only really knew the one way. So while it is important to assess the situation it is also important not to lose sight of what *you* can do in response. As time went on I began to realise that the situation had a bigger influence on me than I could ever have on the situation. But by being aware of the situation I could, more importantly, be aware of what it was doing to me and thus could take the necessary steps to ensure I remained playing my game with, yes that word again, *control*.

I'm not afraid to admit that I could be frightened by a quick bowler (that actually happened a lot!), or perhaps was nervous as hell because I was out of form, or maybe we were six down with not many runs on the board. I was either swinging wildly out of control, or bogged down and not scoring — or occasionally, I might actually be playing well. Whatever the situation, it led me into the third part of my routine, which was 'arousal control'.

Step 3: Arousal control

Acknowledging the situation in which I found myself was a good start in controlling my level of arousal, but I also had to acknowledge what the situation was doing to me. From my analysis I knew what mental state I needed to be in to perform at my best and I also knew that my mental state controlled how well I could effect my techniques and tactics. Before I faced up to the next ball I had to ensure that my arousal was at the level I needed it to be.

Anxiety, the hostility of the bowling, the match situation, the players around you and so on all have a bearing on your psyche. The key is to be able to recognise what these various factors are doing to you and to have strategies to get yourself at your ideal level of mental arousal. This is a hard thing to do and sometimes you simply never gain control. I've had times, mainly in one-day cricket, when my anxiety and lack of ability to get the ball

Allan Border (top left), Chris Cairns (top right) and David Boon (bottom) . . . all appeared to me to be mentally tough.

Right . . .

Wrong . . .

Wrong . . .

Richardson ready to face the unknown

The *New Zealand Herald* reckoned some years ago, in the headline above, that I was 'ready' ... really, I was crapping myself. Clockwise from top: Shoaib Akhtar, Allan Donald and Muttiah Muralitharan.

Akhtar rocks all but Richardson

The *Taranaki Daily News* headline says Akhtar never rocked me . . . but I was most definitely shaken.

The fear of getting hit when batting ...

... and fielding was ever-present ...

. . . and in the nets, no amount of protection ever felt enough.

Sometimes it felt safer to bat *behind* the stumps.

away has led me to go right off the boil and self-destruct in some awful ways. I remember when I played my first test against South Africa. It was my third test and since the first couple had been against Zimbabwe I considered it to be my first *real* test. Between the tours of Zimbabwe and South Africa I'd had a couple of months off while the one-day boys played the ICC knockout tournament, and all I could think about was my impending date with Allan 'White Lightning' Donald and Shaun 'Ritchie Cunningham' Pollock. They were two great opening bowlers and I had plenty of time to contemplate the challenge and to get myself very worked up about it. I made 23 from 22 balls and was completely out of control in the process. Everything was happening at a hundred miles an hour including myself. Not surprisingly, I got bowled swinging wildly. It served as a great lesson.

Consequently I developed several different ways to influence my level of arousal. If I was under-aroused — which didn't happen that often — I would be in danger of playing a lazy shot or leaving a ball that was too straight. To correct that situation I would do some shadow batting, but do it quite quickly, or I would do some calisthenics. It was about getting my heart rate up a little and pumping myself into the challenge. At times I would try to get into a bit of a personal battle with the bowler or start something with a fielder. But if I was over-aroused, which was most of the time, I was in big danger of going way too hard at my shots, over-hitting, and generally losing all shape to my play. In this state I would get out to balls that were there to hit but cock up the execution of the shot. I was also more likely to lose my head and do something dumb in this condition.

So I got very used to trying to calm myself down. What I would do is firstly slow my mind by concentrating on my breathing — not slowing it on purpose but just being aware of it. I would then imagine myself playing a really solid forward defence, at the same time shadow batting it, while all the time doing and seeing it in slow motion. Once I felt I was mentally ready I would then give myself the appropriate cue word and take my stance for the next ball.

Step 4: Cue words

The use of cue words is another popular sports psych technique. These are words that you employ to psych up, focus, keep on task and give direction.

The most important thing with cue words is that they *mean* something. It is absolutely pointless saying something to yourself that has no real relevance to the tasks of the job. There's also no point in saying something you heard another player, such as Brian Lara, say to himself if that word has no relevance to your own game. If you can develop cue words that sum up the important facets of your game and tailor them to the situation at hand you can make life a lot simpler for yourself. This is what I endeavoured to do with my own cue words.

There's a lot that goes through your mind while you bat, and even if it's all good advice you simply cannot operate while telling yourself to do a million and one things — your brain wouldn't cope and you'd most likely self-destruct. On the other hand, you also cannot clear your mind altogether (let's face it, we're none of us Gandhi or the 'Karate Kid'). However, with a little effort it is possible to quiet the mind and channel it in the right direction by giving it one thing in particular to think about.

For instance, early on I played some of my best innings when I focused in on a single little technical tip. During my 162 not out against Central Districts in 1998 all I concentrated on was getting in behind the ball. By focusing in on that one small key I could channel my focus and keep my mind uncluttered. As time went on and my analysis and coping strategies developed I discovered some cue words that were based on the essentials of my game and on the things which I believed I had to do in various situations. I viewed my cue words as being like the tip of the iceberg, with all my analysis and experience providing the body that supports it above water. Each word had a mass of research behind it and therefore held a lot of meaning when I chose to use it. My main word was 'forward' but I also used 'late', 'still' and 'solid'.

'Forward'

I believe that having the intent to play forward was one of the most critical elements in my own successful batting. If you ask Glenn Turner — and I did on many occasions — what the keys to batting are, he would say: 'Score first, defend second, look to play with a straight bat first and have the intent to play forward.' Sound advice, but only if you appreciate the masses of experience that have gone into developing this simplistic philosophy. I'm firmly convinced though, that players need to walk this path themselves — with quality guidance, of course — before settling on their own list of simplistic cues.

For example, I found that if I was looking to get forward, a lot of other important things would fall into line. My weight would be good and going towards the bowlers; my footwork would be sharp both forward and back; and the shape to my shots accurate. It is important to stress that this was an *intent* to get forward not a commitment — at times my intent would turn to a premature planting on the front foot which would cause trouble. The intent to come forward was also a good cue for facing fast bowling. If I felt I was being intimidated by fast bowling — and when you are there is a tendency to get your weight forced back — it became very important to keep my weight going forward. If I got pushed back that is when I tended to shuffle and get caught hovering on the crease, fending at short ones and playing away from my body. By keeping my weight forward I played the bouncers better and was less likely to get out LBW.

'Late/Still'

Playing late was also an important ingredient of success. When I was either nervous or under pressure there was a tendency to push out to meet the ball too early with hard hands. When you open the batting and have to deal with the seaming and swinging ball it's important not to play the first line of the delivery you see as it may still move on you and catch you stranded in the wrong position. By looking to play late I felt I could gear up to play the last line of the ball and thus be in a better position to hit it. I also felt I could time the ball better and avoid over-hitting, which was a big problem for me. If I was bogged down or under pressure I would tell myself to play late. This allowed me a split-second longer to make the right decision and not force that shot and thus reduce errors. The cue words 'still' and 'late' were an effective and often-used combination.

'Solid'

My batting was all about patience and accuracy. I liked to be in control of my actions and deliberate in defence and attack. At times, however, I would lose a bit of control. For instance, if I was approaching a milestone, there was a tendency to get ahead of myself and become a little sketchy. Playing within my game plan was critical at these times and getting out to a shot outside of my plan really pissed me off. When I felt myself in danger of this I would use the cue word 'solid'. It was a reminder to be patient, get back to basics and play each ball on its merits.

Conclusion — Prepared, present and ready . . . ball by ball

Once I had assessed the situation, suitably aroused myself and taken guard, I would say the chosen cue word over and over again in my mind as the bowler ran in — occasionally out loud, which was visually noticeable at times. This was the point: the mind could get away on you, especially against a quality bowler or in a sticky situation; my cue word tried to keep it on task. Once the ball was bowled and my shot played I would go through the 'f**k it, fix it, forget it' drill and scratch my guard, or if all went well just scratch my guard and start over again preparing for the next ball.

While my pre-batting routine was designed to *get me to* my ideal mental state for batting it was also designed to *keep me there* and keep me there for long periods of time. You often hear sportspeople talk about the importance of playing it one ball at a time — well that was exactly what my pre-ball routine allowed me to do. It was a way of concentrating on the things I needed to do right then and there, and thus stay in the all-important 'now'. Ball by ball is the only way to play cricket and 'the now' is just that — the present.

> If you are still batting you have one job and one job alone — and that is to play the next ball as best you can.

You can learn from the past, but you can't afford to dwell on it. The way I played long innings was simply to put all my energy into my pre-ball routine, staying ever-present and doing it one ball at a time until I got out.

Like I said just before, when you're playing really well and know you're in 'the zone' there's obviously no need to 'f**k it and fix it'. The important thing here is to go with it but not get sloppy. Batting in 'the zone' is a great ride and one I'm afraid I never experienced much in test cricket. However, in these rare times I tried to keep my pre-ball routine as simple and brief as possible. My arousal level was good, I was in control of the situation and applying my game well, so all I would do between balls was listen to my breathing and use the cue word 'forward'.

At times I would just enjoy the level of clarity I had within the situation and describe to myself exactly what I was going to do and where I would hit the ball — not premeditating as such, but just reinforcing the level of confidence I had in my game at that time. These were periods of pure positive intent, patience and accuracy which were totally elusive when I was out of form but completely natural when in 'the zone'.

Chapter Twelve

Playing intuitively

By now you're probably thinking, 'Bloody hell, what a ridiculously complicated, analytical, confusing and long-winded process! Why didn't he just go out, watch the ball and simply bat?' Well, to tell you the truth, that is precisely what I was attempting to do. I wanted to be able solely to watch the ball and let it flow. Okay, maybe it never flowed purely in terms of flowing stroke play, but when I got it right it did happen how I wanted it to.

Take the term 'watch the ball', which is one of the most commonly heard expressions in cricket. It's the first thing you tell kids to do when they're learning and it's the very thing you observe countless test-match batsmen mumbling away to themselves — or even shouting to themselves — when some nasty fastie is bearing down on them. It goes without saying that you must pick up the line and length of a delivery quickly to have the time to move into the correct position to play the appropriate shot, and for that it is important to watch the ball closely. Some coaches say you should watch the ball all the way onto the bat as well. While I agree that tracking the ball all the way until it reaches you definitely helps with playing late and timing your shots, I'd also argue that the great players have an ability to use a refined sort of hand/eye awareness that can see them switch their focus from the ball to the area in which they want to hit it right at the very last moment and thus place their shots. I never believed I had that skill myself — for me it was a case of watch the ball all the way and hope I hit it into a gap. Nevertheless, although watching the ball closely is massively important in such a bat versus ball game, the instruction purely to 'watch the ball' is not the be all and end all of successful batting.

When I lost my bowling I was offered the last-resort advice of 'just run in and bowl it'. It was a simple theory in essence — just forget all the bollocks and technique, clear the mind and let my natural ability come through. Although as a bowler with 'the yips' I could never 'just run in and bowl' as my mind kept getting in the way, I found that as a batsman I managed to get the hang of the batting equivalent — 'watching the ball' — quite nicely. What I learnt to do though was watch the ball at the *right time* and understand what I was trying to achieve by watching the ball.

> If at the point of delivery I could focus all my attention towards watching the ball then I could let my intuition take over — and if I had analysed objectively, trained appropriately and had my emotions under control I could trust my intuition.

This is what my whole extensive process was all about. It was about gaining trust. When sportspeople talk about trusting their processes this is what I believe they are referring to. It is the belief that they have built up the correct skill base, have a means of allowing those skills to prevail, and believe that those skills are adequate to get the job done. My batting development and mental management processes of analysis, training goals, pre-batting and ball routines were hugely time-consuming and mentally taxing but were all in aid of enabling clarity and a free mind at the point of delivery — my personal moment of truth. Clarity of focus could only come with trust, and trust for me was very much based on volume and quality of work.

Training for intuitive play

I believe that the game of cricket is played best at an intuitive level. The time you have from the point of release to pick up the line and length of the delivery and then make a decision on how you want to play it is simply too brief for conscious thought. Against spin bowling you maybe have more time, but conscious thought will probably only get in the way of effective decision-making anyway. Rather, the eyes must send the information instantaneously to the brain, which must intuitively make a decision. If you want that decision to be the correct one then you had better have trained your intuition appropriately.

Perhaps those people who pick up a skill very quickly or show an inbuilt aptitude for something have a natural instinct for that particular task, but I believe that most of us can also 'train' that aptitude or ability. When I had throw-downs, net training, or used imagery, what I was trying to do was train whatever I was working on so that it became naturally intuitive. This is why I placed a massive amount of emphasis and importance on my training and trained as much as I possibly could. Rather than having to tell or make myself do something, I wanted it instead to happen as a direct response to a certain stimulus — which was, of course, the ball.

Which is why I have no tolerance for the culture in New Zealand Cricket of preparing substandard practice surfaces. The nets that we trained in here were abhorrent. They were always too fresh and too heavily grassed, and generally the ball seamed everywhere. As for the indoor nets, well they bounced and seamed like buggery. If you wanted to bat against bowlers they had to bowl with very old balls or it became ridiculous. As an opening batsman, over five years I could count on the fingers of one hand the times I could face up to a bowler with a new ball in the nets. It pissed me off because I never got to train against the conventionally swinging ball nearly as much as I needed.

The reality was that I didn't generally face bowlers in the nets because I just felt like a target — and believe me, your own quicks like hitting their own batsmen much more than the opposition! You would hop around, ducking, diving, pushing and fending, which in the end achieved very little except to train poor positions and very undesirable intuitive behaviours. Old balls and dribbly bowlers were my gig for drilling my game. However, every so often I would face the fire, but solely as a means to place myself under pressure and work on mental strategies to try and hold it together. Most of the time I'd just storm out of the net mumbling things like, 'This is bloody ridiculous and unacceptable!' Consequently, I much preferred training overseas!

I would always break my training down into three main categories: *technical, tactical* and *mental*. You'll remember how I've described that I would generally only concentrate on technical development if I had plenty of time before my next bat; however, in and around competition I would do remedial work on small technical issues whenever possible. In training my technique I would start with very slow underarm-style lobs delivered at a pace at which I could consciously move my body parts as I desired. After drilling this I'd slowly move up in pace from throws to bowling only as I felt the technique was grooved and ready to be put under increasing pressure. If the bowling is too fast too soon you will revert to your old, undesirable behaviours and get nowhere at all. Imagery was a great way of trying to groove a feeling and make it intuitive — via imagery you can place yourself at the crease in a test match and see and feel yourself applying the correct technique.

Tactical training involved controlling my game plan. I had my shots that I wanted to play, so I had tailored how I wanted to play within my own parameters of control — which was really a number of ways to block the crap out of it — and would train that way. Ashley Ross had a training technique called 'accountability training' and I found this great from a tactical training perspective. It involved writing down what shots you would play and where you planned to score your runs. You then gave it either to him or a team-mate who would score you on whether or not you backed up your words when you batted in the net.

> The ability to back up your words is a key attribute of quality batsmanship. Many players know what is required in a given situation, but few can actually back it up with actions.

Tactical training was great for building trust. Not only did I hate playing outside my game plan, as a New Zealand opener I was *expected* to remain within it — in fact, if I happened to whack a four or six with a cover drive, pull or hook shot, I always felt a bit naughty. I fervently believed that if I was going to play with discipline in the middle I also had to play with discipline in the nets — one silly shot and I felt my whole net session was ruined. In fact, I threw some great wobblies at net time and was quite a bat thrower and wicket smasher, so it will come as little surprise that I kept having to ask for new bats from my supplier, Slazenger, because I kept breaking the handles. They probably thought they had a problem with their handle strengths when, if they'd seen me at practice, they'd have realised instead that all they had on their hands was a highly-strung contracted player.

In the final analysis, my entire focus was to train myself to be an intuitively defensive player. I never took my responsibility at the top of the order for New Zealand in test matches lightly. I wanted to become tighter and tighter. It was one of the highlights of my career to be labelled 'Mr Reliable' and 'The Rock' at the top of the order and I always wanted to live up to that billing. My defensive play and discipline were my greatest assets, but they were also my biggest downfall in the end because my game became so structured that I couldn't adapt when required.

Being a more attacking player was a very hard thing for me to do, and when I tried to up the scoring my game became very unstructured indeed. My entire game would become extremely self-conscious and inaccurate — I had no trust in myself when it came to breaking the shackles. This shortcoming is nowhere more apparent than in the way my one-day game deteriorated just as my test and first-class game progressed and consolidated. My foray into ODIs was a disaster. I was neither prepared nor organised enough for the differing requirements of opening in ODIs and was a disgrace. I simply hadn't trained for it.

Concentration

I knew from about 1999 what side my bread was buttered on and that was test cricket. I had my chance in the big time and it was in the long form of the game first and foremost, and I wasn't about to blow that chance. So I focused my training on the skills I believed I needed for success in that forum.

Most of my training revolved around developing a sound defence and gaining control over a very restricted and contracted array of stroke play. Then as my career progressed I got more and more absorbed in the mental management side of my game. My mental management was the glue that

I believed held my technique together and allowed me to effect my tactics. As I worked on my routines and processes further I became more and more interested in my philosophy of a totally clear mind and intuitive play. I found the 'Inner Game'-type books absorbing reading and liked the idea of relaxed concentration.

Batting takes concentration, and concentration over long periods of time — or does it? What it really takes is acute concentration over very small periods of time, but often — as well as a general awareness of what is going on around you. To make a hundred I needed to bat for six hours, but there was no way in hell I could keep a quality level of concentration up for anywhere near that sort of time. Instead, the idea was to be generally aware of what was happening to and around yourself and then to channel all your concentration into the *moment* the bowler lets the ball go and you have completed your shot and runs, if any. Sportspeople refer to this as the ability to switch on and off — that is, switch the brain into gear for the delivery and then switch it off between balls. This allows you to rest the mind and thus keep your concentration sharp when required for longer.

Without doubt this ability is a crucial skill to have for batting long periods of time. However, I suggest that switching off is important but *not switching off altogether*. You should remain aware of the game situation, your progress, the bowler's plans and so on but not in a way that is overly taxing. My experience was that keeping connected with the game *between* balls helped channel my focus.

All the routines I've described that I went through to prepare for an innings and each ball of that innings probably sound quite mentally taxing. While the training could be tiring, during an innings my pre-ball routine was all about awareness. It wasn't meant to involve too much concentration, just a quick reflection to assess the situation and my mental level and then steer me towards an action to ensure I was in a state to enhance my level of concentration at the point of delivery.

In retrospect I don't think I ever really got the full knack of switching off. If things were going well, focusing on my breathing between balls did help give my brain a rest, but to tell the truth my limited ability with the bat meant I was always working pretty hard between balls to get through the next one.

Combine that with my slow rate of scoring and you have a large part of the reason I had a poor rate of converting 50s into 100s. Inevitably I would tire around the 80 mark and often make a mental mistake. It would leave me exhausted, disappointed and very frustrated.

During the 2000 'A' tour of England I got to speak with Australian cricket legend Bob Simpson. He was coaching Lancashire who we were playing in Liverpool and I took the opportunity to approach him about batting. He was big on the concept of 'peak concentration' and that you could only peak over a split second and thus that split second had to be right at the point of delivery. His theory was that if you concentrated too hard too soon then you wouldn't be fully focused when it counts. He suggested that if you can't quite see clearly how you got out as you walk off after a dismissal this is a sign that you concentrated too early. Which is a quite brilliant analysis really because that is so often the case. I can recall many instances when I was walking off and puzzling to myself, 'How the hell did that happen?' I couldn't clearly recollect the ball and my shot; it would all be a bit of a haze.

Naturally, I wanted to explore just how good my concentration could get. I knew all the hard work that I was doing with my analysis, training and stringent routines would pay off if I could just let it. That was it though — I had to 'let it'. Under pressure I felt I would force things a little and make mistakes. This was no more prevalent than in the mid to late '90s when I would fail in the big games. After talking to Bob Simpson I decided that during this tour — my make-or-break tour — I would pay close attention to the quality of my concentration. I had read in Galway's *The Inner Game of Tennis* about relaxed concentration and his 'bounce-hit' technique. He encouraged his students to think only of the point at which the tennis ball bounced and the point at which you hit it. You would then yell out 'bounce and hit' at the corresponding times. This was a means of preoccupying your mind with a simple task to allow your skill to show through. He also outlined a concentration technique whereby all you looked for was the pattern on the tennis ball as it came towards you. This was a way to focus the mind on a simple task but also to refine your concentration.

I liked the idea of this and incorporated it into my routine. What I would do was try to pick the exact moment the bowler let the ball go and say to myself the word 'Now'. 'Now' was the key to concentrate on the ball, and not just watch the ball but find the seams on the ball. It was a simple task but refined to an extreme degree. It was a way to pour all my attention into watching the ball as closely as possible — but at the critical time, the 'now' — and then letting my intuition take over. Yes, watching the ball is an important skill, but if you really want it to pay dividends you have to train for correct intuitive behaviour.

It's amazing how clearly you can actually see the ball at times and how useful it can be in allowing your best game to show through. For instance, I've never been a great reader of wrist spinners and by that I mean picking when they bowl their googly, wrong'un, or whatever you want to call it. Martin Crowe told me not to look for the change in action but just to let myself pick them intuitively. At the time, his advice went in one ear and out the other. And then a year or so later I was talking to Glenn Turner about the same problem. Glenn told me I should be capable of seeing which way the ball was spinning as it came at me. Suddenly Martin's previous advice hit home. By looking for the spinning of the ball I could intuitively pick up the variation in ball flight between a googly and a normal leggie. Admittedly, this didn't happen that often and certainly not when my brain was working overtime.

Over the course of my test career I continually tried to develop and refine my concentration skills. I even got into meditation at one stage and would sit in a quiet room with a cricket ball two feet in front of me and stare at it while saying over and over in my mind the word 'now', but I got bored with that quite quickly. I was never particularly into that hippy stuff and practice was my preferred form of meditation anyway. When I was out of form, John Bracewell introduced me to a net training drill that involved yelling out how he had thrown the ball — seam up or scrambled. It was quite useful in keeping my analytical mind out of the act of hitting the ball and allowed me to find a little timing and flow. I also developed a useful technique of channelling my focus from peripheral to narrow and precise. When the bowler was at the top of his mark I would try to be aware of everything around me then slowly narrow it to the bowler in general, then his hand, the ball, and finally down to the seams of the ball. This was a way of letting my eyes send my brain any messages on variations such as the bowler going wide of the crease or changing grip, but then at the moment of delivery channelling my focus right in to the ball itself.

I can almost guarantee that when a batsman is playing poorly the first thing to leave will be their concentration: their quality concentration, their relaxed concentration. This was certainly the case in my ODI play and during my last test tour of Australia. Towards the end of my career I was trying to change my game and become a little more aggressive. It was a forced, self-conscious process and was most definitely not intuitively correct. My game was deteriorating and I never really got back the quality focus and concentration I had achieved over the previous few years. In fact, I didn't *want to* because I didn't want to play that way any more.

Alex McKenzie: Generally speaking, Mark has so far described the mental skills and techniques that he used about as well as anybody could describe them. Rather than making a comment on each element of his programme, I will explain some of the conceptual ideas behind various elements of it, and go into some detail about selected ones.

Mark was regarded as a very mentally tough cricket player. But what does that mean? What characteristics did he possess in order for the media, his fellow players (both team-mates and opposition players), and the fans to label him as 'mentally tough'? There have been numerous attempts to describe these characteristics by various people involved in sports psychology, and one of the simplest is that a 'mentally tough athlete' is one who is

- mentally prepared;
- able to concentrate completely on the job at hand;
- highly motivated and determined to do well;
- confident in their own ability to do well;
- able to control their anxiety and arousal levels; and
- more focused on their own performance than that of other people.

I doubt if anyone in world cricket who knew Mark would question whether he possessed these qualities. Quite simply — he did. His batting record, and the manner in which he achieved that record at test level, would attest to that.

In summary, as a 'mentally tough' cricketer, Mark possessed these attributes (I call them skills), and used various techniques or methods to acquire them. He has talked about things such as mental routines, setting goals, imagery and cue words; all of which are methods or techniques that he used with the purpose of developing particular skills such as emotional control, concentrating on the job at hand, building confidence and maintaining/improving motivation.

Of course, it's all very well to talk about these qualities and how to obtain them, but how do you decide which ones you need to develop, and what methods to use? In other words, where do you start? With Mark, as with many other athletes, the process begins with self-awareness, and discovering the skills and qualities that you already have, those that you need to develop, and the level to which you possess these qualities.

Process

To begin with, Mark talked about his Peak Performance Profile (PPP), which is simply a tool that I have used with many athletes as a means for them to gain some self-awareness. Developing someone's PPP helps them gain an understanding of (a) what skills they need to possess in order to perform well in their particular sport; (b) how good they think they are at these particular skills; and (c) how good they were at these skills when they performed at their best. There is little objectivity to this exercise in the sense that the scores that the athlete gives themself are not based on any measurable parameters apart from their own subjective standards, ranging from 0 (poor) to 10 (excellent). However, it forces them to think about the range of skills that they need in order to perform well, and it usually surprises them when they see how many skills they actually write down. This exercise forms the basis for any change on the part of the athlete, in that it is used to identify areas to work on, and from there, to set some goals.

For Mark, the next step in the process was to compile a batting record that took into account many of the things that he had specifically identified in his PPP. The batting record was actually developed in Perth by Dr Sandy Gordon, a senior lecturer at the University of Western Australia's School of Human Movement Studies, and one of Australia's leading sports psychologists. Sandy has worked extensively with cricketers from around the world for many years, including the Australian and Indian test and one-day teams, and is, quite simply, world class.

Mark kept his various PPPs and batting records as a diary, and would periodically go back over them in order to determine any patterns in his performance, and to gauge whether his training had resulted in any performance improvements. If not, then things needed to change, but if so, then some of his training methods and techniques were reinforced as being worthwhile. Over the years, refinements were made that resulted in the relatively uncomplicated PPP that he developed for the winter of 2004. While this was an apparently simple profile, it represented at least seven years of work, and was a lot more meaningful to Mark than it would have been for any other player who had not gone through the process that he had in order to arrive at that point.

Mark felt that if he got all the various elements of his PPP right on the day, and in harmony with each other, he would give himself a much better chance of attaining the right mindset for batting. In other words, he was more likely to get himself into 'the zone', or, as many like to call it, 'the ideal performance state' for cricket. Mark described his personal experience of 'the zone' as follows:

'It began to dawn on me that to bat well and for long periods of time I needed to find my rhythm as quickly as possible and maintain it. It was also apparent to me that finding my rhythm was not a forced process but had to occur naturally — almost as if I was striking an equilibrium, or balance, between my own game and that which the bowlers were confronting me with. When it all fell into place it was a feeling of being totally immersed in the competition between bat and ball. It was reactive in that my actions were dictated by the nature of the delivery bowled at me and they would be those I trusted and was totally comfortable with. My scoring would be at a pace I felt appropriate for the situation, and I would be quite happy ticking along at *my* pace. I realised that when I had this rhythm and a feeling of total clarity in what I was doing, then I was in "the zone".'

Those who have studied sports psychology would recognise this as a very accurate description of what a very prominent psychologist named Mikhail

Cziksentmihalyi would call 'flow'. This state occurs when there is a balance between the challenge of the task and the ability of the person to meet that challenge. The person feels as if they are immersed in the task, perform as if on autopilot, and feel as if they are in total control of the situation. It is a fickle place, in that sometimes players attain it fleetingly, at other times for longer periods, but by understanding what it feels like, understanding your own game as much as possible, and preparing yourself as well as possible (according to your PPP), then you are more likely to attain it. It doesn't guarantee that you will get there, but it makes it more likely.

Too often athletes (and coaches for that matter) analyse their poor performances to death, but fail to analyse their good performances, preferring instead simply to celebrate them. While this is fine, and people should analyse their mistakes and celebrate when they do well, they should also try to reinforce what it was that contributed to or even caused that good performance, and try and replicate those things so that the performance is repeated. Mark certainly understood what contributed to his good performances as well as his bad, and therefore made it more likely that he was able to get himself into 'the zone' more often.

As Mark appreciated, understanding what it felt like to get into 'the zone' was all very well, but it was a retrospective process, and he needed to figure out how to get himself into that state more often. He worked on a number of techniques to ensure that this was more likely to happen, and described them in some detail. His training goals, his performance, process and outcome goals, his analysis procedures, pre-match and pre-ball routines, imagery training, coping and refocusing strategies, cue words and arousal control techniques were all well documented, and require no further clarification from me.

Developing all of these techniques to the degree that he did enabled Mark to do what every cricket coach tells every batsman: 'Watch the ball!' This may sound trite to many people, but as Mark said, this simple statement meant a hell of a lot more than it appeared on the surface. It was the culmination of all the training that he had done over the years, and was the cue for him to trust that everything he had done in terms of preparing for that moment was able to come to the fore at that time. Therefore, he was focused completely on watching the ball at that specific moment in time.

Consequently, he was able to trust that

    (a) he would recognise the type of delivery that was being bowled;

    (b) he would select the correct shot to play to that ball;

    (c) he would be able to execute that shot without thinking about it; and that

    (d) he was in the right mindset to be able to do so.

All of the work that he had put into preparing himself meant that this was possible, and therefore he was probably better than most players at being able to do what every coach wants a batsman to do when they say, 'watch the ball'. I think this is what he meant when he talked about 'playing on intuition'.

Section Three
Facing the Demons

THE LIMBIC SYSTEM
The centre for emotional control: fear, flight or fight response and anxiety.

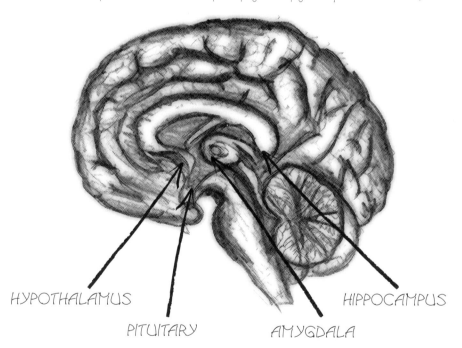

HYPOTHALAMUS

PITUITARY

AMYGDALA

HIPPOCAMPUS

Chapter Thirteen

Anxiety

It's one o'clock in the morning and you're halfway through watching your second DVD. You're tired and you know you should be sleeping but you don't want to because tomorrow you know how you will be feeling and it isn't comfortable. You know the preparation has been done and you've scored runs in the warm-up games, but now they count for nothing and in fact have highlighted a few problems. Your last net lasted for hours and you left pissed off because it wasn't perfect. The thought of failure is prominent and stressful. Stress makes you tired and you can feel yourself drifting off, fighting it all the way because you're questioning just whether you really are ready for tomorrow.

At seven o'clock you're woken by your alarm — well, three alarms really, because you're so anal you've set your watch, cellphone, and asked for a wake-up call. The light framing the edges of the curtains looks ominously bright and your suspicions are confirmed upon opening them — 'Bugger! It's fine, cricket today.' Then you run straight to the toilet.

Your wife laughs at you as you do your tai chi. You've built it into your routine in recent times as you've desperately tried to grab on to anything that eases the nerves and that you think helps you perform.

Breakfast at a five-star hotel is one of the perks of the job, but its novelty has slowly worn off over the years. You eat what your stomach will allow before returning to your room and straight back into the toilet.

In the bus on the way to the ground you listen to your MP3 player. Your usual collection of classic hits soothes the nerves a little and you hope you never quite arrive at the ground.

On arriving at the dressing-room it's straight to the toilet again. God help the dressing-room attendants if the toilet paper hasn't been refilled! On emerging you go to your usual spot in the room — that is if you went okay last time at this ground; if not, you fight it out with the newcomers for a suitable position — it's probably best if it's in close proximity to the toilet.

The whole idea of warm-ups is to get yourself physically and mentally ready to play cricket. In reality though you jog around, silently complaining about how stiff and sore you are, get yelled at for cocking up the warm-up fielding exercise and then throw a tantrum in response.

Even though by this time you're ready for the toilet again your routine dictates you go to the pitch for some shadow batting. The pitch is barren of grass and looks like a 'belter' but in your opinion, and in contrast to the captain's, no pitch is ever flat enough to bat first on. You try hard to imagine yourself middling the ball and playing your flawless game but your mind's eye just keeps on seeing 'jaffas' dismissing you in every possible way. Eventually you give up and head back to the toilet — where the hell is all this coming from, after all you didn't eat all that much for breakfast?!

As Stephen Fleming brushes past you on his way to the toss you say 'Good luck, bro', but really you're thinking 'bad luck' because the bastard plans on batting if he wins it. You watch as the coin goes up, hoping like hell the opposition captain gets interviewed first so you live another day — he doesn't, and you rush back to the toilet.

From this point on you have anywhere between one minute to six hours of worrying about getting out or getting hit. Whatever the outcome, runs or not, upon your dismissal you simply start all over again worrying about your next innings.

This was me — and anxiety, self-doubt, fear and expectation tormented me the whole way through my cricketing career. These foes tried their best to inhibit my ability to apply my processes with far too frequent success. I often thought of them as being like nasty little computer viruses that got into the hard drive of my head and did their best to ruin the smooth running of my cricket program. It was a constant battle, but I wasn't the first and only player to deal with these feelings. Most if not all of us, and from all walks of life and vocations, experience these debilitating feelings from time to time. In cricketing circles they are often referred to as 'the demons' — and if you want to succeed, you need to confront them.

Dealing with anxiety

Nerves, apprehension, butterflies, jitters — call them what you want, anxiety is uncomfortable, and for me it was ever-present. I really can't remember when exactly it first happened but it happened all right! It was that moment when the thought of coming on to bowl or going out to bat turned from being exciting to nerve-wracking. I remember as a kid I would bat at No. 4 in my junior cricket team, and as far as I was concerned the guys who were batting before me were a pain in the arse. They were using up *my* batting time and I couldn't wait till they got out. As for bowling? All I wanted was the ball in hand all day. My first clear recollection of an attack of the butterflies came when I was about 12 years old. I was batting at No. 3 and couldn't quite understand why I was feeling so ill and needed to go to the toilet so much. I went out and got bowled second ball having a wild swing. It was awful and I cried all the way off. In my fragile young mind I associated going to the toilet before batting with getting a low score. It became a superstition and a harrowing one because from that point on all I ever wanted to do was go to the toilet before batting.

I'm no different from most sportspeople — or all people for that matter — I experience anxiety from time to time. Some people deal with it a little better than others. Associating my nervous reaction of wanting to go to the toilet with poor performance was really an example of my inability to deal with my anxiety, but at age 12 I had no real appreciation of the concept. If I'd known what was happening at that early age then perhaps my bowling 'yips' would never have occurred.

Yet the negative effect nerves could have on me was not only confined to cricket; the signs were also there in my other main game as a kid — golf. I loved my golf and would play and practise it almost as much as I would my cricket. It was my winter game and as we lived walking distance from Remuera Golf Club in Auckland's Eastern Suburbs my dad joined me up as a junior member. I quickly got my handicap down to single figures with it sitting most of the time either side of 10. I would play on Sunday mornings with my mates and quite regularly threaten sub-80 scores, but when I was allowed to play with the men in the afternoon my game would fall to bits. For me, playing in the men's field was the big time and I wanted to impress the old fellas but my legs would shake, I'd lose all feeling in my hands, and get that horrible queasy feeling in my stomach. I'd generally smash the ball out of sight from the tee, which of course was adrenalin-assisted, but close to the green, duffs and jerked putts were the order of the day. The same phenomenon would extend to junior tournaments and any important rounds. It upset and angered me and at times I would be inconsolable following another botched afternoon or tournament round. At the same time, throughout my early teenage years, I was bowling, and bowling well — without anxiety — but the signs were there that anxiety and I were not an effective match.

By my mid-teens I was bowling spin and on my way to stardom — well, in my own eyes anyway. I loved bowling and nerves weren't a factor at all. I wanted the ball all the time and when I ran in my focus was on bowling a 'ripper'. When I think back now, there were a few occasions where anxiety got in the way of finding a good length, but I always put it down to some technical fault rather than a mental meltdown.

Like my golfing experience, my first crack at senior cricket didn't go well as I struggled for rhythm and couldn't make it in the Cornwall Cricket Club, but I still had a ton of self-belief and wasn't interested in acknowledging my psychological problems. It all finally caught up with me at age 19 when Auckland captain Jeff Crowe said, 'Next over, that end' and immediately my hands began to sweat, my mind raced, my bladder pressed and the ball went everywhere other than on the right line or length.

My inability to function effectively in a state of anxiety drove me into the cricketing wilderness, but although I was now aware of it, the problem was I had no idea how to deal with it. As I tried to resurrect my career in Dunedin, this inability let me down time and time again. As a bowler it had me well and truly by the balls, and as I became more and more prominent as a batsman, it continued to let me down as I tried to break through into the first-class team, causing me to blow a few of my early chances. The bigger the occasion the more anxiety I would experience. I was blowing my trial situations and then later on when I had finally become established as a batsman I was blowing the big innings, the ones that would really get me noticed. The anxiety was not only frustrating me, I hated it as well.

Through the mid to late '90s the bowling nerves weren't an issue any more because that part of my life was over. I was a good net bowler but a nervous wreck out in the middle with ball in hand, but who cared — I was a batsman now. Unfortunately, I was a nervous wreck before I batted too. I'd find I would be waiting to bat feeling crook, dying to go to the toilet, and often would have to go hoping a wicket wouldn't fall while doing my business. My legs would be moving uncontrollably and I'd be leaning my forehead on my bat handle, too nervous to watch. Other times I would deal with the excessive nervous energy by talking and joking with my team-mates.

Once I got out to the crease the anxiety would settle down after a half-hour or so of batting, but before that it would wreak havoc on my performance. People often talk about pressure making you do dumb things, but really it is the level of anxiety that the pressure produces and your inability to cope with it that triggers the 'brain explosions'. Anxiety would cause me to get too expansive in my play, especially early on in my innings. It was making me a poor starter and my decision-making erratic. Senseless run-outs — usually of my team-mates — and flamboyant strokes were a strong indication that I didn't have my nerves under control. Actually, silly running early in a player's innings is always a good example of someone with a high level of anxiety. Paul Wiseman was a tail-ender but took his batting very seriously and would contribute quite well; however, I always got a little jittery if I was in and he was coming to join me. Paul would come out to bat so hyped up his eyeballs would be vibrating and I knew I was going to be in for some very panicky and rushed 20-yard dashes.

It was my dislike of anxiety that led me to want to open the batting. I didn't cope with waiting to bat very well at all, with my performance frequently determined by my anxiety level when the wicket that brought me to the crease fell. If I was in control and my level okay then there was a good chance I wouldn't do anything dumb; but if the butterflies were out of control I was in big trouble. Simply put, anxiety was controlling me, I wasn't controlling it. It was not knowing the 'when', 'what' and 'who' that would do my head in. When would I be batting? What would be the situation? Who would I be facing? The best way to fix this problem was to open the batting. As an opening batsman I knew exactly when I would be batting, what the situation would be and who I would be facing.

People often say that the opening role is the toughest job but I disagree. Yes, the ball is newer and harder, the bowlers fresh and often the best and fastest, and you may have to deal with early swing and seam. But those challenges paled in comparison to the psychological hurdles I could overcome with a clearer know-ledge of the scenario I was to face. Even though I was still a very nervous player, the day I began to open was the day my consistency improved out of sight.

It was Chris Cairns who really opened my eyes when it came to dealing with anxiety. It was during my first tour with the Black Caps. We had just arrived in KweKwe, a small town in the Zimbabwe countryside, and I was having dinner with Chris in the hotel restaurant when we got talking about it. He said that he always felt nervous before playing but also excited because he just never knew what the day would hold for him. I'd always seen Cairnsy as this sort of larger-than-life cricketer who just went out with total confidence and took the world on; I'd never seen him as a nervous fella. It dawned on me then that everyone experiences anxiety but it is how you deal with it that matters and here is the key:

Dealing with nerves does not mean eradicating them.

In my early years as a batsman I thought great players either didn't suffer from nerves like me or else they had some magical formula that got rid of them. When I first began delving into the realms of sports psych I thought — well, desperately hoped really — that the skills I would acquire along the way would allow me to reduce or even eradicate my anxiety. My discovery that they would not was a major step forward in my maturing as a cricket player. I grew to understand that I would always have a high level of anxiety but that I had to learn how to function while still experiencing its discomforting side-effects.

I've seen many very talented cricketers who have not achieved the heights of which they were capable because they were not prepared to deal with anxiety. I like to define anxiety as a side-effect of committing to a task that is important to you but that challenges you to the point that success is not a given. In a cricketing environment it can strike in many ways. It may be when you take a step up in competition standard, the match situation becomes close, or the batting/bowling conditions grow difficult. Whatever the case, if you are bent on *avoiding* anxiety you are unlikely to succeed. Some individuals are like the great club player who is happy dominating at the lower level but really doesn't want to push himself further; many are like the player who just can't seem to make the step up to a harder grade; and the more subtle one is the one who always blows it in the pressure situation.

In *A Good Walk Spoilt*, a book written by John Feinstein about the United States Professional Golf Tour, I read a great little piece on anxiety. It talked about golf's most pressured environment: the final nine holes in a major tournament. It's written up as if the feelings of anxiety are intolerable, and I'd imagine they are, but through interviews with some of the game's greatest players the book offered a different perspective. It basically said that while these players feel the nerves they see the reason for them — they are in contention down the final stretch of a major. For that reason they are prepared to accept them. That to me is a great way of looking at the reality of anxiety in the sporting arena.

In essence, challenging, foreign and pressure situations produce feelings of anxiety and make you feel uncomfortable, but to be successful you must learn to operate effectively while feeling this way. The trick is not to try and remove the nerves, as that only takes your focus away from the important things, which are the things you must do to succeed. Once I had a handle on those things that I needed to do in certain situations and could focus on them, I then had a means of ensuring that I could operate while under the influence of anxiety.

It was my pre-ball routine that was the critical mental management process when it came to getting the results I wanted when I was basically crapping myself, which was most of the time. The nastier the situation, the more I needed to get absorbed in my pre-balls. It was also my pre-ball routine that

I put my faith in when in a runs slump or dodgy situation. It was invaluable when it came to getting established at the crease, but I have to admit that I still struggled to control my anxiety around milestones like closing in on a century. At first-class level my anxiety often decreased as my innings progressed, but at test level, where the standard of bowling meant I felt under pressure from my first to my last ball, I was invariably highly anxious.

Building confidence

I've said that my mental management plan was devised not to reduce anxiety but rather as a means of enabling me to operate effectively while in its grip. However, that said, there is a way to reduce anxiety to some extent. The way I see it, confidence can be negatively correlated with anxiety — in other words, the more confident you are the less anxiety you will feel, although I still believe that you can have a high degree of confidence and still be extremely nervous at the same time.

'Be confident' were words of encouragement I heard from well-wishers on many occasions and they always made me smirk. Confidence wasn't something I could just pluck from the air, deciding that today I would play with confidence. To me, confidence was misunderstood. Confidence wasn't something I *had* — it was something I *earned*. Perhaps some people possess a higher degree of confidence than others, but does that automatically make them a better or more productive player than the outwardly nervous one? You need to draw a distinction between a confident player and a risk-taker. Hook shots, flowing cover drives on the up, or running down the wicket and smashing sixes over fielders' heads may seem like confident shots and assured play, and maybe they are, but if there is an unacceptably high degree of risk and a lack of control then staying in may be more a case of luck — and I can guarantee you that luck has a tendency to run out. Speaking from my own experience, I know that some of my so-called more 'confident knocks' were played out of simple desperation and a 'you or me' mentality and that I got lucky.

Acting confident is, however, extremely important and something which the Australian cricketers do extremely well. They very seldom look nervous and work hard at establishing a presence on the cricket field that places the opposition under psychological pressure even before a ball is bowled.

This facet of confident play is something that Stephen Fleming talked volumes about during my career and something that I really struggled with. The bravado gained from acting confidently even when under pressure is vital from a competitive standpoint, but confidence can also be gained from accomplishing something you didn't think you could. For instance, facing fast bowling can be daunting, but the more you face up to it and survive, the more confidence you gain in yourself. When Stephen Fleming walked down the wicket in Colombo and told me to use the pad as a defence against Muralitharan, a technique I wasn't comfortable with, I was forced to do it and it paid dividends. I gained a lot of confidence in my defensive technique to the turning ball from that point on. Which is all well and good, but what I was much more interested in was building confidence *before* the event.

Building confidence takes time. Chris Cairns, who can be quite perceptive, noticed how during my short-lived ODI career I was over-hitting when looking to score. He thought that if I used a heavy bat it would mean I would only need to drop it on the ball to find the boundary. Anyone who followed my ODI fortunes would have appreciated that I was open to any kind of advice at this stage and so I gave it a go — in the practice nets. There was no way I had the confidence to take Cairnsy's borrowed three-pounder straight out to the middle so I first practised with it and then practised and practised. When finally I took it out to the middle I got two innings out of it before the middle cracked and the handle broke!

Confidence is also belief. It is the belief that you have the skills to get the job done. I wasn't interested in false belief though — for me to believe in myself I had to work for it. Which, at the end of the day, pretty much sums up the whole rationale for my mental management process. By analysing my game and setting goals I knew what I needed to work on, therefore I could train accordingly; and if I believed I had put the work in — the right work — I could walk out to bat confident in the knowledge that if I could commit to my pre-ball routine then I would give myself the best possible chance of succeeding. When you hear a cricketer say to the media, 'I trusted my processes' this is what they are talking about.

I trained to build trust in my game, and trust at the point of delivery that I could apply that game. Trust, belief, confidence — call it what you want, but it was only ever something I earned through plain hard work. If I walked out to bat confident in the belief I had done the preparation required then I could treat my anxiety as it ought to be considered: a side-effect of the situation and a side-effect that, while it would be ever-present, didn't need to get in the way.

The foundation of my confidence was built in the practice nets and for four years, from 1998 to 2002, that practice was focused solely on being as tight an opening test batsman as I could possibly be. I suppose I started making noises about wanting a go at the one-dayers because I got sick of hearing about how much money Scott Styris was making at that form of the game and realising how little I was making as a test specialist by comparison. I also knew test cricket was coming under a little pressure as a dying game, and with the excessive amount of ODIs being scheduled each year at the expense of test series I thought it wise to expand my outlook. There was one major problem though; there was only one guy around who had any sort of confidence in my ability to play one-day cricket and he wasn't the fella who mattered.

The *New Zealand Herald*'s main cricket writer Richard Boock was at this time testing out his own selecting power, which all media men seem to go through at some time or other, and had decided I was the man for the one-day opening role. While I enjoyed reading how great I would be as the man to anchor the 50 overs I didn't believe any of it. Nevertheless, I was never going to turn down the chance of playing the one-dayers — after all, hitting a six to win an ODI at the MCG was my dream and those new black ODI playing shirts were quite cool besides.

So I made my ODI debut at the MCG, but as I walked out into the centre of the great cricketing coliseum deep down I knew I was lacking the skills for the job. When I walk out onto a test ground I'm as nervous as hell but I know that if I trust my processes I can succeed; but on that day, on my ODI debut, all I was was nervous as hell. I had no processes I trusted and so anxiety ran rampant. It manifested itself in out-of-control batting. My third ODI was possibly my most disappointing day in cricket. I made 26 from 71 balls but I swear I took a swing at every ball. The pitch was seaming, we won the match and my team-mates said I probably did a good job in seeing off the new ball — but I knew in my heart of hearts that the only reason I didn't get out earlier was because I wasn't good enough to nick one.

Chapter Fourteen

Facing fear

Fear comes in many forms and if not dealt with properly has the ability to turn everything to custard very quickly. I feared many things in the course of playing my cricket. I faced my fears on a regular basis and, while never overcoming them, managed to use them to focus my effort.

Fear of failure

Self-esteem, fame, fortune (I picked the wrong game for that!), enjoyment and achievement all played a part in motivating me to play cricket, but from the time I began my resurgence as a batsman and especially during my time as a Black Cap there was one overriding motivator — the fear of failure.

People claim that being motivated by the fear of failure is a negative and ineffectual motivator but I say 'Bullshit!' to that. My dreams of cricketing success had been taken from me in 1992 when I decelerated when I should have accelerated and my first 'yipped' delivery was served up. Why did I keep trying? Well, I covered that in the first section of this book, but now that I was living the life I wanted as a professional cricketer I sure as hell wanted to keep it. One thing could take it from me and that was failure. Failing as a bowler had hurt, and the feelings it left me with were those I did not want to experience again; I desperately didn't want to fail as a batsman. Failure as an Otago player meant loss of future national selection, and failure as a Black Cap meant loss of a job and lifestyle. I would grimly protect what I had and, when it boiled down to it, that was my wicket.

Fear of failure played a large hand in my adoption of a conservative approach to batting. When I went out to bat my motivation was to not get out — that is, to avoid failure. I'll concede that that is not an ideal motivator when it comes to playing attractive cricket and it definitely held me back from getting the best out of myself in terms of quality stroke play, but by God it was effective in ensuring I was a reliable and consistent opening batsman. The best mentality for batting is to look to score first and defend second, as indicated in my PPP. I chose the fact that my scoreable zone would be very small. However, due to my fear of failure, even with very limited options I still looked to defend first too often. The problem was that I associated attacking shots with the risk of getting out and that was risk I didn't really like to take. Time at the crease I associated with runs on the board, slow runs but runs all the same, and so I gritted my teeth, minimised the risk and tried to stay in — well, tried not to get out really.

Fear of failure made me a dedicated practiser. Getting out was awful. After a poor score the feelings of helplessness, frustration, guilt and self-loathing were hard to take (and at times I could sulk for days) but worse still was the nagging thought that another one of those efforts and I'd be dropped. The thought of that was intolerable and so I had to take steps to ensure it didn't happen. Those steps were generally to find the cause of the dismissal and practise determinedly so it was unlikely to happen again. The pain which I associated with getting out cheaply and failing as a batsman was a very strong motivator to get me into the practice nets and take steps towards reducing the chances of getting out for a low score in future. I always drew upon my experience as a bowler to motivate me to succeed as a batsman but I also worried that I had a disposition to fail under pressure. Getting the batting 'yips' was an endless worry of mine and made me shiver every time I played poorly.

Fear of failure eventually played a major part in my retirement. I knew I was lacking the energy and willpower to pull my form around and score against the Australian bowlers. I knew also that a more expansive game was what I needed to rejuvenate my enthusiasm and that it wouldn't happen overnight.

After all I'd gone through to play for New Zealand I wasn't prepared to go out having been dropped, but feared that if I continued to play non-selection was inevitable. The game had finally beaten me, but it wasn't really official unless I was actually dropped, and that was one failure I would not accept. If I walked away now I still walked off with a proud record. I was determined that I wasn't going to leave a bitter and twisted old man as so many had before me.

When I look back now I'd say that while I don't see fear of failure as a bad motivator it is an exhausting one. It's fuelled by enervating emotions such as fear, doubt, anxiety and worry. While these are everyday emotions, it requires strength to overcome them if you are going to use them to drive you on.

> Every time I walked to the wicket I faced failure; it was a risk I had to accept to succeed.

I was only going to accept so much risk though, and while my cautious approach minimised my chance of failure, it just meant I had to wait longer for success. And even though I feared it, cricket is a game in which you must deal with failure on a regular basis. Even the great Sir Don Bradman had his low scores — and I bet he played and missed every so often too — but he faced up and came back for more. As a bowler I couldn't face up to failure but as a batsman I could — well, right up to the bitter end at least.

Fear of getting hit

Cricket balls are hard and it hurts when they hit you, but it's the *thought* of them hitting you that does the most damage. It's also that thought of getting hit that makes people worry for weeks about an upcoming game that involves a fast bowler, wreaks havoc on a batsman's technique, causes players to attempt outrageous shots, and prevents fast bowlers sending down bouncers at other fast bowlers.

I was actually a reasonable little batsman when I was a kid until the guys around me got bigger and stronger and, more importantly, faster at bowling. From the moment I took a backward step out to square leg my batting days were over. I was the first kid in my team to wear a thigh pad and a batting helmet but the extra protection didn't help; getting out of the way was still the number one priority when at the crease. I struggled with my fear of the ball and fast bowling all my cricketing life, and can't quite believe I ended up opening the batting facing the world's fastest bowlers when the ball is at it hardest. Justin Langer once said in an interview that facing fast bowling is never pleasant and anyone who says they enjoy it is lying — I agree and think it was a very brave statement for another test opener to make in public. You can talk it up as much as you like, and many do, but it takes a brave man to admit his fears.

So fear was ever-present when I took on the quicks but I learnt to deal with it, and while I can never say that I enjoyed it I did at times experience feelings of exhilaration. Batting at Perth against Brett Lee was one of the game's great challenges, but it was a once-in-a-lifetime experience and I'm glad I experienced it. So too was facing Shoaib Akhtar who, with a howling Wellington northerly up his arse, was approaching speeds of around 160 kph. There were balls that whistled past that I knew I was simply not capable of playing. I could *see* them but not *react* in time. Sure it was harrowing, but by the same token you are experiencing bowling that is as quick as it has ever got, and that is an experience to treasure. Perhaps this is why I love adrenalin sports. I'm scared as hell of heights and yet I have a pilot licence with an aerobatics rating, and have done bungee jumping as well as a tandem skydive.

However, if you ever want to see the effect fear has on batting watch what happens to a reasonable tail-ender when the slow bowlers are replaced with the quicks. Or for that matter, check out how many big shots are played when the new ball is due in a few overs' time. You see so many tail-end players, even the odd top-order player, who have developed some pretty solid batting techniques and can be seriously hard to remove. Their feet move well, and they have discipline and application — but only up to a point. That point is usually around the 140 kph mark. At that point the footwork seems to go, the solid in-behind style defence becomes a thing of the past, the application is non-existent, and 'hard to remove' becomes 'easy to shift' and it's all down to fear. Which is why it's so important at test level to have a real quick in your team. Many lower-order test batsmen are quite handy with the bat, and when the Black Caps have been without a genuine quick many of them have scored irritating runs against us. Between 1988 and 1994 I was one such tail-ender, but at the first-class level.

I could always handle a bat, but as soon as my physical safety was at risk it was swing hard and hit them before they could hit me.

Then in 1994 I decided I had to grow some balls. If I truly wanted to be a batsman then I had to be prepared to wear the odd one. It didn't mean I had to like it; it just meant I had to be prepared for it. Something I heard from an old team-mate in this regard has always struck me as being very true. I played youth cricket with Blair Pocock, who became a determined opening batsman who played for Auckland, Northern Districts and even a few tests for New Zealand in the early '90s. I was playing against him during the 1994/95 season and was at the non-striker's end while one of our tail-enders was getting worked over by one of their quicks. The umpire looked over at Blair who was at mid-off and said, 'I don't think this guy really fancies it.' Blair responded with, 'No one does but you still have to stand in front of it. Some of us are just better prepared to do that.' It was a fairly nondescript conversation but one that struck me quite hard as a bystander. I too had to be prepared mentally from a bravery standpoint, but I also needed to be prepared technically and tactically to cope with my fear of fast bowling.

By facing my fear head on and deciding not to shy from the ball I immediately became a better batsman. I would not give my wicket away so easily and I began to discover strategies to cope with and counter quicker bowlers. In fact, while I feared it I also started to take a sort of masochistic enjoyment out of taking one on the helmet or body. I was never one to try and cover up the fact that it hurt — everyone knows it hurts — but there was no way in hell I was going to flinch for the next ball. Bruises were cool, they were like having battle scars to show off. They bore witness to how tough you were and proved that you were taking some heat for your country. It even pissed me off that I wasn't a natural bruiser!

With every step up in level though there is always a massive mental battle to be won. In May 2002 I was in Karachi preparing for the second test against Pakistan. We had just suffered our largest ever test loss in the history of New Zealand Cricket courtesy of some ridiculously fast bowling from Shoaib Akhtar. In the course of proving a point to the world media, who were refusing to acknowledge the 161-kph deliveries he'd let fly during the ODIs, he had ripped through us in the first test at Lahore. On the flat surfaces in Pakistan he was the difference between the two teams and we had to find a strategy to deal with him. The strategy was simple: weight forward, low back-lift, watch for the yorker and deny him for his four-over spell. Implementation of the strategy was a little harder because there was always that nagging little thought in the back of the mind that you might just be killed in the process. It was the first time I had been exposed to this level of pace and the experience from the first test was playing on my mind. I'd already had a spat with Craig McMillan over the bizarre closed-off batting stance I had decided to use to counter Shoaib. It made me realise that my fear was controlling me.

Luckily we had the perfect man to speak to in the touring party. Reg Dickson was our security advisor and a former Australian SAS soldier. I figured that when he went to work fear must have been a constant companion, and when it's bullets coming at you and not cricket balls the stakes are a little higher. He was helpful, but not because he gave me some magical formula for avoiding fear, but by reminding me that I had a job to do and that the more I prepared for that job the less my fear was likely to get in the way of me doing it. A few hours later a bomb exploded outside our hotel and we went home without playing the test. People did die that day and it was awful, but deep down inside I had a massive sense of relief.

Preparing for the fear of being hit is a hard thing to do. It takes a hell of a lot of courage to put yourself at peril in a training situation, and to tell you the truth, I never had enough of that kind of courage. While I was a massive practiser and spent countless hours in the nets I was also one hell of a coward in them. If cricket was played solely in the nets I would have struggled to make third-grade club level. I think the problem was that while I was prepared to get hit in a match situation I was certainly not prepared for it at training. All I looked for in the nets was the bouncer and so my weight would get forced back, my feet wouldn't move, I wouldn't get in behind, and basically would play dreadfully. I loved netting against medium pacers, just as tail-enders in general love batting against them, but quicks were simply harrowing.

Still, every so often I would walk in to the nets against one of our quicks knowing I would bat like crap but that I needed to put myself under pressure. The bowlers could smell my fear and loved it so I always got plenty of short stuff. Craig McMillan, who wasn't quick but made up for it by bowling three yards closer, used to have a whale of a time. What I would do most often was bat against a rubber ball. These balls, called 'Incrediballs', looked like real cricket balls but were made of a rubbery plastic. You could get people to bowl or hurl them from close range to simulate quick bowling — really quick bowling — and so sharpen up the reflexes. I would get hit quite often but this way I couldn't do myself any real harm. They were still hard enough that when you did get hit it stung, and this added a little spice, but not enough to force me into practising poor body position and technique. Incrediball training made me feel a little more prepared for actual fast bowling and thus helped with my confidence, but most of all, by getting absorbed in and focusing on my pre-batting and pre-ball routines, I could operate while crapping myself with fear. However, when I analysed many of my dismissals the thought of being hit by a short ball had a hand in a good number of them. By God it would have been good to have been a fast bowler!

As an opening batsman I faced fast bowling on a regular basis, and yes it scared me, but nowhere near as much as fielding at silly mid-off and silly mid-on. As a batsman I could prepare for the job, build my skill and trust in that, but as a close-in fielder I felt like a coconut waiting to be taken out in the shy. On occasions, fielding in close was with without doubt the most frightened I've ever been on a cricket field. It wore me down eventually and made fielding very unenjoyable — it was just more time feeling anxious and frightened out in the middle. The slog sweep and sweep shots are more prevalent in the game today and some players, like Matthew Hayden, hit it extremely hard, low and just in front of square — which is, incidentally, exactly where you stand. I didn't overly mind fielding there against the seamers and Flemo never really used the position much when they were operating. It can even be quite an interesting place to watch a test match from early on the first day, it gives you such a different perspective. You hear the ball coming down the pitch and you can really sense what the batsman is going through. I always thought batting looked really hard when viewed from close in. However, when the majority of the overs were delivered by Daniel Vettori, and he and Flemo insisted on the position constantly, my interest tended to wane a little.

Short leg, under the helmet, silly mid-on, whatever you call it, is generally a position reserved for the youngest team member or the new boy on the block. At 28 years of age I was slightly longer in the tooth than the usual newbie but I actually volunteered for the position. I knew I was a poor fielder but thought I should try and find a role in which to specialise. I had no interest in the ego positions — the slips — so it really had to be the helmet job. Some known players had actually become quite renowned for their work in close, one of them being Australian hard-man David Boon. Boon had a low centre of gravity (that's putting it diplomatically), was well balanced on his feet, had great reflexes, and most importantly was as tough as nails — you couldn't ask for better attributes. I, on the other hand, was old, stiff, poor on my feet and a pussy — it was never really going to work. However, it was tacitly accepted that I would do less harm under there than anywhere else, so I stayed put.

For the record, it's a position where you get no sympathy at all. If you get hit there's always the obligatory enquiry into whether you're all right, but it was the time spent in a crouched position (which could be for days when on the Subcontinent) that I found the most damaging. I never had a particularly healthy back in the first place, but after a day in the field under the helmet I would be in all sorts of trouble. It took some time before my moans were finally taken seriously and I was allowed to get a massage at the end of play, which was a privilege generally reserved for the bowlers. As I got into my 30s it began to wear me down physically and then mentally and all I wanted was to get out of the position. By the end, my attention was more on self-preservation than performance and I really should have been replaced, but by whom? Every younger player that came into the team was a bloody livewire in the field and could be put nowhere other than cover and cover point.

Fear of the unknown

I have freely admitted to being a very nervous player and that my own nervous reaction was to want to go for 'number twos'. Another common nervous reaction experienced by cricketers is nausea. There are many stories about players who were notorious for throwing up before batting, and luckily I wasn't one of them. Instead I would shake, jump around, suffer from bouts of ridiculous negativity and my bum would want to explode — but I very seldom felt nauseous.

There was only really one occasion when I felt a little sick before batting and that was at Perth. It was the third and final test of the 2001 series and my first test at that venue. Perth is renowned as the fastest and bounciest pitch in world cricket and the Australians play on that superbly. The media talk up the Perth game and constantly question your ability to perform on the pitch. The local administration put you in the nets at the top of the practice area that are commonly understood to be a hell of a lot quicker and bouncier than out in the middle, and whenever you walk past an Australian player they comment to whoever's beside them, just loud enough so you can overhear, about how fast this particular pitch is going to be. If it is designed to psych you out, then it does so perfectly. As I padded up to bat in that match I wasn't far from losing my breakfast — and this time out both ends. It was more than the usual case of nerves, it was also a massive case of fear of the unknown. What would facing McGrath, Gillespie and Lee be like at Perth? In my mind it was already going to be harrowing. As it turned out it was nowhere near as bad as I anticipated — it never is — although I don't think the track for this game was a classical Perth flyer.

The unknown is something an opening batsman deals with on a regular basis. You often front up to bowlers you have never faced before or know very little about. While you may have watched them on television, I can guarantee you things always look different facing up from 20 yards away. Even if you know the foe and have faced them before, you don't know whether today they will swing the ball and how the pitch will perform. It was a fear that made me very apprehensive and was hard to control, because as you've read I liked to be as prepared and organised as possible. Possibly this is the reason I never really minded having to go in and bat with a few overs left in the day. Some people hated that situation, but I always looked upon it as a chance to have a look at the bowler and prepare for the next day; providing I survived to stumps of course.

Most of the time I'd say the unknown is never as bad as the mind predicts it will be. Under pressure and when anxious my mind could become a runaway vehicle of dread, but when I finally faced up to the root cause of the concern it invariably brought things under control. My first test against Pakistan was a prime example of this phenomenon. I'd watched and admired Waqar Younis from a distance over the years and now I would have to face up to him.

Waqar had a long and impressive run-up to the wicket and as he sprinted in to deliver his first delivery all I could think was, 'What the f**k is this going to be like!' It only took two balls, two solid leaves outside off stump before the man on my shoulder whispered in my ear, 'You can actually handle this.' I still remained anxious and on edge but can vouch that experience definitely builds confidence.

It was also the fear of the unknown that caused me to bat totally out of control in my first test against South Africa. The long build-up to the series also gave me plenty of time to build up some sort of hysteria about my impending meeting with 'White Lightning' (Allan Donald). I'd faced him before and he'd been too fast for me then, so my experience hadn't helped the confidence much, but that was a long time ago and I knew that circumstances had changed. However, I was so wound up by the time he bowled the first ball of the encounter that my emotions had got well away from me and I failed to get them back under control.

In the end, the only real way to overcome fear, be it of failure, of being hit, or of the unknown, is to face it head-on. The old reflex of 'fight or flight' in the face of fear is a true one and I can guarantee that if yours is always flight then your goals will remain a long way off as you run from the things you need to do to achieve them. I'll concede though that I employed a classic strategy of *get to the non-striker's end* when challenged by Akhtar and Co. It's okay to fear something, that's not cowardly; to admit fear isn't cowardly either; but to run away from it when you know you *must* get through it to achieve the things which you desire is extremely cowardly. Preparing honestly and accurately for the challenge ahead definitely helps reduce fear's grip on you, and confidence can definitely be built on the back of past success even if it never really eliminates the fear completely.

Chapter Fifteen

Self-talk

When I used to run in to bowl as a young spin bowler, all that went through my mind was how great a ball I was going to deliver. I would see myself bowling a ball that dropped sharply out of the air as it drifted in towards leg stump, pitched, spun and hit the top of the off stump. If it didn't happen I would walk back to my mark telling myself it was going to happen next ball. After a few games for Auckland I ran in pleading with myself not to drop it short. If it was short I would tell myself how crap I was, and if it was on a length I would tell myself the short one was only a ball or two away. Later on when bowling in Dunedin there were times when I felt like punching some of my team-mates because following a couple of long hops there would always be someone to offer me advice in the form of 'Pitch it up'. They didn't realise those were words I had grown to fear because they invariably came in response to a load of short shit. Didn't they realise that I had actually been trying to 'pitch it up' in the first place!? When I did get one on a length they had the gumption to yell 'That's better!' As if I didn't bloody know! Running in to bowl saying 'pitch it up' to myself was just another way of saying, 'Don't drop it short'. With thinking like that it isn't hard to understand why my bowling 'yips' just kept getting worse. What does bemuse me now though is that when batting

200

during those same years, as the bowler ran in I would be saying to myself, 'Is this one the bouncer?' Seventeen years later and as a successful test-match opening batsman I was still asking myself the very same question.

Throughout my whole batting career I was a negative thinker, talking myself into failure and predicting my impending doom. Each year when I set my budget, I would factor in an allowance for being dropped halfway through the season. Without a doubt this helped shape the conservative type of player I was, but it still didn't prevent me from achieving my goals because finally I found a way of seeing it for what it was — bullshit!

I was a real worrier. I worried about everything, but most of all of failing. My worry usually manifested itself through negative thoughts and negative self-talk. Anxiety tormented me for many years and I believed that successful sportspeople surely didn't think the way I did. I had to get rid of the worries, but the harder I tried the worse they became. Fortunately, there are a few sports psych techniques designed to cope with this type of thinking. One is to write your negative thought down on a piece of paper and then screw it up and throw it away. Another technique is to say 'Stop!' whenever a negative thought comes into your mind and then replace it with a positive. I developed a technique whereby I imagined it wasn't actually me who was thinking the negative thoughts; instead it was the little man sitting on my shoulder. Whenever he piped up I would simply brush him off my shoulder and reinforce to myself what I was going to do. At the crease, when the little man was at his most negative, I tried to hide what I was doing by pretending I was hitching my shirt or waving away a fly. There were actually times when I pulled away from the crease as the bowler ran in pretending I was being pestered by a flying insect when in fact I was involved in a full-on argument with myself. It got to the point of absurdity, and then when some opposition started noticing what I was doing I had to stop it to avoid ridicule. While this technique didn't seem to stop the negative thinking — in fact, nothing seemed to — at least I made a breakthrough that nullified its destructive impact.

After a couple of years of personal analysis and as I had begun to develop my routines I noticed that my level of negativity really had nothing to do with my performance. My little shoulder-sitter was prevalent in all innings, good or bad, but what mattered was whether or not he had an impact on my behaviour. Immediately I stopped trying to argue with him and learnt to focus on the things I had discovered I must concentrate on to succeed. I like to use the analogy of having a stereo playing in the background as you try to study for an exam. You can choose to listen to the stereo and it can take your focus from the task at hand; or you can focus half on the stereo and half on the job; or better still, you can treat it as only meaningless background noise and continue to focus entirely on the initial task.

Based on the fact that I am a man and theoretically cannot concentrate on two things at once without one of them suffering, it became a question of the quality of my concentration. Quality concentration was correlated to how well I could adhere to my routines. The little man on my shoulder then became a call to attention. The more the pressure the louder he became, so when my mind went haywire it was a warning that I had to get absorbed in my routines — which of course was my mechanism for handling pressure. Unfortunately, the little man didn't really mind being ignored and he never went away. It might take him a long time to win the 'You're going to get out' argument, but he always had the last word on the 'Don't play that attacking shot because you might get out' discussion.

I had the same problem with my imagery. I've talked about how I used imagery to develop new skills and techniques and prepare myself for the upcoming challenge. The little man must have had a mate that lived in my imagination who was adept at throwing the wrong image into my head. It took me some time, but towards the end of my career I got the better of that little bugger. His favourite times for sabotage came when I was working on my balance and shadow batting at the pitch on the morning of a game. When I tried to see myself playing straight with good balance — which is a must for good batting — I found it hard not to see and feel myself toppling and playing around my front pad. More frustrating though was when I was out at the crease trying to image myself playing with control and I would just keep seeing myself getting out to absolutely unplayable deliveries — God it was frustrating! I can say though that the more I practised my imagery the better I became at it. Maybe imagery is a learned skill whereas negative thinking is more innate, but by the end I was able to replace the negative image with a positive one and then get better at seeing positive ones more regularly.

Pressure, anxiety and negative thinking are all related to confidence, and in theory as confidence grows those other factors should subside. It's strange really, because while I cite my second innings 77 in my first test against South Africa as a highlight of my career because it was an innings that indicated to me that I could cut it at the top level, it didn't change the things I would say to myself over the course of my career. I've described how I'd got myself into a frenzy of worry leading up to the South African tour of 2000 and it wasn't helped when upon arriving at my first hotel room on tour I turned on the television and a domestic game of cricket was on. The first over I watched consisted of an over of short balls which the batsman ducked and weaved his way through. At the end of the over, which I thought was terrifyingly spectacular, the commentator observed nondescriptly, 'Another maiden'. I immediately began to tell myself I was going to get seriously hurt over here.

As I walked out to bat in the first test I remember thinking that I was like a lamb to the slaughter. I let the first ball go quite nonchalantly but inside thought, 'Bloody hell that was fast!' While I worked through Donald and Pollock's opening spell in the second innings all I could think about was how much faster Ntini would be. After three tests of telling myself I was out of my league and how much I was going to get hurt, I was on the plane home having scored 232 runs at an average of 46 and reading an article in the *New Zealand Herald* stating that on a difficult tour for New Zealand I was one of the few who had taken up the challenge, stood up to the South Africans and shown real mental strength. How little they knew! Or did they?

Perhaps I was mentally strong after all because I was strong enough to accept that pressure makes you think dumb stuff — that I accepted my negativity and used it to channel my focus. Just like it takes strength to face your fears it also takes mental fortitude to overcome your doubts. I had doubts about myself but I didn't let them rule me, except of course when it came to playing entertaining cricket. Trying to dig out whether or not my idols went through these same thought processes was always a goal of my questioning, and when I learnt that some of those whom I viewed as the most talented and confident-looking players did experience similar thoughts from time to time it gave me the confidence to accept my unruly mind.

Consequently, I couldn't stand overly positive people. All that 'Come on, we can do this!' type stuff really grated on me. Tell me *how* we can do it and then I might get excited. It doesn't even have to be that accurate, but if you're going to open your mouth at least come out with something tangible. I played with many people at all levels who I thought used an outwardly positive demeanour to run from their realities. I'm not saying that I condone doom and gloom but at least I had the courage to face reality. I didn't want to play alongside players who thought that bouncing around, always being 'positive' and ignoring the reality of the situation would achieve the results we desired. I wanted to work with players who were brave enough to admit their own and the team's collective shortcomings and *do something about it*. That, to my mind, meant hard work and discipline.

Okay, I wasn't an optimist, but I sure as hell wasn't a defeatist either. Unfortunately, realism often gets confused with defeatism (which brings to mind a quote someone once told me, although I'm not sure who originally said it: 'Cynic is a word invented by optimists to criticise realists'). And yes, perhaps my negativity *did* stop me from trying to play expansive and entertaining cricket, but I also strongly believe that my realism allowed me to settle on a style of batting that was most likely to achieve results for me. That doesn't mean I decided I couldn't do certain things — that *would be* defeatist — rather, if I decided that I couldn't do it now but needed to in the future then I had to work bloody hard to accomplish it. I still buy into that old saying that 'anything is possible' and I did daydream on a regular basis of achieving some great things, but I also knew that dreaming alone wasn't going to achieve them. My rather fatalistic outlook didn't lead me to shy from a tough challenge, however. If something had to be done, it had to be done, and I would settle on an approach and give it all I had. Sometimes when you give something that you think is too hard a go you find that you surprise yourself. While this does build confidence, whenever it happened I wasn't exactly going to jump around thinking I could do it *all the time*, it just gave me more incentive to continue to improve my skills to compete more regularly.

God, it's all so confusing! As I've been writing this I can't help but think, 'If I had sorted my thinking out I might have been a great player'. On the other hand, I then start thinking, 'Hang on, if you didn't worry about everything that could go wrong perhaps you wouldn't have put the amount of hard work in that was necessary'. One thing I do know though is that if I didn't think the way I did I wouldn't be writing this book — I'd still be playing, but probably averaging 25 by now.

Admittedly, there were times when I really needed to be slapped on the wrist because of my tendency to verbalise my negative feelings. As a result of disapproving of those whom I thought were fooling themselves, I went a little over the top in the other direction. It was my way of dealing with my doubts and frustrations — getting them out and then getting on with it. The problem was that not all people work like me and some probably do need to bullshit themselves. My negativity became more dangerous as I got older and became a role model for younger players. I would bitch and moan about seaming wickets, crap umpiring, how out of form I was, or how good the opposition were, but then go out and graft away in the usual manner. My fatalism was never an excuse or a way out but I do concede that it wasn't the greatest thing to expose younger players to who were dealing with their own challenges in their own ways.

Chapter Sixteen

Expectation

I learnt to operate while feeling anxious, didn't run from my fears, and used my negativity to channel my focus, but expectation had its horrid little way with me time and time again. Of all the pressures I faced during the course of my cricketing life, expectation was the one pressure that made me feel very uncomfortable indeed. It caused anxiety, and while I could cope with anxiety on most occasions, I struggled when the anxiety was caused by expectation. Even though I experienced a lot of negative thoughts I still expected high things of myself. I was fatalistic all right but also quite the perfectionist. There was always room for improvement and I knew that with quality hard work I could always achieve more. Poor training sessions and errors of judgement haunted me for days, even years.

High self-expectation is fine; it motivated me and was quite healthy so long as it was tempered by a good degree of realism. But not living up to your own expectations can be frustrating. Just cast your mind back to John McEnroe — he set high personal expectations and had even higher expectations of the match officials. Such expectations can be destructive if not dealt with responsibly, but having low expectations of yourself is a real pity. The way I look at things, having no preconceived expectations of yourself is the best-case scenario, that is, just focus and see what happens. I tended to expect the worse, hope for the best and, whatever the outcome, want to get better next time. While what I expected of myself was never a major problem, it was when I thought about what others expected from me that the shit really hit the fan. The problem with this kind of expectation is that the better you get and the more success you experience the more you face this horrendous form of pressure. It was pressure that, particularly as I got older, I tried to avoid like the plague. Perhaps self-expectation and public expectation are correlated. If you didn't have any preconceived self-expectation and just got on with it, perhaps you wouldn't really care what others expect. Where I struggled was that I generally had a fair idea of what I was capable of but thought that others expected more.

My first head-on experience with expectation came as a young bowler. I was in the New Zealand Development Squad, which was a team picked from the national Under-18 tournament, and we toured around the North Island playing minor association teams. During this tour a New Zealand under-20 team was selected to tour Australia and I was picked for this squad. The night I heard the team announcement I was thrilled, but the next morning we were playing Hamilton and I felt really anxious because I believed I now had to show everyone how good I was in order to justify my selection, and I bowled really badly in that game as a result.

Fear, anxiety and negative thinking destroyed my bowling, but expectation had a big hand in ensuring I never regained it. The truth was that I never really gave up on my bowling and continued to put a lot of work into restoring it. Even after I was an established batsman, when I did get the ball to bowl I still felt as though I was protecting a reputation as a good left-arm spinner. In later years it was an irrational belief, and many people I played with had no recollection of my early days, but I still found bowling a long hop incredibly embarrassing. In club cricket, where I often bowled, it always frustrated me when some club slogger belted me for six. I used to feel that they thought they were hitting a test player round the ground in a way as if to say 'You're not so flash'. Even though I was a crap bowler, as a test player I always felt that at club level I was excepted to be dominant with the ball as well. In reality I wasn't even senior club level with the ball and there was probably no expectation on me whatsoever, but I still felt that I had to be perfect. As a kid all I wanted to do was show everyone how good I was, but as an adult I wanted everyone to know how poor I was so I could only impress and not disappoint.

If the level of expectation I projected onto myself when bowling was high, it became intolerable when batting. Once I became a test-match batsman I began to loathe club cricket. It wasn't because I was arrogant and felt above it, rather it was because I was expected to be damn good at it. There was a time when I *was* damn good at it because I simply *had to be*. In the mid '90s club cricket was my way into first-class cricket, which was of course my way into test cricket, so I needed to dominate Otago club cricket. I developed the skills to succeed on crap club wickets, but as my game progressed and I started to focus on the requirements of a test-match opener my ability to dominate at the lower level began to diminish. On slow, seaming club wickets you tend to rely on bold drives and pull shots. The outfields, pitches and bowlers are slow and so you must make your own pace and be adept at striking the ball in front of the wicket and also at times go aerial. As a test player, on the other hand, I relied on using pace and working the ball behind the wickets, keeping it along the ground, and considered drives and pull shots the quickest way to get out.

I really should have been good enough to shuttle between the two styles of play and adapt when playing for my club, but was basically too frightened to get out playing a style of cricket that I wasn't known for. I felt I had to score runs, that it was expected of me, but that if I went out and tried to smash cover drives and pull shots I could get accused of not trying — and in my book that kind of arrogance is inexcusable. I think as a young bowler I was guilty of arrogance from time to time and even now I cringe when I think about it. So in club cricket I tried to put my head down and apply my test game. I would leave half volleys, push and prod, and with the ball seaming around be made to look a fool by some pretty ordinary bowlers. It was extremely embarrassing because I thought people expected more and failed to understand.

Some teams had bowlers who were outstanding club bowlers but would never go any further as they lacked pace and bounce for better surfaces — I dreaded playing those teams the most. These bowlers would be all over me and they knew it. I was a prized wicket that was crucial for the development of their egos and I hated giving them that ego rush. At times when I turned up for club games I would be so tense and stressed out that I would have that lumpy feeling you get in the back of your throat just before bursting into tears.

Possibly my most miserable time during my batting days was when I played a season of club cricket for a small English village called Datchet. It was a lovely little place about an hour's drive west of London, right beside Windsor. It was the winter of 2001 and I had just been named New Zealand Cricket Player of the Year. I had a New Zealand Cricket contract, had left my job in Dunedin, and was finally enjoying the life of a professional cricket player I had always envisioned. I'd decided there was no point in staying for the Dunedin winter and spending my contract money when I could bank it and get paid to play in England. Chris Cairns lined me up with Datchet because he was mates with a wealthy expat businessman call Mike Clements who loved cricket and rugby and put a lot of his money into those codes there. Mike 'Animal' Clements was a fascinating character to say the least, larger than life, but most of all extremely generous to me as he paid me a handsome sum to come and play for his cricketing interest. The level of cricket was low — *very low* — and I thought it would be a great holiday swanning around the UK. However, my outlook changed very quickly not long after my arrival.

The club was very excited about having a test-match cricketer playing for them and it was fair enough that they had a very high level of expectation. Things started out okay with a hundred in the first competitive game but I think it astounded my clubmates how scratchy it was and how long it took, and being Poms they let me know. I realised that once again, even though the standard of cricket was woeful, my test-style game was not going to suit the slow, seaming wickets. I tried to hit the ball harder and in front of square to counter the slow bowling and long-grassed outfields and kept getting out for bugger all and in awful ways, steadily becoming more and more embarrassed and frustrated with my returns for the club. I was letting them down and they were getting more and more disappointed with their supposed match-winner. It had been a bit of a coup for them to secure a test cricketer and not really within the rules of the competition and other teams weren't happy about it, but pretty soon they didn't care as I became a bit of a laughing stock.

Each year I'd been to England the summers had been great, and this year was no exception, but all I wanted was rain and plenty of it. I was so stressed out that I was letting myself get involved in some pretty pathetic on-field incidents in an environment that really should have meant nothing to me. On top of this I had been experiencing some domestic problems with my partner at the time and sorting out our difficulties was one of the reasons for going to England, but with the cricket turning me into a nervous wreck this was never going to happen. In the end, I left for home well before the end of the English summer, returning to New Zealand a single man, unsure of my personal future, but positive I would never return to play club cricket in England again. From now on I would take the New Zealand winter over a summer of English expectation any day.

The experience did teach me a valuable lesson in one respect, and that was that whatever the standard at which I played I would always take my performance seriously and the pressure I was placing upon myself in response to perceived expectation was an unnecessary one. I could never just play for fun, so why bother? I faced enough pressure in my own summer or on Black Caps tours so why deal with more when I didn't need it? In fact, the down time could be much better spent in the indoor nets honing my technique. I also promised myself that I would never let money cloud my decision-making again when it came to securing my cricketing happiness.

The real problem I had with expectation was that it took my focus from what I should have been thinking about and doing to what I thought others expected from me. How I thought others wanted me to play or should be achieving became what I expected from myself and was often unrealistic or fostered doubts about my ability to do it. Instead of going through my routine and then focusing my mind to watch the ball, which in fact probably would have produced good results at any level, I began focusing on the outcome and expecting myself to be dominant. When that didn't happen I would get frustrated and things would rapidly spiral downwards.

The unusual thing about my perceived expectation was that it became less the higher the level at which I was playing. During my Datchet experience and about the time I was nearing a nervous breakdown I got the chance to play a first-class game for the MCC against Australia. I hadn't scored runs for ages and my game was not prepared for test-quality bowlers on a faster pitch, but upon arriving at Arundel for the game I felt like I was on weekend leave from prison. There was anxiety about the challenge of facing Australia but no expectation, and as far as a cricket game goes it was one of the very few in which I really enjoyed playing. I held my bat through the entire first innings in making 60-odd not out.

Nor did I ever really feel the pressure of expectation at the test level. Towards the very end I did a little, as I tried to rebel against my expected defensive approach, but for the most part I felt people only expected what I was capable of and that was my trademark, gritty, dour, drawn-out innings. Having the odd failure was expected and tolerated and much of the time I surpassed my own expectations anyway. First-class cricket was a little similar, although I felt more was expected of me in my last few years for Auckland and got frustrated with a couple of lean years. However, most of the players around at that level understood the vagaries of the game and what I was capable of doing. This is not to say that I felt comfortable — far from it, there were always nerves, fear and uncertainty about the result —but they were challenges I was prepared to accept at the test and first-class level because success at those levels held significant rewards for me.

Afterword — Alex McKenzie

From a sports psych perspective, Mark's observations in this last section are the most difficult to write about. This is not because I disagree with anything that he has said, but because I would hate for readers to finish the book with the lasting impression that Mark hated playing cricket, or that the 'demons' he talks about so honestly here (anxiety, fear, negative self-talk and expectation) will eventually get to everyone who plays sport at the highest level and force them out of the game. I'm not saying that everyone doesn't experience these things — they do — but like motivation, it is an individual experience in terms of the level to which each of these demons is experienced, *and* the manner in which each is manifested. In addition, people cope with them in different ways, and in some cases, athletes welcome experiencing these things because it signifies, first and foremost, that they are totally immersed in their sport. It also means that they have an opportunity to overcome these demons and experience the satisfaction of taming them at the highest level of sport in which they will be involved, given their ability. For some this is test cricket, or world championships, or the Olympic Games, whereas for others this might be a local club championship, or even a training session.

Mark's descriptions and explanations of these experiences are personal reflections on how they affected him. He doesn't say that everyone involved in top-level sport will be affected in the same way; it was just how he experienced and dealt with these 'demons', or as he described them, 'nasty little computer viruses [in the] hard drive of my head . . .' I will try to expand on some of the issues that Mark raised under each of the headings that he used.

Anxiety

Quite simply, anxiety is a perception. It manifests itself in different ways. There can be physical symptoms such as muscular tension, increased heart rate and breathing rate, dry mouth, excessive yawning, frequent urination, nausea and so on (Mark describes 'feeling crook, dying to go to the toilet, legs moving uncontrollably'), all of which can be labelled 'physiological anxiety'. This simply means that the person interprets these physical signs as indicating that they are anxious. Another type of anxiety is called 'cognitive anxiety', which is when an individual doubts his or her ability to cope with the situation in which they find themselves, and this causes them to experience anxiety. To make matters more complicated, some people are more likely to perceive situations as anxiety-producing. These people have been described as having high levels of 'trait anxiety', which means that this tendency is part of their personality. Reading this section, I believe that Mark would perhaps describe himself as someone who was high in trait anxiety, which meant that he often got himself into an anxious 'state' when performing, and needed to learn how to cope with those feelings. He openly admits that he 'was still a very nervous player', even when he converted to opening the batting in an attempt to exercise a greater degree of control over his anxiety.

However, getting back to the notion that anxiety is a perception, it is probably useful at this point to differentiate between some key concepts that are often confused. 'Arousal' is a term that is often used to describe a level of physiological activation in the body, and there are numerous theories relating to the arousal/performance relationship. One of the most well known of these is the inverted-U theory, which states that as arousal increases, so too does performance, up to a point where further increases in arousal cause performance to decrease. The relationship can be illustrated as follows:

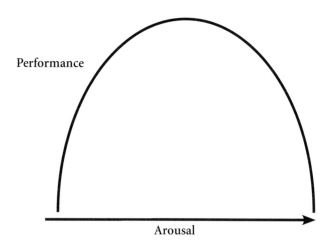

When a person's arousal level gets to the stage where their performance starts to decrease (that is, over-activation), then this is often interpreted as anxiety.

While this theory may be oversimplistic, it does help to explain the phenomena where athletes can experience poor performances by being under- or over-activated, and that by being able to control their activation levels, they may be able to control how well they perform. In addition, while some athletes may interpret their physical arousal levels as signs of anxiety, others may choose to interpret them as signs of excitement and challenge. Physically the signs are the same (for example, elevated heart rate, muscle tension, wanting to urinate), but the person's *perception* of those signs can make quite a difference as to how they perform.

The key element in all of this is the ability to bring the level of activation under control, so that performance is maximised. For those who interpret this activation level as anxiety, this means bringing their anxiety under control. It was interesting to read about Mark's conversations with Chris Cairns, who had said that he felt nervous (which perhaps meant that he experienced the physical signs of activation), but also excited because he never knew just 'what the day would hold for him'. In other words, he interpreted the physical indicators of 'nerves' as both anxiety and excitement at the same time. In both instances though, these feelings needed to be controlled in order to be able to perform well. You cannot eliminate them altogether, but need to accept that they are going to occur, and learn how to deal with them. In some cases you can use them to your advantage, in the sense that you could (a) learn to interpret them as excitement rather than anxiety (that is, as a positive rather than negative feeling — easier said than done of course — but possible nonetheless), and/ or (b) use the feelings as a cue to focus on ' . . . the important things [that] you must do to succeed', as Mark goes on to state. For him, his anxiety acted as a cue for him to use his pre-ball routines, which was the 'critical mental management process' that he used while batting in this state.

Building confidence

It seems logical to assume that there is an inverse relationship between confidence and anxiety, in that the more confident you are the less anxiety you will experience. While this may be true for some people in some circumstances, there are also plenty of examples of people who experience huge amounts of anxiety prior to doing things that they have done successfully dozens of times, and of which they are confident that they can perform well. Athletes, musicians, after-dinner speakers, comedians, teachers and all manner of other people who 'perform' in public in some way often get anxious before and during performances, despite being confident in their ability to perform well. However, they must still have the ability to control their anxiety in order to perform to the best of their ability. Thus the relationship between confidence and anxiety is more complicated than it might at first appear.

So what exactly is confidence? For most people, confidence is belief in one's own ability to do well at a particular task. In other words, it is when you expect to be successful when you attempt a particular skill. If you *expect* to succeed, then you are confident. However, there is a difference between confidence in your ability to perform certain specific skills (for example, a hook shot to Brett Lee or Shane Bond), and a general belief in your overall cricketing ability. These two forms of confidence can be labelled specific and general self-confidence respectively. Those who have studied sports psychology have also called specific self-confidence 'self-efficacy'.

So how do you become self-confident? As Mark rightly pointed out, you can't just pluck it out of the air, it has to be earned. However, you can act confidently even when you're not feeling confident, and this can help to change an opponent's perception of you. This can be to your advantage. Mark talks about the Australian cricketers 'very seldom looking nervous' and establishing a presence at the crease that 'places the opposition under psychological pressure even before a ball is bowled'. What psychological pressure is he talking about here? Perhaps by acting as if you are supremely confident, your opponents start to worry that they can't intimidate you or place you under pressure, and it reduces their confidence and alters the way that they play against you. For example, if a batsman looks as if he is playing very confidently, the opposing captain or bowler might decide that placing fielders in close as a ploy to put him under pressure won't work, and therefore they set a more defensive field. This has the effect of placing less pressure on the batsman, and he may in fact be able to 'play himself in' a little more easily than he might have been able to do if he showed visible signs of anxiety and lack of confidence to his opponents. Indirectly then, acting confidently can have the effect of actually developing confidence for real!

What are some other ways to develop confidence? By far the most important source of confidence in a particular situation (that is, specific self-confidence/ self-efficacy) is knowing that you have succeeded before when you were faced with the same task. As Mark stated, 'Facing fast bowling can be daunting, but the more you face up to it and survive the more confidence you gain in yourself.' This doesn't mean that you won't be anxious about facing fast bowling; it just means that you know you have the skills to cope with it. You can also gain confidence from the fact that you have done as much work as you could possibly have done in preparation for a particular performance, and you believe in the processes that you have put in place to help you perform. Again, Mark put this very succinctly when he said, 'When I walk out onto a test ground I'm as nervous as hell but I know that if I trust my processes I can succeed.'

So what are some other sources of confidence for a player? As we have already stated, previous experience is the most important source of confidence, but people can also gain confidence from watching other people succeed. If you see someone performing well at a task, and that person is very similar to you in many respects (for example, age, size, shape, experience), then you might think 'if they can do it, so can I!' Psychologists call this 'vicarious experience', and it can be an important source of specific self-confidence (self-efficacy) for performing a particular task. However, if you were watching someone who was totally dissimilar to you performing a particular task, then you will probably be much less confident in your ability to perform that task. So, if you have never performed a particular skill or task before, and you wanted to boost your confidence about performing that task, you would gain a lot more from watching someone very similar to you performing that task, and performing it easily, than you would from watching someone who wasn't like you at all performing the task, especially if they were having difficulty doing it well. This is where your imagery skills can come in handy. If you are good at imagery, and can vividly imagine yourself performing a particular task with ease, then you are likely to boost your confidence levels about being able to perform that task successfully. After all, there is nobody more similar to you than you! Imagery is simply another form of vicarious experience.

A further source of confidence is called 'verbal persuasion', which is simply another way of saying that your confidence can be boosted if someone tells you that you can successfully perform a certain task. It will be boosted even more if that person is someone that you trust and whom you believe knows what they are talking about. If my mother told me that I would make a great fast bowler when I was 17 years old, it would have been unlikely to have boosted my confidence as much as Richard Hadlee telling me the same thing (sorry Mum!). Similarly, my wife (who is Canadian and struggles to understand cricket, having been brought up with baseball and softball) telling me that I could be a great opening batsman would probably do little for my confidence about being able to become such a batsman, whereas if Mark Richardson told me the same thing, I would think 'Hmm . . . he knows what he's talking about . . . maybe I can do this!'

The final major source of information regarding a person's self-confidence is their ability to interpret their feelings, both emotional and physical about an upcoming performance. If your heart starts to race and you get butterflies in your stomach whenever you think about an upcoming performance, your confidence in your ability to perform well is likely to be much less if you interpreted these feelings as being indicative of anxiety and pressure rather than ones of eager anticipation, excitement and challenge. If you interpreted these physical feelings as anxiety, then in order to boost your confidence to perform, you could try to reduce the intensity of these physical symptoms by learning how to bring them under conscious control. This can be achieved through the use of techniques such as relaxation, imagery, or stress management techniques (including routines, such as the pre-ball routines used by Mark before each ball he faced). If you know that you are capable of bringing these feelings under conscious control, then you are likely to feel confident that you can perform, and your anxiety levels will reduce. Mark summed up both perspectives nicely when he said:

> 'When I walk out onto a test ground I'm nervous as hell but I know that if I trust my processes I can succeed; but on that day, on my ODI debut, all I was was nervous as hell. I had no processes I trusted and so anxiety ran rampant.'

Fear

Mark's observations on fear were by far the most interesting to read from a sports psychology perspective. I have no doubt that his fear of failure was an extremely effective motivator for him, as it is for many sportspeople at the elite level, but as he admitted, it was *'not an ideal motivator when it comes to playing attractive cricket and it definitely held me back from getting the best out of myself in terms of quality stroke play'*. However, he also stated emphatically *'that it was effective in ensuring I was a reliable and consistent opening batsman'*. In other words, for the role that he played in the team, his response to this form of motivation was ideal.

However, I wonder whether it would have been as effective if he were *expected* to be a risk-taker and an attacking stroke player? After all, he also admitted that it led to his conservative approach to batting, in that he looked to defend first, score second. It's a moot point I guess, because that wasn't his role in the team, and his style of play was extremely effective for the role that he *did* play. Unfortunately, it was a double-edged sword for Mark, in that he used that fear as a reason to develop and refine the mental, technical and tactical processes that he went through in order for him to reach the level that he did, and yet it was the effort that he had to put into going through those processes in order to be able to cope with all the negative emotions associated with fear that played a major role in his decision to retire from the game.

Many would say that this was a premature retirement, but after reading this book I believe that a lot of these people would change their minds.

I also think that one of the reasons that fear, and fear of failure especially, was such an exhausting motivator for Mark, was due to the nature of the game itself. Cricket is a game that is defined by failure! In most circumstances, at test level anyway, ten batsmen are expected to fail at some stage in their innings, and most of the time that happens! Even if you score 200 runs, and are dismissed on the boundary attempting a six, the bottom line is that at that particular moment, you failed! In other team sports, failure is not so individually defined, or as noticeable. In games such as rugby, soccer, netball and also cricket, one person's performance often depends heavily on the performance of his or her team-mates, yet a *batsman* in cricket is largely on his own, and one small mistake in judgement can lead to his dismissal. In contrast, in these other team sports there is always an opportunity to make up for a mistake because you can still continue to play. The consequences for making a mistake as a batsman are often far greater for that person than they are for a rugby, soccer, hockey or netball player.

So what's my point? In a nutshell, all test opening batsmen must approach each test match knowing that if they get two opportunities to bat, that they are probably going to fail at some point, in both innings, no matter what score they make. If you are a batsman who is motivated by fear of failure, as Mark was, then it is no wonder that having to cope with the fear, and then dealing with the fact, is exhausting.

A final note on fear: I was always interested to see that Mark almost always fielded in close for New Zealand, and after reading his explanation that he volunteered for the position I must admit to being a little perplexed. While I understood his rationale, the fact that fielding in this position essentially meant that his anxiety and fear were exacerbated, and that the physical toll on his body was increased, was something that seemed counterproductive to him being in the best possible physical and mental shape for opening the batting. I would have thought that the powers that be in the New Zealand team at the time might have recognised this and taken him out of that position. The situation was undoubtedly more complicated than this, but it did strike me as odd all the same.

Self-talk

Mark's point that you cannot eliminate negative thoughts completely is a good one. If a person says to himself or herself that they are not going to let any negative thoughts creep into their mind when performing, and then one does, they have immediately failed! A better strategy would be to either (a) eliminate the negative thought and replace it with a positive one, or (b) use the negative thought as a cue to focus on some other strategy (for example, your pre-ball routine) that will not only distract you from that thought, but also reduce the anxiety that the negative thought may elicit because you are confident in the processes that you have put in place to counter the thought. This is what Mark talked about when he said:

> The little man on my shoulder became a call to attention. The more the pressure the louder he became, so when my mind went haywire it was a warning that I had to get absorbed in my routines . . .

The bottom line is that an athlete in any sport invites failure by saying that he or she will not think negatively leading up to and during a performance. The mere fact that they say this to themselves means that they are thinking about thinking negatively — if that makes sense! It's like telling someone not to think of their mother — the first thing that usually comes to mind is their mother. Having said that, there may well be some athletes who never think negatively at some point, but I have yet to meet them. The important point in all of this, and Mark makes this point well, is that it is not so much whether you *have* negative thoughts, it is what you do in response to them that influences how well you perform.

Expectation

The difficulty about worrying about other people's expectations of you is that you have no control over them. Mark stated that coping with his own expectations wasn't a problem for him: 'It was when I thought about what others expected from me that the shit really hit the fan'. Other people's expectations caused him a great deal of anxiety, not only because he had no control over them, but also because he probably perceived that they were greater than they really were.

If, as a sports psychology consultant, I am confronted with an athlete who worries about other people's expectations of them, I usually ask them a series of questions that go something along the lines of:

Who are these people who have these huge expectations of you?

Have you actually asked them what their expectations are?

Do you know them personally and are they important figures in your life?

Usually these people are not members of the athlete's immediate circle of friends or family, so the next question is usually:

Why should you be worried what they think?'

And if they are friends or family, I ask whether they will still support the athlete if he or she doesn't perform well. Usually the answer is 'yes', and that seems to ease the perceived pressure somewhat, and reduces the athlete's anxiety.

However, Mark himself best sums up the crux of the whole matter when he says that:

'The real problem I had with expectation was that it took my focus from what I should have been thinking about and doing to what I thought others expected from me. How I thought others wanted me to play or should be achieving became what I expected from myself and was often unrealistic or fostered doubts about my ability to do it. Instead of going through my routine and then focusing my mind to watch the ball, which in fact probably would have produced good results at any level, I began focusing on the outcome and expecting myself to be dominant. When that didn't happen I would get frustrated and things would rapidly spiral downwards.'

In other words, other people's expectations can take control of an athlete, instead of the other way around, and can distract him or her from focusing on their own performance routines and processes. They project themselves into the future by thinking about the outcome of the performance or competition, and therefore are not focused on what they need to do at that particular moment. Consequently, their performance suffers.

Finally, Mark's admission that the pressure of expectation became less the higher the level of cricket that he was playing is not unusual. It would have been a bigger blow to his ego if he failed when playing at a lower level, where others' expectations would have been perceived to be higher, and therefore his anxiety levels would have been higher as a result. He would not have been expected to play as well as often at test level, therefore the expectations would have been less, the perceived pressure and anxiety of these expectations would have been less, and therefore his ego would not have suffered as much if he performed poorly. In other words, it would have been less of a blow to his ego if Shane Warne, Shoaib Akhtar or Steve Harmison dismissed him, than if Warwick Larkins, the local part-time spinner for the Albion President's Grade team, dismissed him for a low score. People would expect him to struggle against international test bowlers more than the club-level bowlers, and therefore the perceived pressure to perform well that Mark experienced would have been greater.

Conclusion

In my opinion Mark Richardson underestimates his contribution to, and place within, New Zealand's cricketing history. He may not have been the most elegant stroke-maker, or most agile fieldsman, but his mental game was exceptional. To me he ranks as one of the most gifted athletes that I have ever worked with in terms of the way that he thought about, and worked on, his mental skills. That doesn't mean that he always conquered the 'viruses' that lurked in the hard drive of his brain, but that the processes that he went through, and the techniques that he used to try and overcome them, meant that he was more likely to be successful than anyone else who experienced the same things.

He understood himself and his game, knew what he needed to do to succeed, trained according to those requirements, remained focused on them, and allowed them to take hold during competition. He was careful to treat the development of his mental game as a process that would take time, and understood that there was no substitute for preparation in this phase of his game. He also took responsibility for the further development and refinement of his mental game, and took it upon himself to listen to people whose opinions he respected, thought about what they had to say, and either rejected or amended their advice to suit his purposes.

I never played test cricket. In fact, I barely played senior club cricket, so I can never presume to truly understand the emotions and thought patterns that players at that level go through. However, I feel that my discussions with Mark over the years, and the observations I have made while reading this book, have provided me with the greatest possible insight into what it takes to become a truly mentally tough batsman at the highest level of the game. That's not to say that Mark's experiences are indicative of all test cricketers in terms of the processes, routines and thought patterns that he used and experienced; they are not; but after reading what he has had to say in this book, I believe that athletes from any sport will be able to appreciate what it is possible to achieve if you literally 'put your mind to it'.

Alex McKenzie, 2005